THE POTSDAM CONFERENCE VILLAS AND THEIR HISTORY

Lilian Harvey photographed in front of her house by Griebnitzsee, March 8, 1936

THE POTSDAM CONFERENCE VILLAS AND THEIR HISTORY

A beautiful idyll, steeped in history

C. J. Partsch

© 2022, Elisabeth Sandmann Verlag, Munich
1st Edition
All rights reserved
ISBN 978-3-949582-19-6
Design: Schimmelpenninck.Gestaltung, Berlin
Lithography & Production: Jan Russok
Printed and bound by: Pustet, Regensburg
Visit us online at www.esverlag.de

Contents

7   Foreword by Thomas Harding
11 Introduction

Rudolf-Breitscheid-Strasse
19 Ufa-City and the Kayser Villa
27 The Stern Villa

Karl-Marx-Strasse
36 The Truman Villa
48 The Herpich Villa
56 The Mosler Villa

Virchowstrasse
61 The Stülpnagel Villa
71 The Schade van Westrum Villa
82 The Urbig Villa
90 The Saltzmann Villa
98 The Goldschmidt Villa

Spitzweggasse
112 The Heidmann Villa
117 The Riehl House
126 The Sarre Villa

Griebnitzstrasse
141 The Schleicher Villa

147 Conclusion

149 Acknowledgements
149 Index of Names
151 Picture Credits

Postcard, around 1920
(Published by: Kunstverlag J. Goldiner, Berlin)

Why the place where we live is so important for our identity and for our sense of belonging.

My grandmother Elsie grew up in a small house by one of the lakes in Brandenburg. The house overlooked Groß Glienicker See, just a short drive from Potsdam city centre. She called it her 'soul place'. Her father, Dr Alfred Alexander, was a prominent physician in Berlin, with clients who included Albert Einstein and Marlene Dietrich. The family would go out to the house for the weekend and would spend the summers there. When the Nazis rose to power, my grandmother and her family were forced to flee Germany and found refuge in England. The subsequent fate of the house mirrors the turbulent historical events of the time. As part of the Aryanisation process, the house was transferred to a Nazi family who ran their music publishing company from there during the Second World War. In April 1945, the Red Army fought the Wehrmacht in the grounds around the house—the external walls are still pocked with bullet holes—and then occupied the village. Following the division of Germany in 1949, two families shared the house. Then, in August 1961, the GDR erected the Berlin Wall between the back of the house and the lake.

  When I came to the house in 2013, it was near collapse. The windows were broken, the walls covered in graffiti, and my grandmother's parents' bedroom was being used as a drug den. With the support of local residents and various members of my family, I set about saving the house. First, we won support from the City of Potsdam Assembly. Then the State of Brandenburg awarded the house 'Denkmal' or historic monument status. We began raising money to restore the house to its former glory and received funding from the Federal government, the State of

Brandenburg and from individuals and foundations from around the world. Today, the house is a Centre for Education and Reconciliation. Though the journey has not always been easy, thanks to creative thinking and the support of the local community, politicians, lawyers and journalists, it has been possible to protect this historic building. Details of the 'Alexander Haus' project can be found at www.alexanderhaus.org.

My family's house is just one of the many homes, dachas, villas and mansions that were built around the beautiful lakes of Brandenburg such as Griebnitzsee, Wannsee, Sacrower See, and many others. Each building has its own unique story, filled with love, celebrations, tragedies, losses and personal dramas. Each shows us the power of home, and why the place we live is so important to our sense of belonging and identity. But why are these stories important? Is it because we can only avoid repeating the mistakes of the past if we understand where we come from?

Christoph Partsch's book tells the stories of the people who lived at Griebnitzsee; it tells of the rise and fall of their families and of the many vicissitudes of life.

Thomas Harding, British writer, journalist and documentary film maker, author of the bestselling novels *The House by the Lake* and *Hanns and Rudolf*

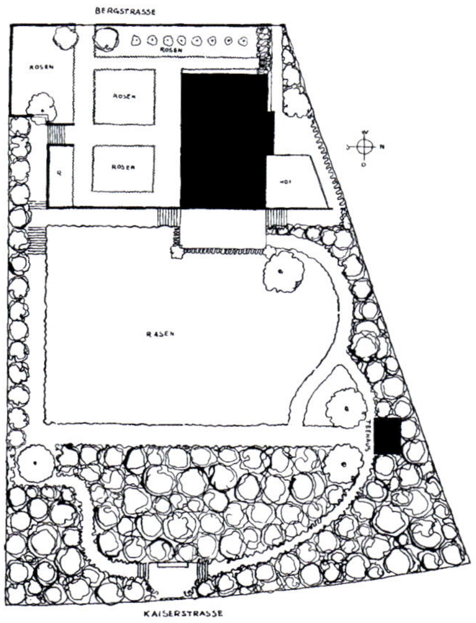

The Goldschmidt Villa

The Riehl House

The Truman Villa

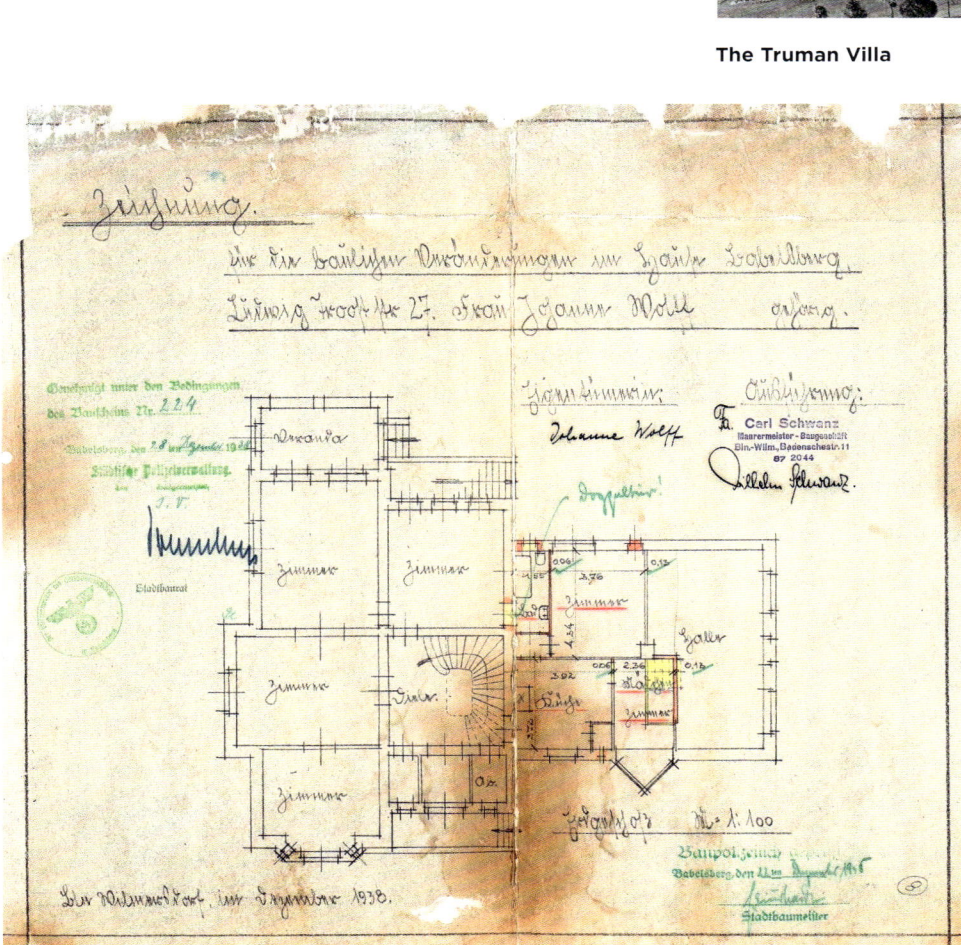
The Saltzmann Villa

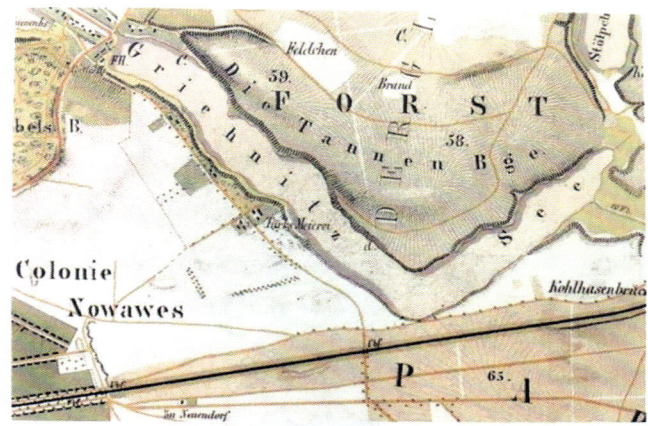

"Plan of Potsdam including the surrounding area based on the original records of the topographic department of the ordnance survey of 1848", scale 1:25000 (excerpt)

Erwin Albert Barth: "Villengarten am Griebnitzsee, Potsdam-Babelsberg", plan of the garden with the terrace complex 1:200, planting list, décor, scale, Karl-Marx-Strasse 34

Introduction

Over the last 150 years or so, the lakeside at Griebnitzsee has been the location of choice for the rich, the beautiful and the powerful. Here, far from the bustle and noise of the capital, Berlin, they could relax in the scenic surroundings of the peaceful countryside and enjoy life at a more leisurely pace. At the same time, key events in German history were concentrated here as if under a magnifying glass: all of its happy times, but also all of its terrible catastrophes had direct consequences—some auspicious, some tragic—for the fates of the people who lived here.
It was also always a place of contradictions: of generosity and greed, of honourable deeds and transgressions, of worldliness and narrow-mindedness, of heroes and hypocrites.

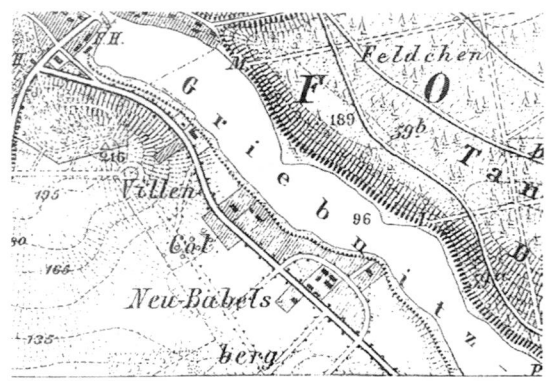 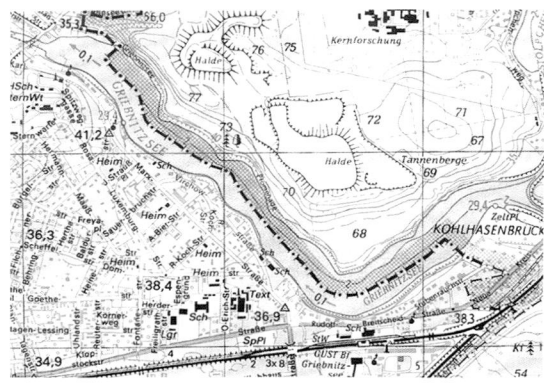

left: Griebnitzsee and the beginnings of the villa settlement in Neubabelsberg, topographic map of Potsdam (excerpt), 1877

right: Griebnitzsee and the surrounding area, topographic urban map (excerpt), 1989

The cultivation of the area began with the small mulberry tree plantation for the orphanage established in 1827 by educational reformer Wilhelm von Türk in the Glienicke Hunting Lodge. Türk, himself an orphan, came to Potsdam in 1817 as the School Councillor and Royal Councillor of the Kingdom of Prussia following the Wars of Liberation against the French occupying forces and used his fortune to finance orphanages. The mulberry plantation was intended to provide jobs and a source of income for the orphans.

In 1871, city planners and architects Hermann Ende and Friedrich Wilhelm Böckmann founded the planning company "Societät Neubabelsberg", through which they purchased the land between Griebnitzsee railway station and the park grounds of the Emperor's Babelsberg Palace. To the south of Griebnitzsee, the area they acquired reached as far as what is today Rosa-Luxemburg-Strasse. However, contrary to expectations, development of the area was so slow that by 1900, only ten villas had been built.[1]

1 Kurt Weiden: Neubabelsberg. Die historische Entwicklung der Villen-Colonie Neubabelsberg und der Filmstadt Babelsberg (Brandenburgische Ortsgeschichte) Potsdam 1984, p. 150.

left: Erwin Albert Barth: "Villengarten am Griebnitzsee, Potsdam-Babelsberg", view of the terrace complex with residential building 1:100, Karl-Marx-Strasse 34

right: Erwin Albert Barth: "Villengarten am Griebnitzsee, Potsdam-Babelsberg", cross-section of the terrace complex 1:100, Karl-Marx-Strasse 34

Consequently, Ende and Böckmann sold the land in 1902 to the Neubabelsberger Terraingesellschaft. This company was smarter and more successful in their marketing: among other things, they emphasised the excellent train service to Berlin—53 connections daily![2] As a result, a number of splendid villas were built in the historical style popular among the upper-middle classes at the time, which played with a variety of architectural forms from the Gothic and Renaissance styles and entertained the classically educated audience with quotations from and allusions to literature and art. The proximity to the imperial residence held a particular appeal for many developers, who hoped with their stately villas to attract the attention of Wilhelm I as he travelled from Griebnitzsee station along Kaiserstrasse (today Karl-Marx-Strasse) to his English neo-Tudor-style Babelsberg Palace. Kaiserstrasse twice intersected a street that curved towards Griebnitzsee and was named after the Prussian princess Luise, today Virchowstrasse and Robert-Koch-Strasse. The semi-hippodrome shape was intended to be reminiscent of Rome. All this drew in the industrialists and their heirs, who had become rich during the construction boom following the Franco-Prussian War of 1870/71. A splendid half-timbered villa at what is today Virchowstrasse 25 is a reminder of the heiress of building councillor Wentzel, Elise Wentzel-Heckmann, an important women's rights activist and philanthropist.

Wentzel-Heckmann not only financed the archaeological expeditions of her nephew, Professor Friedrich Sarre, but also the construction of his Tuscan-style villa at the end of what was at that time Kaiserstrasse. When the street was renamed "Strasse der SA" in 1938, Professor Sarre changed his address to Bergstrasse 6 (today Spitzweggasse 6).

Just a few houses along in Spitzweggasse, Mies van der Rohe's 'Landhaus Riehl' illustrates the architectural transition from classical temple references to the new country house style favoured by the likes of Hermann Muthesius. Below it, closer to the lake, stands the Herpich villa, constructed in 1911 and designed by Alfred Grenander, the inventor of the colour coding system for Berlin's underground rail network, which used different colours to make it easier to navigate the U-Bahn stations.

2 Ibid., p. 149.

At Griebnitzsee: Landhaus Wentzel-Heckmann, Virchowstrasse 25, with boathouse, Kunstverlag J. Goliner, Berlin C. 25, around 1915

Following the end of World War I, the imperial system of names remained in place, but a number of villas changed hands, including that owned by Carl Saltzmann, artist to the imperial navy, in what is today Virchowstrasse 27. The new leadership of the Weimar Republic acquired the existing villas or built their own prestigious homes to which they could retreat with their families. The chairmen of nearly all of the major banks, such as Jakob Goldschmidt of the Danat Bank, Franz Urbig of the Deutsche Bank or Georg Mosler of the Dresdner Bank, built their homes by Griebnitzsee. With the arrival of the Ufa film studios in the south of the villa colony, they were followed by media stars such as Lilian Harvey, Marika Rökk, Brigitte Horney, Heinz Rühmann, Willy Fritsch and Emil Jannings, as well as director Georg Jacoby, the man behind epic 1923/24 historical drama film *Quo Vadis?*

The Great Depression and above all Adolf Hitler's seizure of power in January 1933 also led to fundamental changes for most of the wealthy occupants of the villas. Kaiserstrasse was renamed 'Strasse der SA'; Luisenstrasse became 'Ludwig-Troost-Strasse'—Paul Ludwig Troost was Hitler's favourite architect. Hitler did not hesitate to cement his power by all available means. At 12.50 a.m. on June 30, 1934 (the Night of the Long Knives) SS officers forced their way into the villa of the last Imperial Chancellor of the Weimar Republic, Kurt von Schleicher, in Griebnitzstrasse 4 and shot both von Schleicher and his wife.[3]

The systematic terrorisation of the Jewish residents had already begun prior to this. At first, the Jewish owners, like the merchant Leon in Lindenstrasse, today's Rudolf-Breitscheid-Strasse 180, were offered money in exchange for the sale of their houses:

"Luckily, my father's own encounter with a Nazi intruder ended less tragically. In the early 30s he owned a villa on the shores of Griebnitzsee, one of the lakes just outside Berlin. The villa had been designed in imitation of an English country house and prided itself on a large and most attractive fireplace in the lounge. ... One sunny afternoon in May 1936 the family was sitting on the porch, when a small boat landed on our motorboat quay. One of the passengers came ashore. He limped across our lawn and disappeared into the house next door. We recognised him as none other than the Propaganda Minister, Josef Goebbels,

3 Documentation. Zur Ermordung des Generals Schleicher, in: Vierteljahreshefte für Zeitgeschichte, volume I (1953), issue 1, p. 71–95.

whose wife's relations, the Quandt family, owned the adjacent villa ... Next morning my father received an offer for his property. It was made clear to him that this was an offer he should not refuse. He took the hint and agreed to sell. Payment was in cash and, not surprisingly, the buyer's name was not disclosed. Now, Goebbels was no longer forced to walk across a Jewish lawn when he came on a visit to his wife's relations."[4]

The systematic "Aryanisation" of all of the villas, without any compensation whatsoever, followed. Furniture, works of art and other furnishings were in part publicly auctioned. For the remaining Jews, it soon became a matter of simply saving their lives. The banking families with their international networks often managed to escape to the Netherlands, Switzerland or the USA. Institutions of the Nazi regime moved into their villas, such as the *Bund Deutscher Mädel* (League of German Girls) which took up residence in the Goldschmidt villa. The villas were converted without any regard for their original functional contexts and in some instances had already been partly destroyed by this time.

Refugees who had not made it further than the Netherlands, such as the merchant Max Stern and his wife, soon met with the Nazis' thirst for extermination.

The genocide against the Jews also had a local offshoot in Griebnitzsee. At the beginning of the 1940s, the National Socialists forced the remaining Jews in Potsdam into a "Jewish Home for the Infirm and Elderly" at what was once Bergstrasse 1 (now Spitzweggasse 1, 2-2a). Those who didn't die there as a result of their inhumane treatment, were soon deported to the concentration camps. Among the last forty people removed from the home on January 16, 1943, was the last cantor of the Jewish community in Potsdam, Samuel Guttmann.[5] He was murdered in Theresienstadt on May 17, 1943.

Of the non-Jewish residents who did not have to leave their villas, some actively supported the regime, while others resisted—some tentatively, some more forcefully. The Nazis targeted those who resisted, among them the children of Friedrich Sarre who lived at what is now Spitzweggasse 6, and General von Stülpnagel of Virchowstrasse 15, who survived only by lucky coincidence.

The allied bombing that devastated Potsdam at the beginning of 1945 without any military purpose, left the villa district almost entirely unscathed.

However, many of the houses were damaged during the last defensive battles of the German forces. When the Soviet troops moved in, there was mass rape. The villas were plundered, their precious furnishings, including all of the works of art, were destroyed or scattered, marking an abrupt end to the last vestiges of traditional upper middle-class culture.

The occupants and owners, if they hadn't fled, were usually given no more than twenty-four hours by the new Russian rulers to vacate their villas. During the Potsdam Conference, Joseph Stalin, Harry S. Truman and Winston Churchill and then, following Churchill's election defeat, Clement Atlee, resided at the stately houses by Griebnitzsee. The owners were not permitted to return to their homes after the Potsdam Conference. In some cases, formal expropriation never took place, or not until much later, to facilitate the construction of the Berlin Wall.

4 Gary Leon: The Way It Was: A Jew's Struggle Through Two World Wars, Avon 1997, p. 17f.

5 Kurt Baller, Marlies Reinholz: Potsdam im Zweiten Weltkrieg. Eine Chronik, Magdeburg 2010, p. 209.

left: Watchtower of the GDR border troops at Griebnitzsee, July 13, 1990

right: NVA border troops with boat on Griebnitzsee, June 25, 1966

During the GDR era, 'Strasse der SA' was renamed 'Karl-Marx-Strasse', and 'Ludwig-Troost-Strasse' became 'Virchowstrasse'. State institutions such as the Ufa-Filmhochschule and the Academy of Political and Legal Sciences of the GDR, a talent factory of the workers' and farmers' state, moved into the empty buildings. Only those who were loyal to the state and "completely dependable" in political terms were permitted to live in the beautiful villas. The construction of the border fortifications went hand in hand with the destruction of the remaining splendid gardens, together with their magnificent boathouses, including that designed by famous architect Alfred Breslauer for the Goldschmidt villa.

Countless people who tried to cross the walls and fences put up by the GDR were murdered at Griebnitzsee. A concrete patrol route dissected the gardens, preventing access to the lake. The city authorities of Potsdam surreptitiously ordered the demolition of the towering villa that had once housed the "Jewish Home for the Infirm and Elderly." There was to be nothing in this state that saw itself as anti-fascist that could act as a reminder of the death of its Jewish citizens.

After the Fall of the Berlin Wall, the regional capital of Potsdam left the street names as they were. This ought to have been a warning sign for the citizens who had been robbed of their rights and had had their property expropriated. Their hopes for the return of the property or any kind of compensation went unfulfilled for many years, even after the disintegration of the GDR. Initially, between 1990 and 1996 a strange interregnum took hold at the lakeside: the Federal Republic paid their ownership of the villas barely any heed. The remaining occupants who had been

"... in line with the political views ..."

"Life on our street was very quiet. Its name changed depending on the political views of the city administration, from Luisenstrasse during the monarchy, to Ludwig-Troost-Strasse under the National Socialists after Hitler's favourite architect and today, in keeping with the communist iconoclasm, it bears the boring name Ringstrasse."

Joachim von Stülpnagel, 75 Jahre meines Lebens. Private publication, Oberauerdorf am Inn 1955, p. 318.

Views of Griebnitzsee, 2018

loyal to the state were happy at the low rents and soon took this to be the norm. While the Bundeswehr took down some of the border fortifications, the city of Potsdam insisted that the concrete patrol route be left intact, since they already had plans to build a public walkway along the lakeshore.

At the same time, the previous owners, irrespective of whether or not they had been the victims of "racial persecution", were fighting for ownership of this valuable real estate against the winners of the Aryanisation process of the 1930s, as well as against claimants who, in the dying days of the GDR, had used their proximity to the regime to cheaply acquire properties or conclude long-term leases at rock-bottom prices. The courts, which had intentionally been poorly appointed under the regional government led by Manfred Stolpe, were completely overwhelmed, resulting in delays to restitution cases that lasted for years. Many Jewish claimants turned their backs in disgust and sought purchasers for their claims. Only very slowly were the villas returned to their rightful owners. The return of the 'Wall land', which had been used for the construction of the Berlin Wall, took even longer.

At the lakeside in particular, where there had already been two expropriations, by the shore of the Griebnitzsee, the regional capital of Potsdam made two further attempts by means of renewed expropriation to acquire the properties that had only just been returned to their rightful owners for the creation of a lakeshore park and walkway. Twice it submitted its building plans, and twice these were declared invalid by the Higher Administrative Court of Berlin-Brandenburg—first in 2009 and then in 2019.

Today, nearly all of the villas have been restored in line with the various tastes of their new owners. The styles range from an elaborate reconstruction, complete with a Norwegian-style boathouse, to the creation of an apartment complex in what was once the Quandt villa, to the complete gutting and destruction of the original villa or avantgarde new builds. In the majority of cases, the previous relationship between the villa and the garden is barely evident; the boathouses, some of them modern, look like foreign objects. The educational canon of the nineteenth century is nowhere to be seen.

Nowadays, just as it was at the beginning of the 20th century, the narrow, L-shaped Griebnitzsee, which is around three kilometres long, is a tranquil oasis between Berlin and Potsdam. It is a beautiful, if deceptive, idyll. The Goldschmidt family's plot of land by the lakeside was the subject of a protracted legal battle. The city of Potsdam finally wrested it from the Goldschmidt family in 2019. Once again, the Goldschmidts did not receive any compensation.

top left: Meta Lewandowsky, photographer: Anton Sahm, Munich, Vintage, 1920s

centre left: Magda Schneider, photo: Anton Sahm, Munich, Vintage 1920s

bottom left: Hedy Velmy, photo: Anton Sahm, Munich, Vintage 1920s

right: Katharina Stern, known as Katta Sterna after her escape to Sweden, and her sister Maria Stern in costume, photo: Atelier Badekow, January 1, 1928

Ufa Film City and the Kayser Villa

Babelsberg's ascent began when it was connected to the railway network in 1874 and Neubabelsberg station was built. Babelsberg found international fame in the next century, thanks to the film industry established there in 1917 by forward-thinking military leaders and bankers. During the Weimar Republic era, the productions of Universum-Film AG opened up entirely new aesthetic dimensions for film and a number of its actresses became global stars. The National Socialists used the Ufa's films for propaganda purposes and had plans to create a colossal media city. This drew the crème de la crème of Germany's directors, scriptwriters and actors (both male and female) to Babelsberg—many of whom were forced to flee after 1933 while those that remained faced other momentous decisions.

In 1874, the railway station was built to serve the villa settlement under construction at Griebnitzsee, which is why it was named "Neubabelsberg". A wooden pavilion designed by Berlin architects Kyllmann & Heyden, which had been shown to great acclaim as the "German House" at the Vienna World Fair a year prior functioned as the first station building. The pavilion ensured that Emperor Wilhelm I could be provided a befitting welcome when he travelled to his Babelsberg Palace. However, the railway station can also be seen as an expression of the swift industrialisation of Germany, which was met with general approval and enthusiasm, and the planned development of an efficient infrastructure for the German Empire. In 1931, the chief architect of the imperial railway, Günter Lüttich, built the elegant brick building in the modernist style fashionable in the Weimar Republic that still stands today.

 Of all people, it was the Chief of Staff of the German Army, Erich Ludendorff, together with the chairman of the Deutsche Bank, Emil Georg von Stauß, who in December 1917 planned and founded the film production company Universum-Film AG, which later came to be known across the globe as Ufa. They had recognised how cinema could be used to influence political opinion among the population, as exemplified by the Danish Nordisk Films Kompagni in films in neutral foreign countries.[1] When a hostile takeover of the Danes proved too expensive, the general and the banker decided to start their own film company. In addition to Stauß, its

[1] Klaus Kreimeier: Die UFA-Story. Geschichte eines Filmkonzerns, Frankfurt am Main 2002, p. 34. Cf. on the Ufa in general: Friedemann Beyer: Die Gesichter der UFA. Starportraits einer Epoche, Munich 2015 (2nd ed.); Valerie Weinstein: Antisemitism in Film Comedy in Nazi Germany, Indiana University Press (IPS), Illustrated Edition, March 5, 2019.

board members included, among others, the chairman of banking house Jacquier & Securius, Hermann Frenkel, the chairman of Dresdner Bank, Herbert Gutmann, as well as the chairman of Schwarz, Goldschmidt & Co., Jakob Goldschmidt, who built his own villa at Griebnitzsee a short time later. Their goal had been to cultivate the Germans' willingness to fight with their hastily produced films, but they failed to reach the military and financial elite of the empire and the war was lost.

In spite of this, Ufa became the most successful film company in Europe. Directors such as Fritz Lang, Friedrich Murnau and Ernst Lubitsch used the technical possibilities on offer to instigate an artistic revolution. Actresses like Pola Negri and Marlene Dietrich became world stars. In addition, due to the poor economic situation, the harmless, enjoyable entertainment films epitomised by Heinz Rühmann and Hans Albers developed into a successful genre of their own.

left: The first arrival hall of Neubabelsberg train station, postcard, publisher: Max Hochgeladen, Potsdam, around 1915

right: S-Bahn station Neubabelsberg, photographed and published by: Max Hochgeladen, Potsdam, around 1930

"A blonde dream"

Lilian Harvey, born in London in 1906 is *the* face of Ufa-Film. She had barely finished her 'Abitur' in Berlin in 1923 when she landed her first role in Robert Lands film *Der Fluch (The Curse)*. She successfully made the leap from silent movies to sound and first appeared alongside Willy Fritsch in the operetta film adaptation *Die keusche Susanne (Chaste Susanne)*. In 1930, she and Fritsch became the dream couple of German film in the romantic film *Liebeswalzer (The Love Waltz)*. *Der Kongress tanzt (Congress Dances)*, in which she sang evergreen hit *Das gibt's nur einmal (Just Once For All Time)* followed in 1931. Due to her language skills, Harvey also sang and spoke the English and French versions of the film and became an international star as a result. In 1932, Lilian Harvey successfully arranged for her partner, the as-yet unknown Paul Martin, to direct her new film *Ein blonder Traum (A Blonde Dream)*. The film, a banal comedy, became the greatest box office success of the late Weimar era. In addition to Harvey, it's likely that the music of Werner Richard Heymann for 'Schlager' hits *Wir zahlen keine Miete mehr, wir sind im Grünen zu Haus* and *Irgendwo auf der Welt gibt's ein kleines bisschen Glück* perfectly reflected the mood and yearnings of the time.

Lilian Harvey, photographer: Anton Sahm, Munich, Vintage, 1920s

Following a first visit to Hollywood, Lilian Harvey returned to Germany in 1935 and bought the villa in Griebnitzstrasse 5a at the most north-easterly shore of the lake. The last imperial chancellor of the Weimar Republic, Kurt von Schleicher, had been murdered at the neighbouring property just a year earlier. One has to assume that Lilian Harvey knew this but was not concerned by it. Perhaps she was naïve enough following her return from the USA to believe that she would be able to escape the harassment of the National Socialists because she was a global star and, in some respects, a darling of fortune. Her first film after her return to Germany was *Glückskinder (Children of Fortune)*, in which she again starred alongside her dream film partner Willy Fritsch. The film was directed by her partner, Paul Martin. Curt Goetz wrote the screenplay. The film, released in 1936, was a huge box office success. Film expert Karsten Witte attests the comedy a *"crazy harmlessness"*.[2]

[2] Träume Bilder. Bilder Träume. Die Geschichte der Ufa von 1917 bis heute, published by Ufa Film & TV-Produktion GmbH, Berlin 2007, p. 55.

When Harvey invited Jewish friends to her house, the Gestapo was quick to demonstrate the limits of her good fortune. In 1939 the actress decided to leave Germany again and moved to her house in the South of France. In 1942 she fled Vichy and escaped to Hollywood. She never saw her villa in Griebnitzstrasse 5a again; it fell into disrepair and was demolished after the construction of the Wall.

"The woman of my dreams"

For actress Marika Rökk, born in Cairo in 1913, however, proximity to the new regime did not give rise to any moral conflict. She became the mega star of revue film. For the regime, she was a propagandist godsend. Ufa signed her in 1934. Her films bore superficial titles like *Heißes Blut* (*Hot Blood*, 1936) or *Hallo Janine* (1939). She played the lead role in the first German colour film, *Frauen sind doch bessere Diplomaten* (*Woman are better Diplomats*). In *Die Frau meiner Träume* (*The Woman of my Dreams*), first screened in 1944 in a Berlin already devastated by bombing, Rökk sings: "Don't look this way, don't look that way: look only straight ahead / and whatever may come / don't worry about it!"[3] The regime had ordered light-heartedness, and Rökk sang the accompanying melody.

In 1935 Rökk played in *Leichte Kavallerie* (*Light Cavalry*), produced by Alfred Zeisler. Zeisler began his career in 1921 as assistant director to Fritz Lang in classic film *Der müde Tod* (lit. *The Weary Death*, English title *Destiny*). Films like 1932s *Schuss im Morgengrauen* (*A Shot at Dawn*) with Heinz Rühmann made him famous. When Zeisler was forced to leave Germany in 1935 on account of his Jewish roots, Marika Rökk and her husband Georg Jacoby purchased his beautiful villa with the hipped roof in Domstrasse 28, which leads to Griebnitzsee. Zeisler never received any payment or compensation.

After the war, Marika Rökk was able to continue her career at public service broadcaster, the ZDF (*Zweites Deutsches Fernsehen—Second German Television*) free from any accusations or pangs of conscience. After the fall of the Wall, she even blithely applied for the restitution of the property in Domstrasse, contesting the claims of Zeisler's heirs.[4] This time, however, Rökk lost. She died in 2004.

A strong woman

Brigitte Horney, who was born in Berlin in 1911, began her impressive acting career during the Weimar Republic in 1930. Her success meant she could afford to make a film in London in 1936 about the Spanish Civil War, *The House of the Spaniard*, and another, *Secret Lives*, in 1937 about French spy, Claude France.

Neither was ever screened in Germany. She nevertheless returned to Germany to serve the propaganda machine of the 'Third Reich'. In 1943, she played Catherine the Great in *Münchhausen*. It was one of the biggest budget and last films of the Nazi regime.

The role Horney played under the Nazis is ambiguous. While on the one hand she attempted to help the Jewish wife of her acting colleague, Joachim Gottschalk, on the other, she profited from the 'Aryanisation' process, through which she was

Actresses Lilian Harvey, Magda Schneider and Gretl Theimer along with actor and screenplay writer Franz Zimmermann (from left to right) on a boat on Griebnitzsee, photographer: Artur Grimm, around 1930

3 Cf. Ibid., p. 67.

4 Cf. on this: Villenkampf in Babelsberg, in: *Der Spiegel* 4/1996 (https://www.spiegel.de/spiegel/print/d-8870830.html).

able to inexpensively acquire the lovely house at Johann-Strauss-Platz 11 in 1938. It had been built for silk manufacturer Hans Guggenheim in 1921/22 by the most well-known representative of the country house movement, Hermann Muthesius. Guggenheim fled to Switzerland in 1936. He, too, had to fight for the restitution of his house following reunification, first against the heirs of Brigitte Horney, and then against the city of Potsdam, who initially refused to let Hans Guggenheim, by that time an old man, into his house and then failed to protect the house against vandals, who squatted at the property and left it in a terrible state.

left: A popular postcard motif: The Kayser villa, beginning of the twentieth century

right: The Kayser villa, located directly by Griebnitzsee

Goebbels' dream woman

Neither Brigitte Horney nor Marika Rökk and especially not Lilian Harvey fitted the National Socialists' image of women. Officially, they promulgated the blonde wife and mother who obeyed her husband and happily birthed many children. In Magda Goebbels, divorced Quandt, Reich Minister of Propaganda Joseph Goebbels had selected precisely this kind of woman as his official partner. Unofficially, however, the fanatic Nazi, also known as the *"Bock von Babelsberg" (the Babelsberg stud)* had numerous affairs with actresses—his own undersecretary, Karl Hanke, meticulously counted thirty-six names at the behest of Magda Goebbels. He had a particular penchant for foreign beauties. Czech actress Lída Baarová signed with Ufa in 1934, aged twenty, gaining a reputation as a vamp with an exotic charisma through her roles in films such as *Barcarole* (Barcarolle, 1935), *Leutnant Bobby, der Teufelskerl* (Lieutenant Bobby, the Daredevil, 1935 and *Die Stunde der Versuchung* (The Hour of Temptation, 1936).[5] The affair between Goebbels and Baarová lasted two years, until Magda Goebbels and Adolf Hitler himself intervened. Hitler demanded that Goebbels end the relationship and Baarová returned to Prague.[6] Magda Goebbels, who lived at what was at that time the Quandt villa, today Virchowstrasse 1–5, had prevailed over her strongest rival.

5 Kreimeier 2002 (see note 1), p. 288f.

6 Cf. Beyer 2015 (see note 1), p. 28.

top left: Front view of the main building of Griebnitzsee S-Bahn station, 2018

top right: Former 'death strip' at the lakeside of Griebnitzsee on a level with Griebnitzsee train station; soldiers of the National People's Army dismantle the border fence, July 13, 1990

bottom: View of Griebnitzsee station from the lake, at the lakeside with the border fortifications, 1987

Great plans

In 1938, the Reich Minister of Propaganda had great plans to build a film and propaganda city of gargantuan proportions. Neubabelsberg station was renamed Babelsberg-Ufastadt. While the nearest train station, Bahnhof Grunewald, began transporting Jews to the extermination camps in 1941, the *Deutsche Reichsbahn* provided stars of politics, film and trade swift transportation from the Babelsberg-Ufastadt station to Berlin, the capital of the Reich. Goebbels' delusional dreams for the 'film city' were thwarted by the outbreak of the war.

Goebbels' plans included, for example, turning the Kayser villa into a huge brothel to serve Babelsberg's film city. Passengers leaving the railway station in around 1900 would immediately see this neo-renaissance style villa, which architect Heinrich Kayser had built for himself. Like a kind of pattern box, the villa boasted every iteration of the markers of upper-middle-class architecture—a tower, bay windows, a walkway, a loggia and a gatehouse, as well as a stepped gable. It was an enormous advertising installation that won the architect many contracts in Neubabelsberg. Together with his colleague, Karl von Großheim, Kayser built the nearby villa of bookseller Carl Müller-Grote in Karl-Marx-Strasse 2 as well as the Wentzel-Heckmann villa in Virchowstrasse 25. The Kayser villa itself became a popular postcard motif.

However, Goebbels' planned brothel ultimately fell victim to the prudishness of the National Socialists and the war they were waging. Following war damage, the GDR authorities removed the remains of this once proud villa in 1961 to make way for the construction of the Berlin Wall. The site became a restricted area and is now home to a rather plain-looking hotel.

The Stern Villa

There is barely any trace left of the original owner of this villa, Max Stern—his fate is one of the many historical blank spaces left behind by the National Socialists' extermination policy. The life path of another of its residents, however, is well documented: leading chemist Otto Liebknecht, son of Wilhelm Liebknecht and younger brother of Karl Liebknecht, communist member of the Reichstag, was banned from teaching under the Nazis and was monitored by the Gestapo. When the war ended, the tide turned—courted by the Socialist Unity Party of Germany (SED), Liebknecht was allowed to resume his academic teaching activities and was finally appointed a full professor at the Friedrich Wilhelm University in the Soviet-occupied sector of Berlin. However, this bold individual of independent spirit also came into conflict with the new government.

Rudolf-Breitscheid-Strasse 182 (formerly Berliner Strasse)

The villa was built in 1926 for Jewish merchant Max Stern. The original architect of the plans for this two-storey country manor is unknown. The perfectly symmetrical façade facing the street echoes traditional architecture and only the gently sloping hipped roof, which projects slightly, reveals the influence of modern construction methods. The side of the house facing the lake dispenses with the symmetry of the front and a semi-circular projection (an 'avant corps') with a row of tall, narrow windows, protrudes from the cubical main body of the house. It extends from the basement level up to the lower edge of the second floor, where it is topped with a semi-circular terrace.

left: The Stern villa, front façade, 2018

below left: The Stern villa, side view with views of Griebnitzsee, 2018

below right: The Stern villa, garden side with the avant-corps that extends out from the building on the right-hand-side, 2018

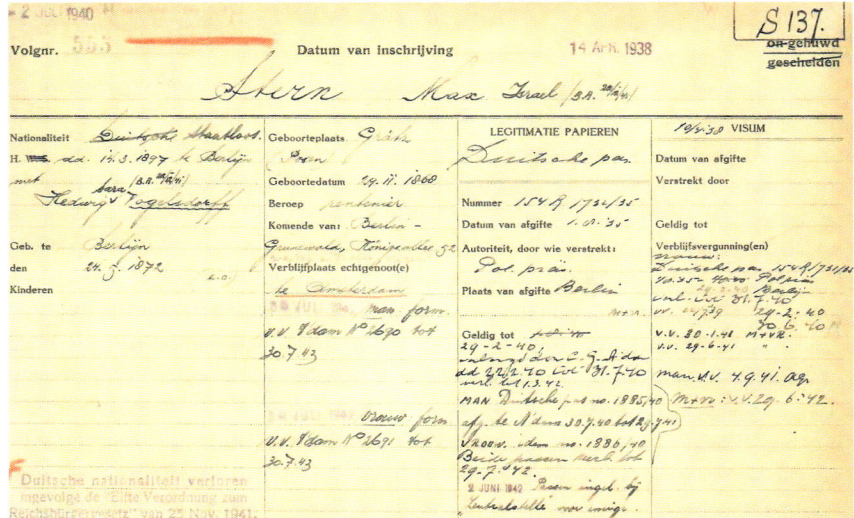

Official index card with personal details of Max "Israel" Stern and his wife Hedwig, created upon his registration on arrival in Amsterdam on April 14, 1938

Disenfranchised, persecuted, murdered

The little information to be found about Max Stern and his wife Hedwig, née Vogelsdorff, stems for the most part from an index card from the Amsterdam City Archives, created in April 1938 and later added to. It states that Max Stern was born on November 29, 1868, in Grätz (today Grodzisk Wielkopolski) in the province of Posen, his wife Hedwig on May 24, 1872 in Berlin. The couple was murdered in Sobibor in 1943.[1]

When Max Stern wrote his will in 1920, he and his wife were still living at Lützowstrasse 107 in Berlin, a genteel residential area that was home to many affluent Jews. There was a synagogue at Lützowstrasse 16, built from red bricks in the neo-Romanesque style, where the congregation met for common prayers according to the liberal rite, accompanied by organ music. The Jewish community centre was on the corner of Potsdamer Strasse, and the Jewish religious school was located at Lützowstrasse 16. The Wertheim family, who owned several large department stores in Berlin and other cities, lived next door to the Sterns, in Lützowstrasse 111; they had set up a synagogue for Sephardic Jews in their flat.

In 1925, Stern bought the property directly next to Griebnitzsee in Babelsberg. Construction work on the house began a year later. The Sterns' happiness at Griebnitzsee was short-lived, however—even before the Nazis seized power, National Socialist publications such as '*Der Stürmer*' had begun agitating against the Jews in Potsdam. After the seizure of power, life in Potsdam quickly became unbearable for the Sterns and they returned to Berlin, to Königsallee 52 in Grunewald. Sadly, their hopes of a more undisturbed life as Jews in the capital, which many considered to be more liberal, did not come to pass.

In 1934 the Sterns, like many German Jews, fled to the Netherlands. However, the National Socialists had already put everything in place to make it increasingly difficult to transfer assets from the German Reich to the foreign countries that provided refuge. The instrument designed to do so was the 'Reich Flight Tax'. The Nazis swiftly amended the rules to make the tax, introduced in the Weimar era during the Great Depression, yet more draconian by lowering the tax-free threshold

1 Cf. LABO Berlin, BEG-Akte Reg.-Nr. 346.131.

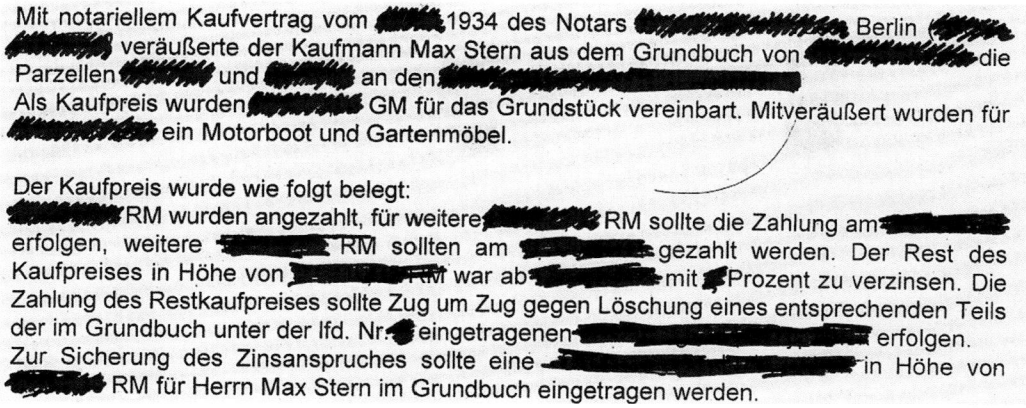

Restitution notice issued by the Regional Capital of Potsdam dated March 31, 1998, sent to the property owner by notice dated April 20, 2020 (excerpt)

and applying the tax in a targeted manner to plunder the assets of emigrating Jews especially. The tax continues to apply today as an 'exit tax', albeit without the anti-Semitic targeting. As recently as 2019, the Federal Ministry for Finance (*Bundesministerium der Finanzen*, BMF), again attempted to further intensify exit taxation with the Anti-Tax Avoidance Directive Implementation Act. The fact that this would undermine economic freedom of movement appeared not to bother the officials at the BMF who, it would seem, have a limited memory for historic events.

Limiting economic movement had been precisely the goal of the Reich Ministry of Finance in 1933. As early as April 8, 1933, the President of the Regional Tax Office of Dresden *"sincerely"* announced that, in addition to the civil service trainee Fritz Friedensohn, the engineer Robert Baruch and the married couple Grobtuch, the merchant Max Stern of Nowawes by Berlin, Berliner Strasse 96, had been apprehended in the night from March 31 to April 1, 1933, in the course of a train inspection en route to Prague and that these persons had been found to be in possession of *"domestic and foreign means of payment"* that exceeded *"the legally permissible maximum amounts for emigration to Czechoslovakia"*.[2] On May 12, 1933, Dresden District Court issued a penalty order against Stern in the amount of 5 Reichsmarks, or one day's imprisonment, and ordered the seizure of the confiscated foreign currency. This marked the failure of Stern's first attempt to save his assets by moving capital abroad.

Max Stern was forced to sell his house considerably below value—as was the norm in such cases—in order to be able to pay the high flight tax. The Jewish Claims Conference, which supports Jewish victims of National Socialism in their efforts to obtain compensation, provided the precise figures: *"Regarding the withdrawal, I can inform you that the purchase contract was dated 15.2.1934 and the purchase price was RM 54,000 with a taxable unit value of RM 90,000."*[3]

Having already been forced to sell their property under value, a series of perfidious mechanisms then prevented the transfer of the sales price and other assets to the Sterns in the Netherlands. First, their bank balance was transferred to frozen emigrant accounts to secure the Reich Flight Tax. Stern had to pay RM 40,000 of his total assets of RM 160,000 in flight tax. In addition to the Flight Tax, there were repeated arbitrary charges, fees and delays to the disbursement. On December 9, 1940, the Moabit Tax Office advised the Department for the Confiscation of

2 BLHA, Rep. 36 A, no. G 2880, p. 23.

3 E-mail from Mr Peter Heuss, Jewish Claims Conference, dated March 18, 2020.

Forfeited Assets (*Dienststelle für die Einziehung verfallener Vermögenswerte*) that, in addition to the Jewish Capital Levy of RM 23,874.95, an overdue payment surcharge of RM 690 and fees of RM 119.86 were also payable. No justification was provided for these sums. Their sole purpose was to seize funds from the emigrants' frozen accounts.

In addition to the legislative and administrative chicanery of the German tax administration, there were plenty of other people who sought to exploit the plight of those who had fled. The Sterns had appointed Berlin auditor Alfred Schulte as trustee. In many letters, Stern, who was running out of funds in Amsterdam, implored Schulte to send money to the Netherlands, but to no avail. It is not clear exactly why Stern had chosen this particular auditor—perhaps he knew him from Galerie Flechtheim. Schulte had already been instructed in 1933 to liquidate the famous gallery at Lützowufer 13, in the course of which all of the valuable paintings and drawings, including many by George Grosz, disappeared. Neither Flechtheim's widow, nor her heirs following her suicide, not to mention George Grosz himself ever received any money. In 1954, Schulte claimed before a Restitution Chamber that there had been only *"a number of objet d'art and old furniture"* left at the Flechtheim's; he made no mention of the paintings.[4]

In a circular dated September 24, 1940, the Reich Security Main Office ordered the seizure of all domestic assets *"in the course of an intended expatriation"*; in a letter of November 19, 1941, the Reichsführer SS notified the Moabit tax office of the execution of the order pertaining to Max Stern.

Following the German Wehrmacht's invasion of the Netherlands in 1940, there was no escape from Amsterdam either. The Sterns had their German citizenship revoked pursuant to the *"Eleventh Ordinance to the Reich Citizenship Act"* of November 25, 1941, as a stamp in the index card kept in the Amsterdam City Archives attests. On June 2, 1942, the two were required to appear at a *"Zentralstelle" (central agency)*, from where they were deported to the extermination camps. Max Stern and his wife Hedwig were declared dead on July 30, 1943. It was Alfred Schulte of all people who enquired to Potsdam District Court in 1948 whether the Sterns had left a will there.[5]

The Stern villa was purchased in 1934 by a Major a. D. Kurt Neumann, who was born on December 20, 1884, on his father's estate in Semerow, West Pomerania. His daughter Jutta, born on September 27, 1914, married Georg Schulze-Büttger, an officer with the General Staff's First Department (Operations) under Major General Henning von Tresckow in 1934. Like von Tresckow, Schulze-Büttger was a member of the resistance and was executed following the failed assassination of Hitler. What little is known about Kurt Neumann includes the fact that he chose death for himself, his wife and his second daughter Sibilla when the Red Army closed in on them in 1945.[6]

Neumann soon resold the land and what had once been the Stern villa by deed of December 14, 1936. The purchaser was chemist Otto Liebknecht. Pursuant to a notice dated April 20, 2020, the City of Potsdam did not wish to provide details of the time of sale, the purchase price and purchaser: *"If the personal information in*

4 145 WGK 1 WGA 2792/50.

5 Letter from Alfred Schulte dated April 16, 1948, to Potsdam District Court, BLHA File Rep. 5 E Local Court (Amtsgericht) Potsdam (no. 4281).

6 Cf. Antje Vollmer: "I knew that I very much wanted to keep living" [translation: author's own], in: *Die Welt*, July 20, 2012.

left: Otto Liebknecht and his wife Elsa. On the front, a handwritten menu, on the back the words: "In memory of the wedding celebrations of their children Elsa and Otto, Charlottenburg, 6.III.1901" [translation: author's own]

right: Otto Liebknecht, around 1920

the restitution file refers to deceased individuals, it is also to be considered personal insofar as the information in question also has a reference to living persons, such as the heirs or family members of the deceased."[7] If one were to follow this line of pseudo-legal gobbledygook reasoning, historical research would no longer be possible. It is clear that, in Potsdam, such research is welcomed only to a limited extent.

A Career fraught with Obstacles

The third of the five sons of Wilhelm Liebknecht, co-founder of the Social Democratic Workers' Party of Germany (*Sozialdemokratische Arbeiterpartei Deutschlands*) and his second wife Natalie, Otto Liebknecht, studied chemistry in Berlin. He was awarded his doctorate in 1899 by Arthur Rosenheim, head of the private institute *Wissenschaftlich-chemisches Laboratorium Berlin N*. It took another year before he found employment commensurate to his training. This was his first experience of his family name standing in the way of his personal advancement. In addition, he was also a member of the SPD, which, though it had no longer been prohibited since 1890, was still seen as a threat to the state by many in the Wilhelmine monarchy.

In July 1900, Liebknecht was given a post in Frankfurt am Main at Degussa (*Deutsche Gold- und Silber-Scheideanstalt*); he began investigating the colouring agent indigo at the research laboratory there. It was in 1904 that he landed a great coup—which also proved highly lucrative for his employer—with the development of a process for the manufacture of sodium perborate, which was used as a bleaching agent in the first self-acting laundry detergent "Persil" (the name was created from the components *Perborate-Silicate*). Henkel launched it on the market in 1907. While Liebknecht was not active in the SPD, he was an enthusiastic advocate of social democratic values in his professional environment: having been promoted in 1905 to the post of head chemist in the research department, he always had an eye on the concerns of the employees; In 1920 he was appointed chairman of the first Works Council at Degussa.[8]

7 Notice issued by the Regional Capital of Potsdam on April 20, 2020, relating to the freedom of information request pursuant to the State of Brandenburg's Act on the Inspection of Files and Access to Information (*Akteneinsichts- und Informationszugangsgesetz*, AIG).

8 Cf. Der streitbare Forscher: Otto Liebknecht, Chemiker, in http://history.evonik.com/de/persoenlichkeiten/liebknecht-otto.

For reasons unknown, Liebknecht had a dispute with the management of Degussa. He left the company in 1925 and went to Berlin, to take on the position of head chemist at Permutit AG, a company that manufactured water treatment systems. From 1931 to 1935, he also held a teaching position at the Friedrich-Wilhelm University in Berlin, which is today the Humboldt University.

Liebknecht moved to Neubabelsberg with his wife Elsa in 1925, to a villa at Domstrasse 10. The villa had been built in 1898 by the architect Emanuel Heimann, who had previously constructed a similar residence for himself at Virchowstrasse 45. The two-storey house in Domstrasse was renovated by its owner at the beginning of the twentieth century to allow easier access to the garden at the rear, which also made the demarcation between house and garden more permeable in line with the ideas of the country house movement. The alterations made by Berlin architect Paul Karchow in 1922 first and foremost served the purpose of returning, in part at least, the original character of the building as a classic villa based on formal symmetry.[9]

"... I seek only to protect the law"

When the National Socialists came to power in January 1933, Otto Liebknecht and his wife Elsa, who was Jewish, became increasingly exposed to mistreatment. He was forced to stop teaching at the university in 1935 and was summoned to the Gestapo headquarters in Albrechtstrasse for interrogation several times. The fact that their son, the architect and committed communist Kurt Liebknecht, had been in the Soviet Union since 1931 made their situation even more perilous. What saved Otto Liebknecht and his wife from worse during this time—alongside his fearless stance—was above all the fact that he was essential to the regime in his capacity as a chemist of outstanding skill. He stayed at Permutit AG until 1939, and from 1943 worked as a freelance scientific adviser to Th. Goldschmidt AG in Essen.

After the end of the war and the fall of the "Third Reich", the situation for Liebknecht and his wife changed fundamentally. That which had previously been a disadvantage was transformed into an advantage: All of a sudden, his membership of a socialist family of the highest reputation made him a respected person—as, of course, did his expert skills as a chemist, which those in the pro-

9 Cf. Villa Liebknecht: Landhausbewegung, Otto Liebknecht und die Perborat-Entwicklung. Potsdam, press release no. 611 of September 7, 2017 (http://www.potsdam.de/611-villa-liebknecht-landhausbewegung-otto-liebknecht-und-die-perborat-entwicklung).

Excerpt from Elsa Liebknecht's diary

"As the Liebknechts were assumed to be Jews, I barely played any role when the Gestapo suddenly came, asking me: Your husband is Jewish, where is he? … Our radio was to be confiscated on account of our being Jewish, they said. Otto, who was anything but cowardly, banged his fist on the table with such force that they [the Gestapo officers—author's note] literally winced. I was afraid something would happen … We were reproached about why Curt was in Russia! Otto replied: Have you always done what your parents wanted you to do? This was the response he had given the Gestapo in Albrechtstrasse. Since I had gone with him, I waited around two hours for Otto. I almost collapsed with fear he had been abducted in one of these grey cars that kept driving past. But finally, he reappeared. It seemed he had won through …"

Passage from Elsa Liebknecht's diary, in: Kurt Liebknecht: Mein bewegtes Leben, Berlin 1986, p. 110. [translation: author's own]

cess of establishing a socialist German state were keen to harness. In spite of this, the initial period in the largely destroyed Berlin was anything but easy. At least he was soon able to teach at the Friedrich-Wilhelms University, which had *"newly opened"* in January 1946. The Soviets avoided using the term *"re-opened"* since this would have meant involving the other   or which he had worked until 1939 had not sided with the National Socialist regime. On the contrary—despite the *"extremely exposed position"*, he had found himself in as the son of Wilhelm Liebknecht and the brother of Karl Liebknecht, the company had *"not only continued to work with me, but also stood in front of me protectively"*. They had done the same for the commercial director, *"who is a recognised victim of fascism"*. He argued that, based on this clear *"antifascist stance"* of the company management, expropriation was not justified.[10]

Liebknecht's courageous defence of his former employer shows how steadfastly he stood by his convictions. This was true regardless of on whose behalf he was fighting for justice at any given time. He confirmed this in an exemplary manner in another letter concerning the "expropriation of Permutit AG":

"The law was abused for twelve years, and justice replaced with despotism. The National Socialist principle that the law is what is useful for the German people, has always been branded by all anti-fascist circles as one of the greatest crimes against the soul of the people … I would not even remotely think of protecting some capitalist …, I seek only to protect the law. I have always done so, even at the risk of being exposed to misinterpretation and even slander."[11]

In 1949, Liebknecht was appointed Professor of Inorganic and Organic Chemistry at the Berliner University, which was renamed Humboldt University not long after. He died the same year after a lengthy and serious illness.

Restitution despite resistance

After 1990, the regional capital of Potsdam initially attempted to delay restitution of the former Stern villa. In response to the inquiry of the Jewish Claims Conference as to what had happened to their request of 1992, the city did not reply until April 1995, citing the enormous number of requests and a catalogue of priorities. One year later, research began in Potsdam. Not until August 1998 did the City of Potsdam announce that the property would be transferred back. One of the reasons the decision took so long was surely that the former GDR customs administration continued to operate their crèche there under new management.

Another reason was that the city councillors had already decided on February 28, 1990, to build a public lakeside walkway on the former border strip. The city councillors gave little thought as to whether the Stern heirs, the Jewish Claims Conference or the heirs of the Liebknechts would agree with this. Nor was this of any interest to the municipal administration of the city of Potsdam, who sought to implement the wishes of the city councillors through a number of cunning tricks. In February 1992, the deputy mayor at the time, Ute Platzeck, first attempted to prohibit the clearance of the property by the Bundeswehr.[12]

Specifically, the lawn grids and the former border patrol road, made of meter-

10 The quotes (translated into English by the present author) are taken from the letter written by Prof. Otto Liebknecht on September 24, 1946, to the Provincial Administration of Mark Brandenburg, Commission for the Sequestration and Seizure of Industrial Assets concerning the expropriation of Permutit AG, Ruhlandwerk Department, Rathenow/Havel, BLHA, Rep. 203 Amt zum Schutze des Volkseigentums, BET 1056; Evonik Industries AG, Konzernarchiv Hanau, biographical documentation Liebknecht, Otto.

11 Letter from Otto Liebknecht to the Provincial Administration of the Mark Brandenburg, F.A.O. Oberregierungsrat Weidenbach, re expropriation of Permutit AG dated October 29, 1946, quoted based on: Birgit Bertsch-Frank: Otto Liebknecht – eine ungewöhnliche Karriere, in: Chemie in unserer Zeit, volume 32, issue 6, December 1998, p. 302–310, here p. 302, 308 [translation: author's own].

12 Letter from the municipal administration of the City of Potsdam, Mrs Ute Platzeck, sent on February 27, 1992.

```
Professor Dr.phil.Dr.ing.E.h.,      Potsdam-Babelsberg, 30. Januar 1947
Otto  L i e b k n e c h t ,         Berlinerstr. 96.
                                    Telefon: Potsdam 5196.
```

An die

R e g i e r u n g der Mark Brandenburg,
Kommission für Sequestierung und
Beschlagnahme von Industrie-Vermögen,
z.Hd. von Herrn Oberregierungsrat W e i d e n b a c h ,

P o t s d a m .
Friedrich Ebertstrasse.

Dr.L./Rü.

Betr: P e r m u t i t Aktiengesellschaft,
      Abteilung Ruhlandwerk, Rathenow (Havel).

Sehr geehrter Herr Weidenbach !

Nachdem die Angelegenheit P e r m u t i t nunmehr ihre Erledigung gefunden hat, möchte ich im Anschluss an mein Schreiben vom 29.Oktober 1946 Ihnen noch folgendes sagen, wozu mir die Verhandlung nicht der richtige Ort zu sein schien.

Ich habe für mein Eintreten keinerlei irgendwie geartete finanzielle oder sonstige Vorteile gehabt, sondern habe vollständig ehrenamtlich, wenn der Ausdruck gestattet ist, gehandelt, um zu vermeiden, dass ein Beschluss gefasst wird, der den tatsächlichen Verhältnissen nicht gerecht wird. Auch für die Zukunft sind mir keinerlei irgendwie geartete Versprechungen gemacht oder in Aussicht gestellt worden. +

Ich wäre Ihnen dankbar, wenn Sie hiervon auch die Kommissions-Mitglieder in Kenntnis setzen würden und den Durchschlag dieses Briefes Herrn Minister R a u , der ja auch Abschrift meines Schreibens vom 29.Oktober erhalten hatte, mit meinen besten Empfehlungen übergeben würden.

Allerdings hat die Sache doch einen Vorteil für mich gehabt, als sie die Veranlassung war, dass ich Sie kennen lernte und einen Begriff von Ihrer unermüdlichen objektiven Arbeit erhielt. Ich würde mich freuen, wenn wir uns wieder einmal sehen würden.

Ich begrüsse Sie mit meinen besten Empfehlungen als

+ nicht einmal meine   I h r
  Auslagen liess ich
  mir erstatten.

Letter from Otto Liebknecht to the senior civil servant Weidenbach, January 30, 1947. In the letter, Liebknecht assures that he did not receive "any financial or other benefits whatsoever" in return for speaking up in support of Permutit AG.

The Stern villa (centre) from the lakeside, with the border strip at the lakeshore, around 1966

thick perforated concrete slabs, were to be left on the properties. She was advised by the Bundeswehr that the border fortifications not only posed considerable risk, but that such installations, be it border patrol road, wall or vehicle barrier ditches, could be left on the properties only if the owners of the property consented to this.[13] *"The other owners/legal entities received the prepared declarations of consent and release from the municipal administration for signature. Unfortunately, we have not received any response"*,[14] Ms Platzeck swiftly responded. None of the current owners and none of the former owners received any such declaration. Nevertheless, in 1996, the Federal Republic of Germany ceded the riverbank properties that had once belonged to Max Stern to the Potsdam municipal authorities under a usage agreement.

In 2003, the Jewish Claims Conference sold the property, including the villa, to the present owners, who are very committed to remembering the fate of Max and Hedwig Stern and commemorating them. Only in 2009, following numerous embittered legal disputes were the owners able to take full possession of the lakeside properties. Today, a small, park-like garden again leads from the villa directly down to Griebnitzsee.

[13] Letter from the Military District Administrative Office VII of May 27, 1992, File ref. IV B 2 – File Ref. 45-10-00.

[14] Letter from the municipal administration of the City of Potsdam, Ms Ute Platzeck, to the Military District Administrative Office VII dated June 19, 1992.

The Truman Villa

Although US President Harry S. Truman actually only stayed here for around two-and-a-half weeks in the summer of 1945, this house is still widely known as the "Truman Villa". In fact, it had been owned for more than fifty years by a successful publishing family who supplied literary works to a wide readership. In terms of publicity, however, the publishing of fine literature is not nearly as impressive as the events that are said to have taken place in the "Little White House" at Griebnitzsee in July 1945. It was from this villa, so the reports go, that the President of the USA gave the order for the atomic bombs to be dropped on the Japanese cities of Hiroshima and Nagasaki. There is not, however, any direct evidence of this.

Karl-Marx-Strasse 2 (before 1938: Kaiserstrasse, after 1938: Strasse der SA)

Books for an audience with an appetite for education

In 1865, Carl Müller-Grote, who came from an old-established publishing family, relocated to Berlin from Hamm in Westphalia together with his G. Grotesche Verlagsbuchhandlung. Thanks to shrewd decisions as to which works to publish, he succeeded in just a few short years in firmly establishing the publishing house as a commercial success. Müller-Grote had—to put it into today's terms—a clear idea of his target audience, namely the gradually emerging bourgeoisie who were coming to appreciate the value of education. Müller-Grote landed his first major

The Truman villa, garden side, 2018

coup with the affordable illustrated classical volumes published from 1868, which included works almost exclusively by German authors (Goethe, Schiller, Lessing, Körner, Chamisso, Hebel, Hauff, Bürger) and thus, also satisfied the demand for a strengthening of the national consciousness. In 1875, he launched another series featuring works by contemporary writers, some of whom, such as Theodor Fontane and Wilhelm Raabe, for instance, are still counted among the greats of German literature today, though most have long since been forgotten. It was precisely these authors who achieved gigantic sales successes in some instances. The old-fashioned novels and epic poems of Quedlinburg poet Julius Wolff, for example, had total sales of 570,000 copies.[1]

Müller-Grote soon expanded the publishing programme to include schoolbooks and works on history and history of art. These included magnificent large-format collections, for example those showing works from the royal art gallery or Albrecht Dürer's drawings. One especially ambitious project was *Allgemeine Geschichte in Einzeldarstellungen (General History in Individual Depictions)*, edited by Wilhelm Oncken, Professor of History at the University of Gießen. The first volume was published in 1878; by 1892, a total of forty-four volumes had been published. This monumental publishing venture was, as the editor and publisher saw it, spurred on by the Zeitgeist of the time; it *"sprung from the fresh stream of the new, powerful intellectual life that was beginning to emerge across the most diverse fields during the first years after the establishment of the new empire"*, as the epilogue of the last volume puts it.[2]

A prime example of architectural historicism

Müller-Grote's decision to build a prestigious summer house at Griebnitzsee was also a very of-the-minute move. The villa colony that was being established also owed its existence to the founding of the new empire, or to be more precise: *"the fresh stream"* of money flowing into Germany in the form of reparations payments from the defeated France, which made the *"Gründerzeit"* (the period of rapid industrial expansion in Germany) possible in the first place. In view of the favourable prospects, the two government architects Hermann Ende and Wilhelm Böckmann, who ran a joint architectural office in Berlin, had immediately taken the initiative and, as early as 1871, had purchased land directly next to the lake, Griebnitzsee, in order to build grand villas there for wealthy citizens of Berlin and Potsdam.

The plans for the Müller-Grote family villa were drawn up by the architects Heinrich Kayser and Karl von Großheim, and it was built in 1891 and 1892. The two-storey "Erlenkamp House", as it was referred to by its owner, is a typical example of architectural historicism, which imitates the building styles of previous epochs—in this case primarily the German renaissance—and, in some instances, positively luxuriates in the use of different construction elements. The façades of Haus Erlenkamp, too, feature various structures and sculptural forms, with red sandstone cornice bands on the horizontal plane, and three imposing avant-corps on the vertical: a central one on the façade facing the street and one on each side on the short ends of the building. All three avant-corps have their own gables and

1 Cf. the details provided in the article on Gustav Grote in: Rudolf Schmidt: Deutsche Buchhändler. Deutsche Buchdrucker, book 2, Berlin/Eberswalde 1903, p. 338–342 (http://www.zeno.org/Schmidt-1902/A/Grote,+Gustav).

2 Quoted based on ibid.

roofs, while the roofs on the sides of the building are half-hipped, and the avant-corps on the side facing the street is finished with a half barrel vault roof. There are also dormers recessed into the roof on either side.

The side facing the lake features a number of other elements from the architectural repertoire: two false gables located on either side dominate the façade. Between them, at the centre, a small tower with three windows rises up from the roof, above which there are two shed dormers. At ground level, a wide loggia with red sandstone pillars leads into the park-like garden, allowing the eye, looking onto the lake, to recover from the exuberant diversity of shapes present in the villa.

left: The "Erlenkamp House", later referred to as the "Müller-Grote villa" and today known as the "Truman villa", garden side 1895

right: The Müller-Grote family

Providence gifts the people a leader

Following the death of Carl Müller-Grote in November of 1904, his son Gustav moved to the summer house at Griebnitzsee with his wife Friederike, their six daughters and two sons. One of their daughters, Gabriele, married the son of the architect and designer Peter Behrens, who from 1907 had his office and atelier in the villa of former Imperial Court Sculptor, Erdmann Encke in Steinstücken and often visited the Müller-Grote family at the nearby Haus Erlenkamp.[3] Gustav and Friederike Müller-Grote kept an open house—among the many people from the publishing industry, the art and literature scenes, who often and gladly visited the noble villa at Griebnitzsee was the art historian, museum director and cultural policy maker Edwin Redslob, who as representative of the Reich Ministry of the Interior in the Weimar Republic had been in charge of all administrative issues relating to art, as so-called *"Reichskunstwart"* (Imperial Art Protector). In March of 1933, Redslob was forcibly retired by the Nazis but participated in the reconstruction of cultural life in various capacities after the war ended. Together with two journalists and a paper merchant he founded daily newspaper *Der Tagesspiegel* and was appointed Rector of the Free University of Berlin in 1949 and 1950.

Gustav Müller-Grote had joined the publishing company as a partner on May 11, 1896, and successfully continued the business. The lavishly designed art volumes with their outstanding print quality, for example, were held in high esteem by the readership. However, unlike his father, things didn't always go well for Gustav and

3 Cf. Jörg Limberg: Potsdam. Die Villen- und Landhauskolonie Neubabelsberg, in: Brandenburgische Denkmalpflege, year 2, Berlin 1993, issue 1, p. 44.

there were challenging times. In a speech marking his father's hundredth birthday on October 31, 1933, he complained that his generation experienced countless failures and disappointments, and had suffered through many disasters and catastrophes, though the tide was now changing. *"But now we are experiencing it, hoping and longing that Providence remembers us again in our deep depression and has gifted us a man, a leader of the people, whom we can trust to guide Germany upwards once again."*[4] While the trust Müller-Grote placed in this *"leader of the people"* appeared not to be so great that he would join the NSDAP, it can be assumed that he was not entirely opposed to National Socialist ideology, given that his publishing house had offered an intellectual home to writers such as Gustav Frenssen, who had already revealed his anti-Semitic and racist tendencies at the beginning of the century in his highly successful novels and writings and later became an enthusiastic supporter of Hitler.

Having abandoned his studies in history, art history and history of literature, Hans-Dietrich Müller-Grote, the publisher's son, joined his father's publishing house as a trainee in 1932 and became a partner in 1935. He did not hesitate to declare his support for National Socialism. As a service report reveals, he had already joined the SS ("*Schutzstaffel*", the protective echelon of the NSDAP) in October 1933. The report attests that his National Socialist convictions were *"firm"* and that he performed his *"SS service with great enthusiasm and love"*.[5] However, he only made it to the rank of *"Rottenführer"* (Corporal of the Waffen SS), a crew rank, while his brother Gottfried became an officer and fought against the Spanish Republic as a lieutenant in the air force and squadron leader in the Condor Legion from 1936 onwards.

Throughout the period of National Socialist rule, the publishing family was able to enjoy their private life largely undisturbed. On June 1, 1935, Hans-Dietrich Müller-Grote married Ursula Kolck, the daughter of a Potsdam lawyer. The wedding celebrations were suitably extravagant, and the many illustrious guests included some from the neighbourhood, like the family of industrial magnate Günther Quandt, whose second wife married Reich Minister of Propaganda and Public Enlightenment, Joseph Goebbels, after her divorce from Quandt. By that time, some other residents of the villa district, first and foremost its Jewish residents, had long since been forced from their homes.

Favourable "service report" for SS-Rottenführer Hans-Dietrich Müller-Grote, March 29, 1935

4   Quote [translated by the author] based on Robert S. Mackay: This Mr. President is the story of the little White House ...: Das Truman-Haus in Potsdam 1892–2002, published by the Friedrich-Naumann-Stiftung, Berlin 2002, p. 23.

5   See service report for SS-Rf. Müller-Grote dated March 29, 1935, Bundesarchiv, Bestandsignatur: VBS 1013 (NS 34), archive shelf number: ZB 0199 A.04 (image shown above).

The beautiful setting, intended to obscure the all-too-clear view of such ugly events and preserve as much light-heartedness as possible in social life, remained intact for some time. A photograph published in 1937 in the illustrated fashion magazine *Die Dame* shows Ursula Müller-Grote, née Kolck, in relaxed, jovial mood, wearing *"a summery evening dress"*. The shadow of the guitar player on the wall is a precisely considered counterpart to the woman in the foreground, who appears all the more radiant as a result. However, this cheerful exterior concealed the darker reality. In the same year, 1937, Ullstein Verlag, which had been "Aryanised" three years earlier, and which published the magazine *Die Dame*, was renamed *Deutscher Verlag* and integrated into Franz Eher Verlag, the central publishing house of the NSDAP. At this point at the latest there was no longer much scope for the culturally discerning, free-spirited stance that had characterised the magazine during the Weimar Republic. Imre von Santho, the much sought-after Hungarian photographer who took the picture of Ursula Müller-Grote is likely to have left Germany and settled in Vienna in 1933, when Hitler was named Reichskanzler. Since several of the photographs he took in Berlin are dated in the late 1930s, it can be assumed that he returned to Berlin at several points in between; perhaps Magda Goebbels, with whom he had been friends, provided assistance.

When the war ended, the Müller-Grotes shared a similar fate to many of the other villa owners at Griebnitzsee. Their house was plundered, the furnishings partially destroyed. At the beginning of June, selected villas were seized as accommodation for the delegations of the victors—the USA, the Soviet Union and Great Britain, who from mid-July to the beginning of August would be negotiating at the Potsdam Conference to decide how to deal with Germany in future. The Müller-Grote family villa was to be home to US President Harry S. Truman and his closest staff. Like the other families in the neighbourhood, the Müller-Grotes were given only a few hours to leave their home. *"For a number of days"* as the seizure notice often stated, though barely any of the residents ever returned to their homes.

The "Little White House" at Griebnitzsee

Harry S. Truman was less than enthusiastic about the prospect of travelling across the Atlantic to the conference in Potsdam. *"How I hate this trip"*, he confided in his diary.[6] The sights he was met with in Europe and in particular in the devastated Berlin left him deeply shaken. By contrast, the villa district in Neubabelsberg, where he took up accommodation in the house of the Müller-Grote family, was a tranquil idyll.

However, here, too, there were unusual circumstances to cope with. The villa had been stripped bare by the Soviet occupying forces, *"not even a tin spoon left"*.[7] The American Commander had subsequently succeeded in gathering together enough items of furniture that had been stolen from various houses as to be able to furnish the rooms that were in use. *"Nothing matches"*, Truman complained. It was comfortable enough, but *"what a nightmare it would give an interior decorator"*.[8] This was a true luxury of a problem, however, given the conditions under which the majority

Hans-Dietrich Müller-Grote and Ursula Elisabeth Kolck before they were married in June 1935

6 Diary entry, Potsdam July 7, 1945, in: Off the Record. The Private Papers of Harry S. Truman, edited by Robert H. Ferrell, New York 1980, p. 49.

7 Diary entry, Potsdam, July 16, 1945, in: ibid., p. 50.

8 Ibid.

Ursula Müller-Grote, photograph by Imre von Santho, published in *Die Dame,* January 1, 1937

Eviction

Gustav MüllerGrote contacted Truman directly, in broken English, in a letter. The letter never reached the President.

"It was a most bitter sentiment for us to see, while we removed, that our large house was not cleared but really emptied by hundreds of Russian soldiers and that our whole property was loaded on trucks and driven away, we did not know where. There were furnitures of considerable worth, paintings, sculptures, antiques, drapes and linens perhaps lost forever, while all carpets, curtains, linen, silver had already been taken away by the troop. Could you, Mr. Truman, help me to get back my house after the depart of the High Commission? So that I am not forced to leave it perhaps again … ?"

Letter from Gustav Müller-Grote to Harry S. Truman, quoted based on: Steffi Pyanoe: Trumans "kleines Weißes Haus", in: Potsdamer Neueste Nachrichten of July 18, 2015, (https://www.pnn.de/potsdam/70jahrepotsdamerkonferenztrumanskleinesweisseshaus/21495528.html

above left: Living area in the "Little White House", the residence of US President Truman during the Potsdam Conference, June 12, 1945

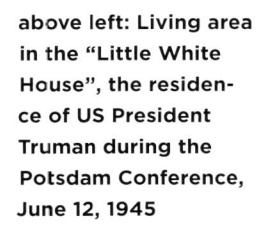

above right: Piano room in the "Little White House", July 13, 1945

below left: President Truman's bedroom in the "Little White House". The bed is made with G.I. bed-linen, July 13, 1945

below right: Dining room of the Müller-Grote villa, 1891/1920

of people were struggling to survive at that time, and also in view of the other problems that the US President had to deal with.

After all, the issue was not only to agree with the Allied Forces, the Soviet Union and Great Britain as to how to manage and rebuild Germany; the Soviet Union's colossal reparations claims against Germany were not yet off the table, the question of the future order of Europe was still unresolved, and a common organisational concept for the planned "United Nations" was yet to be agreed upon. Above all, however, the war was not over for the USA and American troops were still fighting the Japanese in the Pacific. As a result, Truman was not able to give the negotiations his full attention.

Moreover, Truman had only been President of the United States for a brief time—his predecessor Franklin D. Roosevelt had died suddenly on April 12, 1945, and Truman, as Vice-President had had to take over all official duties. He did not have much experience in international negotiations and was said to be correspondingly nervous when the conference began at Cecilienhof Palace.[9] His main goal, as he had himself stated, was to win the Soviet Union as an ally in the fight against Japan and to obtain from Stalin a renewed personal commitment that Russia would join the war against Japan.[10] Truman was therefore at pains to build a good, even trusting, relationship with Stalin.

Invitations to lunch or a celebratory dinner and a friendly gesture here and there were intended to help achieve this. During a luncheon on July 17 at the Müller-Grote villa, Stalin praised the wines that had been served. Two days later,

9 Cf. Philipp Gassert: Im Schatten von Jalta und Hiroshima: Potsdam 1945 aus Sicht der USA, in: Potsdamer Konferenz 1945. Die Neuordnung der Welt, published for Generaldirektion der Stiftung Preußische Schlösser und Gärten Berlin-Brandenburg by Jürgen Luh with the assistance of Truc Vu Minh and Jessica Korschanowski, n.p., n.d. [Dresden 2020], p. 36–61, here p. 49f.

10 Harry S. Truman: Memoirs by Harry S. Truman. Year of Decisions, 1945, New York 1955, p. 454.

left: A patrol boat on Griebnitzsee opposite the "Little White House", July 13, 1945

right: Relaxing by the lake: Sir Charles Portal, chief of the British air staff (front) and Henry H. Arnold, General of the US Air Force fishing in Griebnitzsee, July 1945

twelve bottles of 1937 Niersteiner—a top vintage that is still rated today—, twelve bottles of Port and six bottles of Moselle wine were delivered to Stalin at the Herpich villa with best regards from the American president.[11]

On the evening of July 19, Truman hosted a State Dinner at the "Little White House" attended by Stalin and Churchill together with the highest-ranking members of their delegations. The menu was meticulously recorded: *"pâté de foie gras, caviar on toast, vodka, cream of tomato soup, celery, olives, perch saute meuniere, chilled Rhine wine (Niersteiner 1937), filet mignon, mushroom gravy, shoestring potatoes, peas, carrots, Bordeaux wine (Mouton d'Armailhacq), lettuce and tomato salad, French dressing, Rocca cheese, vanilla ice cream, chocolate sauce, champagne (Pommery 1934), demi-tasse, cigars, cigarettes, port wine, cognac, and vodka."*[12] According to the log, the celery, lettuce, tomatoes and ice cream had been flown in especially for the dinner from the *"USS Augusta"*, a heavy cruiser anchored at Antwerp.

The American hosts' musical programme went down particularly well. Generalissimo Stalin was so impressed by the Tchaikovsky piece that he stood up from the dinner table, walked over to the pianist, shook his hand, and drank a toast to him. President Truman himself took part in the musical programme and sat down at the piano to play Beethoven's Minuet in G. It is doubtful whether these trust-building measures in a relaxed atmosphere did, in fact, succeed in influencing Stalin's political plans in any way. While the Soviet Union did, in fact, declare war on Japan on August 8, 1945, just a few days after the Potsdam Conference had ended, this had already been held out in prospect at the Yalta Conference and linked with Russia's territorial claims (South Sakhalin, Kuril Islands).

In any case, at this point in time, on August 8, something else had already occurred that, on the one hand, made Japan's surrender inevitable and, on the other hand, was to have enormous military and political consequences for years to come, as Stalin was well aware. The USA had dropped an atomic bomb on the Japanese city of Hiroshima and another hit Nagasaki a few days later. The day before the Potsdam Conference was due to begin, Truman had received news that the first atomic bomb had been detonated at the atomic testing site in Alamogordo, New Mexico; the USA were now in possession of the most dangerous weapon in human history—and they were prepared to use it.

11 Cf. Log of the President's trip to the Berlin Conference (July 6, 1945 to August 7, 1945), written and compiled by Lieutenant William M. Rigdon, U.S.N., https://studylib.net/doc/8414894/log-of-the-president-s-trip-to-the-berlin-conference, p. 29.

12 Ibid.

In Potsdam, Truman first told Churchill that the USA was in possession of the atomic bomb. He spoke with Stalin about it a few days later. Stalin, whose spies had more than likely already advised him of this, did not betray how alarmed he was in the light of this development. However, he then ordered that the Soviet's research into nuclear weapons, which had been underway for some time, be pursued more forcefully.

Whether, as has often been written, the specific order to deploy the atomic bomb was, in fact, issued at the "Little White House" by Griebnitzsee, or not until Truman's journey back to the USA remains unknown. Harry S. Truman, Winston Churchill and Chinese president, Chiang Kai-shek, called for the unconditional surrender of the Empire of Japan in the Potsdam Declaration of July 26. Overestimating their options entirely, the Japanese refused. On July 31, 1945, President Truman approved a press release with a notice that read: *"Suggestions approved. Release when ready, but no sooner than August 2, HST."*[13]

This handwritten note, which refers to a press release has—erroneously—been understood to be confirmation of the approval of the bombing. On August 2, the president left Potsdam at 8:00 a.m. and headed for the war ship "Augusta" to take him back to the USA. It is more likely that the president issued the command from there, beyond the reach of Potsdam, which was under Russian control. The first bomb exploded over Hiroshima on August 6, the second over Nagasaki on August 9. When and where the president issued the command is unknown and no document that would confirm this has been found to date. In light of the catastrophic consequences for the civilian population in Hiroshima and Nagasaki, it is also possible that the president falsified his records after the event in order to obfuscate his accountability.

While such a macabre version of events may help to boost the present-day attractiveness of the Truman villa for tourists, the issue is ultimately of little import. What is certain is that the decision was taken during the Potsdam Conference to force Japan to surrender swiftly with the aid of the bomb. On July 25, Truman wrote: *"The weapon is to be used against Japan between now and August 10th."*[14] The pre-

The first meeting between Joseph Stalin and Harry S. Truman at the "Little White House", the residence of President Truman during the Potsdam Conference. From left to right: Vyacheslav Molotov, Soviet Foreign Minister; Secretary of State James Byrnes; Charles Bohlen, interpreter for President Truman; Harry S. Truman; Admiral William Leahy; W.N. Pavlov, interpreter for General Secretary Stalin (partially obscured); Joseph Stalin, July 17, 1945

13 Approval by Harry S. Truman of a press release, George M. Elsey Papers. Truman Library-US Army, quoted based on: Mackay 2002) see note 4), p. 50

14 Diary entry, Potsdam, July 25, 1945, in: Off the record 1980 (see note 6), p. 55f.

cise date had not yet been decided, and the location was also still under discussion; the suggestion to bomb the ancient imperial city of Kyoto was rejected as they did not want to destroy this location, so steeped in history and of supreme importance for Japanese identity. *"The target will be a purely military one"*, notes Truman on July 25[15]—it is common knowledge that this is not what came to pass.

In retrospect, Truman revised his opinion of Stalin and conceded that he had probably been somewhat naïve and gullible during the conference in Potsdam. Although it had been possible to reach some agreements under adverse conditions, these had been immediately broken, *"as soon as the unscrupulous Russian dictator returned to Moscow!"*. With obvious regret, Truman adds: *"and I liked that little son of a bitch."*[16]

Governmental machinations

When the Potsdam Conference ended, it was not the Müller-Grote family who returned to the house; the new man of the house was Georgy Zhukov, Commander-in-Chief of the Soviet occupying forces in Germany. It was he who had signed the Instrument of Surrender of the German Wehrmacht in Berlin Karlshorst on May 9, 1945. When he was recalled from his post in March 1946 and ordered back to Moscow, Soviet authorities impounded copious quantities of furniture, carpets and other valuable objects that had been looted in Germany, which Zhukov had wanted to take back with him to his home country in seven rail carriages.

Meanwhile, Gustav Müller-Grote sought permission to reopen his publishing company in the US-occupied zone in Berlin. As the American authorities correctly assumed that the 79-year-old was, in fact, applying on behalf of his son, Hans-Dietrich, former SS Rottenführer, he was refused a licence. Gustav Müller-Grote died in 1949. The same year, his daughter Lore was finally successful in her efforts and was granted a licence. Describing the publishing house, she had pointed out that its program was *"non-political"* and *"tolerant"*, and that the *"Catholic authors based in Southern Germany and Switzerland [...] had gladly entrusted their books to the care of the publishing house"* and that they had many Jewish authors *"in particular in the area of the arts"*, *"who had been on very friendly terms with the owner, Dr. Gustav Müller-Grote"*.[17] From 1949, the publishing house was again headquartered in Hamm, Westphalia, where it had originally been established. Hans-Dietrich Müller-Grote was also a co-owner.

The GDR authorities made the family's villa available to public institutions. It housed the SED Party School and a Polytechnic Secondary School from 1961 to 1974. For a brief time, it was also used for furniture storage. The fate of the property is also a perfect example of the kinds of measures employed by the administrative bodies in the GDR to override legitimate legal ownership while maintaining the appearance of legality.

Citing Section 6 of the *Verordnung zur Sicherung von Vermögenswerten* (Decree on the Securing of Assets) of July 17, 1952, the Müller-Grotes property was placed under *"provisional administration"*, as entered in the Land Register. The municipal housing

15 Ibid., p. 56.

16 Diary entry, March 15, 1957, in: ibid., p. 349.

17 Typewritten, undated letter, hand-signed by Lore Müller-Grote, Bundesarchiv, Bestandssignatur: R/9361/V, archive shelf number: 148193.

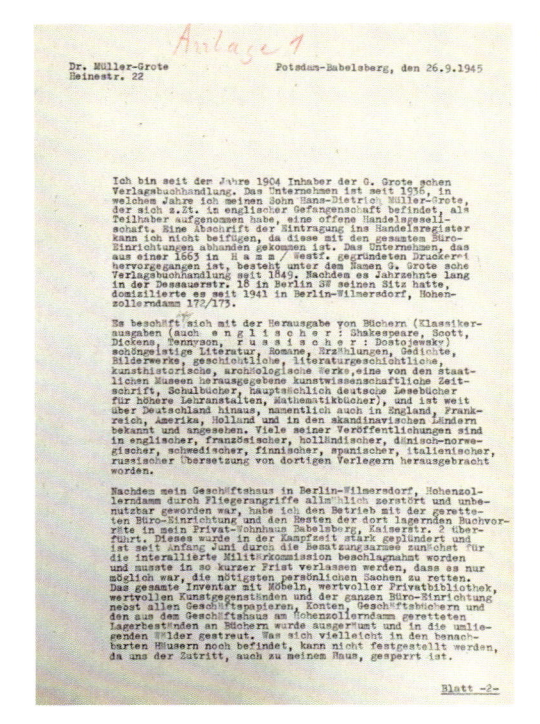

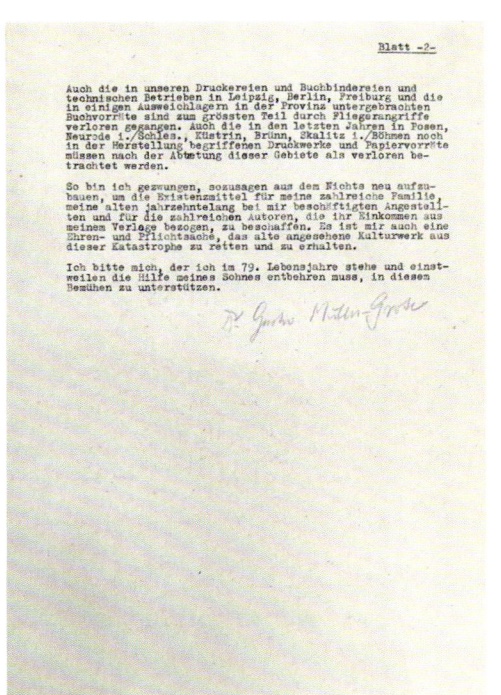

authority and the Council of the City of Potsdam concluded a property purchase agreement on July 12, 1962, which provided that a strip of land with an area of 1,632 sqm, located directly by Griebnitzsee, on the property at Karl-Marx-Strasse 2, was being *"claimed"* in accordance with the provisions of the *Verteidigungsgesetz* (Law on the Defence of the German Democratic Republic) for the purposes of the construction of the Wall and with effect from August 13, 1961, would be transferred to public ownership. The appointed legal owner was Potsdam City Council.

One expropriation followed the next: On September 25, 1965, an additional area measuring 1,792 sqm was "claimed" and passed to public ownership. Again, Potsdam City Council was appointed as the legal owner. On December 1, 1983, the remaining property was transferred to public ownership pursuant to Section 14

Gustav Müller Grote's application for recovery of his publishing licence, September 26, 1945

Changing street names

Street names are also a reflection of the time at which they are decided. This was especially evident in the villa district by Griebnitzsee. The prestigious avenue that led from the railway station Neu Babelsberg to Babelsberg Park and the palace erected for German Emperor, Wilhelm I, was originally called Kaiserstrasse. By renaming the avenue "Strasse der SA" in around 1938, the National Socialists made it amply clear that a new era had begun, in which a different, harsher, tone would prevail. It is logical that people wanted to change that name when the "thousand-year empire" had ended. Following the end of World War II, the powers in charge then lodged their claim to make clear which path history would be taking from that point on: the municipal authorities of the City of Potsdam decided on August 28, 1945 "unanimously, to rename the streets in Potsdam and Babelsberg, that currently have names 1) commemorating National Socialists, 2) in memory of the monarchist period". Ever since, the main street in the residential district at Griebnitzsee has been called Karl-Marx-Strasse. This name was retained even after the end of the GDR.

Quote from: Minutes of the meeting of the municipal administration of August 28, 1945, 3:00 p.m., Potsdam City Archives, Decision of the municipal authority on the naming of KarlMarxStrasse from File A1./0007 (Microfilmno. 146).

Aufbaugesetz (National Reconstruction Act) of September 6, 1950, in conjunction with Section 9 of the *Entschädigungsgesetz* (Compensation Act) of April 25, 1960. This time, the Publicly Owned Enterprise for Building Services (*Volkseigener Betrieb Gebäudewirtschaft*) assumed the legal ownership. According to the files, there was no calculation of a compensation amount or distribution thereof.[18]

After reunification, restitution to the heirs of Müller-Grote was smooth and took place on November 23, 1992. Having been on the market for several years, it was purchased by the Friedrich-Naumann Foundation at the end of 1998. The Foundation is based on the principles of liberalism and in 2007 added the suffix "For Freedom" to its name. The entry into the Truman villa of the employees of the foundation, which has close ties to the FDP, was delayed as a result of fire damage in September 1999. The fire, set by unknown individuals, took place shortly before the extensive renovation work was completed and destroyed almost in their entirety the historic interiors, the staircase and part of the roof. In 2000, a modern office building was built next to the villa.

18 Municipal administration of the City of Potsdam, Office for the Regulation of Unresolved Property Claims, Potsdam, November 23, 1992, Re.: Implementation of the Act on the Settlement of Unresolved Property Claims (VermG), here: Notice pursuant to Section 33 subsection 3 VermG, application dated August 17, 1990, August 27, 1990, and September 11, 1990.

The Herpich Villa

For more than 30 years, the Herpich family, who had made their fortune selling fine furs and elegant ladies' and men's fashion, enjoyed a comfortable life in their genteel villa by the lakeside at Griebnitzsee. Then, at the beginning of 1945, by order of the Soviet officers, they were forced to leave their home within the space of just a few hours—never to return again. The requisitioned property was then made ready for one of the most powerful men in the world: the Secretary General of the Central Committee of the Communist Party of the Soviet Union, Joseph Stalin, who lodged here for around three weeks during the Potsdam Conference.

Karl-Marx-Strasse 27 (before 1938: Kaiserstrasse, after 1938: Strasse der SA)

C. A. Herpich Söhne. Specialist Purveyors of Furs and Fashion

The company grew from humble origins at the centre of Berlin, not far from Alexanderplatz, where C. A. Herpich, founder of the entrepreneurial dynasty, founded a furrier's, a craft atelier where furs are made into garments, in 1835. The workroom was attached to a small shop that sold the finished products. Over the following decades, Herpich successfully established the shop as a permanent fixture in Berlin's commercial sector. With this secure basis, his sons were able to find success beyond the bounds of the Prussian capital: one set up a branch in Leipzig, while another emigrated to New York, where his ready-to-wear fur business was remarkably successful.

The Herpich villa, frontage with main entrance, 2020

The business in Berlin, which was managed by third son, Julius Herpich, profited from the favourable economic situation at the end of the nineteenth century and continued to grow. The business relocated to a spacious new property in Leipziger Strasse and continued to expand the range of this long-established and "distinguished" fur house. In 1910, the founder's grandchildren, Paul and Julius junior, celebrated the company's seventy-fifth anniversary. To mark the occasion, the winter collection 1910–1911 was presented in a brochure described as the *"Anniversary Issue"*. In addition to Berlin, the title page also listed Paris and London as company locations. The brochure comprised thirty-four pages for interested readers featuring images depicting not only all manner of items of clothing made from fur—such as *"fur coats, overcoats and jackets"* for the lady with evocative product names such as *"Geisha"*, *"Medea"* and *"Salome"*—, but also accessories including feather boas, bags, umbrellas, skirt suits, dresses, blouses, dressing gowns and 'jupon' (elegant ankle-length underskirts). The offerings for gentlemen were not quite as extensive and imaginative, though they, too, could rely on Herpich to outfit them with walking, travelling, driving and hunting furs, with suits and dinner suits, with liveries, as well as with hats, braces, ties, jerseys and much more besides—all of outstanding quality, naturally. Those who were so inclined could, of course, avail themselves of the opportunity to purchase *"elegant made-to-measure items produced in our in-house atelier"* all made using *"excellent German and English fabrics"*. C. A. Herpich's grandchildren dressed the high society of Berlin and the surrounding area and, in the meantime, had themselves become a part of those circles.

A Country House designed by the architect responsible for Berlin's underground rail stations

In 1910 and 1911, just in time for the company anniversary, Paul Herpich and his wife Luise ordered the construction of a villa in the upper-class neighbourhood by Griebnitzsee. And they didn't commission just anyone to design their country house—the architect in question was Alfred Grenander, from Sweden. Grenander had worked at the offices of Alfred Messel and Paul Wallot, the architects behind the Reichstag building. Grenander himself had found fame primarily for his design

left: Title page of the winter collection brochure 1910–1911, and the anniversary issue marking 75 years of the furrier's C. A. Herpich Söhne, 1910

centre left: C. A. Herpich Söhne, Berlin, winter brochure 1910/11, p. 29: coats and overcoats for ladies

centre right: C. A. Herpich Söhne, Berlin, winter brochure 1910/11, p. 19: ready-to-wear menswear

right: C. A. Herpich Söhne, Berlin, winter brochure 1910/11, p. 5 (excerpt): style "Tristan", "Elegant, slightly curved. Overcoat with very wide fur trim, 135 cm long."

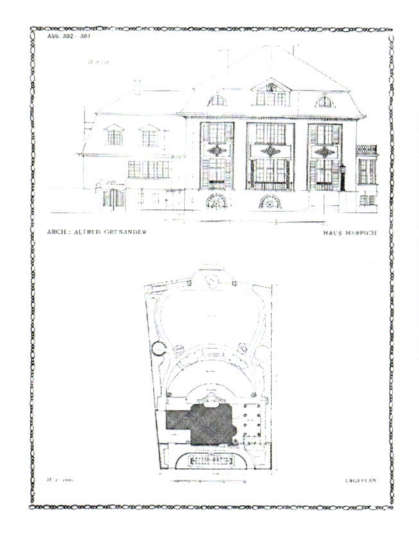

of Berlin's underground and overground railway stations. By the time of his death in 1931, he had designed around seventy train stations. It was also Grenander who invented the colour-coding system for the city's rail network: the various bright colours were intended to help travellers immediately recognise which underground station they had arrived at. He also supplied plans for several residential and country houses, as well as for administrative buildings, factories and bridges. He had presented two interiors at the Louisiana Purchase Exposition in St. Louis in 1904 that caused quite a stir with their clear, straightforward design. In addition, he was also a successful furniture designer. Journalist Robert Breuer wrote of Grenander's designs, with obvious pleasure in his own wording: *"Though the motifs are reminiscent of late German Empire, they have a forged suppleness, a flexibility, a flow of lines that is mathematically perceived."*[1]

The design of the two-storey villa for the Herpich family cannot be reduced to a single concept either; here, various opposing principles interlock in the construction. The refined sense of proportion softens the heaviness of the boldly placed main structure while the richly decorated façades also ensure that the house does not at any point appear bulky.

left: The Herpich villa, cross-section of the front and site plan with garden, 1912

centre: The Herpich villa with park-like gardens and lakeside terrace, date unknown

1 Robert Breuer: Alfred Grenander in: Moderne Bauformen, year 12, issue 6, June 1913, p. 273–295 (quoted based on: http://www.u-bahn-archiv.de/geschichte/bio-grenander-1913-06_mb.html).

"Architectural Civilisation"

"Grenander built country houses, a larger type of single-family dwelling, with particular success. In doing so, he made a significant contribution to the process of architectural civilisation in the greater Berlin region. Anyone familiar with the 'Grunewald masonry workshop' will be aware of the importance of this. The few whose work seeks to combat the tide of mediocrity cannot be praised enough: Muthesius, Paul, Riemerschmied, Taut, William, Müller, Baumgarten. They also include Grenander. One can enjoy an experience both terrible and pleasing in equal parts if one, arriving from Wannsee, takes the steamer across Stolpersee, and then Griebnitzsee towards Potsdam. As far as the architecture is concerned, the lakeshore is almost fatally desolate. Rich people live there; they use their money to erect the most ridiculous monstrosities, veritable hordes of hideousness. Anyone trying to describe it would require a dictionary of the absurd. And into this, Grenander placed the Herpich house, the only decent building for kilometres around."
Robert Breuer: Alfred Grenander, in: Mcderne Bauformen, year 12, issue 6, June 1913, p. 273-295 (quoted based on: http://www.ubahnarchiv.de/geschichte/biogrenander191306_mb.html [translation: author's own].

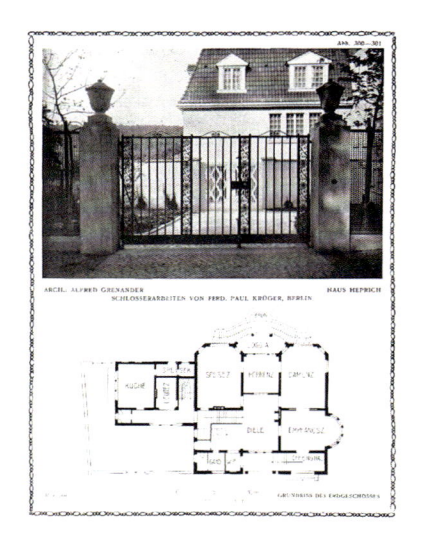

The façade facing the street is broken up by the wide staircase and the large windows with their wooden shutters. A three-window gable dormer and two smaller batwing dormers add further formal accents on the mansard roof. This approach is continued unswervingly on the lakeside façade: sculptural elements like the protruding oriels, the two-winged staircase swinging wide to the sides and the oval balcony supported by four columns, break up the main body of the building. This creates a flowing transition to the garden, which slopes down to the lake. Directly on the shore, a lakeside terrace with surrounding columns once again provides an architectural counterpoint. This is one illustration of how Grenander conceived and composed the house and garden as a cohesive ensemble.

Descriptions of Grenander's construction style always point out that he resolutely turned his back on historicism and its opulent and arbitrary use of ornament; instead, he tailored the design to the purpose and function of the building, which is to say, he developed a functional aesthetic so that the transition *"from artistic craftsmanship to industrial design is evident in his work"*.[2] The term *"functional elegance"*—a descriptive category that perfectly describes the interiors of the Herpich villa, is also sometimes used when referring to Grenander's work. While the rooms were arranged according to the traditional pattern, with a spacious hallway for receiving guests, leading to the parlour and the drawing room, the study and the dining room, all of which enjoyed views of the garden. To the left, a corridor led from the hallway to the single-story annex that housed the kitchen, a pantry and a *"Leutezimmer"*, a room, not much larger than the pantry, for the staff.

One piece of technical equipment that, at the time, was at the cutting edge, demonstrated how a functional aesthetic could be expressed in a highly practical fashion. In the basement, Grenander had built in a vacuum cleaning apparatus that when operated via the connection points on the various levels of the house, created a vacuum. This made it considerably easier to clean the villa.[3]

Progressive and successful

The Herpichs again demonstrated their reliable good taste and awareness of quality when they commissioned architect Erich Mendelsohn to renovate and substantially

left-hand page, right; this page, left and centre: The Herpich villa, photographs of interiors: Billiard room, entrance and hallway, 1912

right: The Herpich villa, entrance gateway and floorplan of the ground floor, 1912

2 Heiko Schützler: Ein meisterlicher Modernist. Der Architekt Alfred Grenander (1863–1931), in: Berlinische Monatsschrift, issue 7-2, 2001, p. 103–113, here p. 113 [translation: author's own]

3 Cf. Nadine Fabian. Ein Besuch in der Stalin-Villa in Potsdam, in: Märkische Allgemeine of August 23, 2017 (www.maz-online.de/Lokales/Potsdam/Ein-Besuch-in-der-Stalin-Villa-in-Potsdam).

enlarge their store, 'Kaufhaus Herpich' in Leipziger Strasse. Mendelsohn was also an important proponent of modernism; his recently completed 'Einstein Tower', the observatory of the Potsdam Astrophysical Institute, had caused quite a stir.

One of Mendelsohn's most challenging tasks when redesigning the department store was creating a uniform façade that also incorporated the two former residential buildings that comprised part of the department store complex. The new shopfront on the ground floor was fully glazed, to ensure that the sales rooms were well lit during the day. At night, the opportunities provided by the electrification of the city were used to illuminate the horizontal bands of travertine under the windows, which marked the floors, and also illuminated the lettering with the company name. Mendelsohn's concept was so unusual, indeed revolutionary, that it was only approved by the construction authorities following a public discussion and with the support of other architects.[4] The Herpichs' entrepreneurial dynasty again set the standard, proving itself both progressive and sophisticated in equal measure: *"a department store by star-architect Erich Mendelsohn, a refrigeration chamber for furs to protect the expensive pieces against pests in the summer, fine plaster from Terranova for the villa in Neubabelsberg … whatever was the latest and most modern—the Herpichs were on board."*[5]

And the Herpichs carried on. They not only survived the difficult years of the Great Depression, but also National Socialist rule. Unlike many of their Jewish competitors, they were not subject to ill will or persecution and their store was spared the Nazi's destructive furore. On October 13, 1930, the day the newly-elected

4   See the relevant details in: Bauen in Berlin 1900–2000, published by Josef Paul Kleihues, Jan Gerd Becker-Schwering and Paul Kahlfeldt, Berlin 2000, p. 108. Cf. also Janos Frecot, Klaus-Jürgen Sembach: Berlin im Licht. Photographien der nächtlichen Stadt, Berlin 2002, with an image of the illuminated façade of the C. A. Herpich Söhne department store in Leipziger Strasse in 1928 (p. 81).

5   Fabian 2017 (see note 3) [translation: author's own].

With fur or without

Dancer Anita Berber, whose performances were always met with rapturous applause, proved at the Hotel Adlon in Berlin in the roaring twenties that a fur coat can not only be worn as an elegant and warm cover-up, but can also be removed to great effect. Actor and cabaret artist Hubert von Meyerinck describes the scene in his memoirs entitled "My famous friends":

"So Berber swept into this opulent dining room where an illustrious group was dining; actually, she didn't so much swish as glide in. She wore a sumptuous mink coat, fastened up to her neck, and gold shoes with very high heels, but no stockings, which was unusual at the time.

She sat down at a table with her companions. Her hair glowed a hellish red over her green-painted mermaid face. 'Waiter,' she called, 'three bottles of champagne, please, Veuve Cliquot!

And that's when it happened. She fiddled at her fur coat … and it fell to the ground. A hushed gasp went around the room—for there she sat—stark naked.

All the guests sat transfixed at their tables. Only the elderly Countess Clothilde, a humorous woman, said to her husband in a very loud voice: 'Am I mistaken, Eberhard, is this lady naked or am I hallucinating? 'You are not wrong, Clothilde, she is naked', he said, and wedged his monocle with a grin.

The management did not rush to intervene, the police were not called, nothing out of the ordinary happened. Only the head waiter came over: very gently, he put the fur around the naked lady and just as gently moved her chair back so that she could stand up. She walked out, followed by the two ephebic young men. A queen of sinfulness …"

Hubert von Meyerinck: Meine berühmten Freundinnen. Erinnerungen, Düsseldorf/Wien 1967 [translation: author's own].

left: The lady stepping aboard a hackney cab wears a travel outfit in lavender-blue jersey with a modern three-button fastening, outfit by: C. A. Herpich Söhne. Photograph by Yva, published in the fashion magazine *Mode-Express,* April 1937

right: On deck aboard the "Bremen Europa": lady in dark-blue pullover with white horizontal stripes (by: Rochlitz) and dark-grey flannel trousers (by: C. A. Herpich Söhne). Photograph by Karl Ludwig Haenchen, January 1, 1939, published in *Die Dame,* 11/1939

Reichstag opened, with the NSDAP as the second-strongest party, Count Harry Kessler described in his diary the demonstrations by *"mass demonstrations by the Nazis": "The destruction in Leipziger Strasse [...] confirm that the mischief was organized. Only businesses with Jewish names suffered. Christian ones (like Herpich, the Porcelain Manufactory, and the Goethe bookshop) were ostentatiously left untouched."*⁶

The business continued to flourish until into the 1940s. National and international trade in furs continued to be the core business, but other areas were added, such as the sale of carpets and rugs from Persia and the Arabic countries at the beginning of the 1920s. The ladies' fashion division was expanded considerably. In this area in particular, advertising was breaking new ground: the models presenting the latest collections were no longer photographed in the studio, but in situations in keeping with the clothing in each case—setting off on a journey or in a relaxed pose on a boat, for example. The photographs then appeared in the appropriate illustrated magazines.

The ongoing commercial success meant the company was able to open a new branch on Tauentzienstrasse in West Berlin in 1937. The tide only turned during the war years with the death of the third generation of the entrepreneurial family. Paul Herpich, who had commissioned the construction of the villa by Griebnitzsee, had already died in 1923. His younger brother Julius died in January 1944. Part of the department store in Leipziger Strasse and the building in Tauentzienstrasse, built just a few years earlier, had been destroyed in 1943 and 1945. Only Luise, the elderly widow of Paul Herpich, was left behind. Immediately after the end of the war, she was forced to vacate her villa in Neubabelsberg from one day to the next to make way for one of the "Big Three" who were preparing to decide on the fate of the defeated Germany in Potsdam.

Comrade Stalin in a bourgeois setting

The meeting of the three victors, the USA, the Soviet Union and Great Britain, took place in Potsdam, at the Hohenzollern Palace, Cecilienhof. Since this area was controlled by the Soviet occupying forces, it was they who decided which of the undamaged houses within easy reach of the conference site was to be made available to the delegations. The spacious Herpich villa was reserved for the Soviet head of

6 Berlin, October 13, 1939. Monday, in: Berlin in Lights: the diaries of Count Harry Kessler, 1918–1937, Grove Press, New York 2000, p. 400.

state, Stalin. At the beginning of July 1945, the head of the Soviet secret services, Lavrentiy Beria, informed Stalin, who was still in Moscow, of the measures that had been implemented thus far: *"62 villas (10,000 sqm) have been prepared and a two-storey detached house for Comrade Stalin, with 15 rooms, an open veranda, attic (400 sqm). The detached building is fully equipped. There is a post and telegraph office. Supplies of game, poultry, culinary and colonial goods, as well as other products and beverages have all been catered for."*[7]

Beria also mentioned the security situation at the Herpich villa and Cecilienhof Palace, to reassure Stalin, who perceived danger everywhere and at all times: *"Seven regiments of NKVD troops [troops of the Ministry of the Interior] and 1,500 members of the operational team are available for guard duty. The guard is organised in three rings. The head of the bodyguards for the detached house is Lieutenant General Vlasik. The guarding of the conference venue will be taken over by Kruglov."*[8]

This arrangement was not without symbolic meaning: of all places, the head of the Communist Party of the USSR was lodging in the luxurious villa of an entrepreneurial family who owed their wealth to capitalist business methods and the decadent bourgeois consumption habits of their customers. It also constituted a triumphant act that has manifested itself in various different forms throughout history: by preference, the victors pitch their tents in the most sacred spaces of those they have vanquished. In Stalin's case, the tent was his camp bed, with which he is said to have moved from room to room, to make it as difficult as possible for any would-be assassins.[9]

Even before Stalin arrived, the Soviet troops had removed all of the furnishings from the house, throwing it on rubbish dumps or simply disposing of it in the woods; all that remained was a large sideboard in the dining room, which was connected to the wall panelling. It was put to good use, for example at a banquet that Stalin hosted on July 21, 1945, for President Truman, Prime Minister Churchill and members of their delegations. As Truman, suitably impressed, wrote in a letter to his mother two days later, there was caviar and vodka for starter, while the main course consisted of smoked fish, chicken, duck and game, followed by watermelon and champagne for dessert. *"With a toast every five minutes"*, where everyone raised their glasses to everyone else.[10]

When the Potsdam Conference ended, Stalin left on August 2, pleased at having achieved his main objective of securing the Soviet Union's sphere of influence, which had expanded considerably over the course of the Second World War. This provided far greater scope for the pursuit of great-power politics in the future.

Conflicting Memories

The cultivation of memories is also always a child of its time. Soon after the conference attended by the "Big Three" in Potsdam ended, a commemorative plaque adorned the Herpich villa, where Stalin had resided for a little more than two weeks. It read: *"Joseph Vissarionovich Stalin, the great student of Lenin and perpetuator of his work, lived and worked in this house."*[11] This could not be left to stand when Stalin's horren-

---

7 Stefan Gehlen: Zur Verortung der Berliner Konferenz in Potsdam, in: Potsdamer Konferenz 1945. Die Neuordnung der Welt, published for the Generaldirektion der Stiftung Preußische Schlösser und Gärten Berlin-Brandenburg by Jürgen Luh with the assistance of Truc Vu Minh and Jessica Korschanowski, n.p., n.d. [Dresden 2020] p. 20–33, here p. 26f. [translation: author's own].

8 Ibid., p. 27.

9 According to: Martin Klesmann: Der sowjetische Diktator wohnte während der Potsdamer Konferenz 1945 in der Villa Herpich: Wo Stalin residierte, arbeitete später Lothar Bisky, in: Berliner Zeitung of July 18, 2005 (www.berliner-zeitung.de/der-sowjetische-diktator-wohnte-waehrend-der-potsdamer-konferenz-1945-in-der-villa-herpich-wo-stalin-residierte-arbeitete-spaeter-lothar-bisky-li.9344).

10 Cf. ibid.

11 Klesmann 2005 (see note 9).

dous crimes came to light after his death. Just as hastily as the plaque had been put up, it was removed again by the GDR administration. Nowadays, the house bears a plaque with a text formulated to be as neutral as possible: *"The Soviet delegation headed by J.V. Stalin lived in this house from July 17 to August 2, 1945 during the Allied negotiations on the Potsdam Agreement."*

The rest of the story is quickly told. Part of the garden that originally led all the way down to the lake was destroyed and the antique terrace on the bank demolished in 1961 to make way for the construction of the Berlin Wall. The Academy of Legal Studies and Political Science of the GDR, the most important academic training centre for state functionaries, and the Academy for Film and Television took up residence at the Herpich villa. Following reunification, the villa was returned to its rightful owners. In 1994, the heiress sold the house to the Berlin-Brandenburg Construction Industry Association, which renovated the building in keeping with its status as a historic building. Again, as customary at the time, the stately home was transformed into an imposing office building. Nowadays, there is no longer any reminder of the Herpich family and their achievements.

left: The Herpich villa, garden side, photograph from 1949

right: The Herpich villa, stone plaque noting Stalin and his delegation's stay at the house during the Potsdam Conference, 2020

The Mosler Villa

The villa that belonged to banker Georg Mosler, which was built in the mid-1920s, survived World War II unscathed. Its subsequent use as a children's hospital and as a residential home for the disabled during the GDR era did not cause any serious damage to the building either. Extensive and fundamental damage was caused only by a construction company hoping to use the villa as its future company headquarters. During the "renovation" work in the year 2000, the original parquet flooring, the elegant wood panelling and the expressionist-style ceramic tiled walls and floors, along with a sizeable proportion of the other furnishings, were all destroyed. The entrance hall with the elegantly curved staircase remains in its original form solely due to the fact that the company abandoned its plans and stopped work on the property.

Karl-Marx-Strasse 28/29 (before 1938: Kaiserstrasse, after 1938: Strasse der SA)

T he original plans for the villa were drawn up by Ludwig Mies van der Rohe, with whom Georg Mosler had previously had dealings in 1923 when he was looking to commission van der Rohe to convert a building in Große Weinmeisterstrasse in Potsdam. The Mosler house was Mies van der Rohe's third project in the villa district in Neubabelsberg by Griebnitzsee. Unlike the other two contracts, the Riehl house in 1907 and the Urbig House in 1917, when work began on the Mosler villa in 1924, the architect had already completed his first buildings applying the principles of modern design. With its simple cube-shaped main body and a low-pitched roof, the Ryder House in Wiesbaden, dating from 1923, is a well-known example of this. As such, the neoclassical-style country house that he designed for Georg Mosler can be viewed as an excursion back to an earlier phase in the creative development of Mies van der Rohe's design language.

Tradition with style

The two-storey house with its hipped roof and hipped dormers represents traditional architecture not only in terms of design, but also as far as construction techniques are concerned: the building material used by Mies van der Rohe was not reinforced concrete like in his other projects, but clinker brick. He did, however, select a special Dutch clinker, which is slightly narrower than that fired in Germany, and opted for the Dutch bond, an elaborate ornamental arrangement of the bricks in the masonry.

The meticulous approach employed on the façade continued in the design of the interior rooms of the house. In the large, imposing hall, finished in Carrara marble, the solid walnut staircase leading to the first floor was an appealing eye-catcher

1 Cf. the extensive explanations provided by Martin Gaier and Claudia Mohn in: Mies van der Rohe. Frühe Bauten. Probleme der Erhaltung – Probleme der Bewertung, edited by Johannes Cramer and Dorothee Sack (Berliner Beiträge zur Bauforschung und Denkmalpflege, volume 1), Petersberg 2004, p. 71ff.

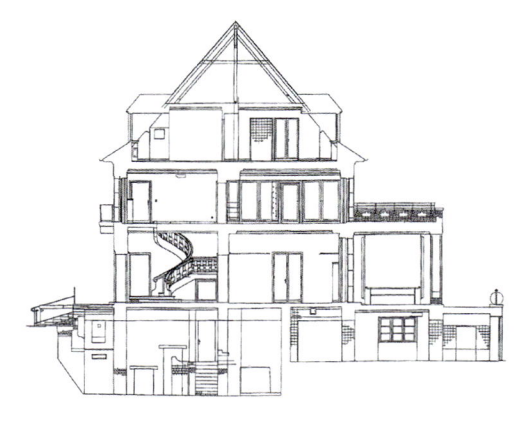

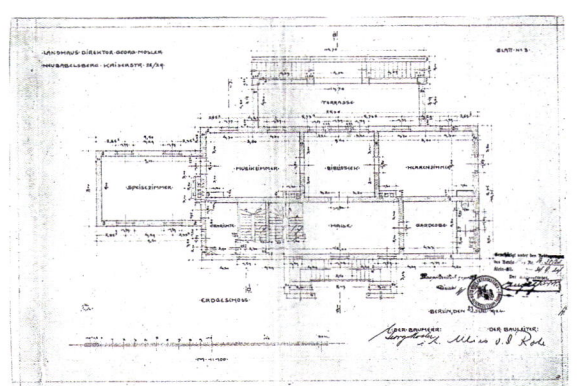

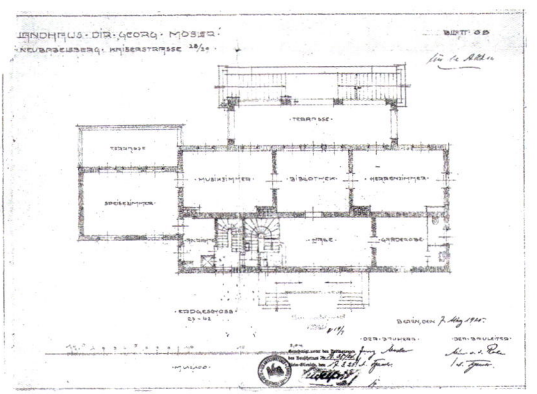

to the left of the entrance. Straight ahead was the library, which, with its coffered ceiling made of Circassian walnut veneer, also fulfilled the master of the house's desire for something prestigious. Like the music room and the study, which flanked it on either side, the library provided wonderful views across the terrace to Griebnitzsee. Mies van der Rohe created a special effect in that, when looking towards the lake from the library, the little park was concealed by the balustrade of the terrace, making it seem as if the villa was located directly by the water.[1] Based on amended plans of the ground floor dated March 7, 1925, a separate terrace facing the lake was built in front of the grand dining room in the annex to the side which, it seems, had not originally been part of the plans.

The villa, ambitious in every respect, also boasted two extra features: a passenger lift—a technically challenging and at the time highly unusual feature in a residential building, and a walk-in-safe for the owner. Even the tax officers who inspected the property in order to calculate the property tax, were impressed. They wrote: *"The Mosler property at Kaiserstrasse 28/29 has an area of 8,672 sqm at a prime location by Griebnitzsee. The site alone represents a value of at least RM 175,000. On it is built a very noble villa, the construction costs of which amounted to at least RM 300,000 in 1926."*[2]

above left: The Mosler villa, front view from Karl-Marx-Strasse, 2018

above right: The Mosler villa, cross-section facing north, building survey 2000, scale 1:200

below left: "Landhaus Director Georg Mosler", floorplan for ground floor, 1924

below right: "Landhaus Dir. Georg Mosler", floorplan for ground floor, 1925

2 Statement relating to the objection concerning the property at Kaiserstrasse 28/29 in Neubabelsberg (W.W. Bg. III 83 Neubabelsberg), Potsdam City Archives, shelf number 1-13/0822/15m Film 2977.

left: Georg Mosler, portrait by W. V. Krause, 1928

right: The former caretaker couple of the Mosler villa, photographs presumably from 1939

An emigrant's fate

Alongside Herbert Gutmann, Henry Nathan, Wilhelm Kleemann and two other bankers, Georg Mosler, who was born in 1872, was a member of the board of the Dresdner Bank for many years. As such, he was among the most successful German bankers in the Weimar Republic. However, the Dresdner Bank also became caught up in the maelstrom of the global economic crisis. Next to the Danat Bank, it was hit the hardest when major textiles company Nordwolle (Norddeutsche Wollkämmerei & Kammgarnspinnerei) went bankrupt in 1931; shortly after Danat Bank, it, too, had to file for insolvency. In order to save the Dresdner Bank, by government decree under Reich Chancellor Heinrich Brüning, the Reich acquired the majority of the shares. The government thereupon ordered not only a merger with the Danat Bank, which in 1930 already formed a "community of interests" with the Dresdner Bank, but also that the board of the Dresdner Bank step down. Georg Mosler was among those who were not appointed to the new board.³

Soon after the National Socialists took over the government, the Mosler family, who were Jewish, fled to Switzerland. For many years, they stayed in touch with the married couple who had worked as janitors at the villa; in 1939 they sent greetings from Mosler's old home in the form of portrait photographs taken on the shore at Griebnitzsee. Georg Mosler was officially expropriated in 1941.⁴ The authorities entered the State of Prussia as the new owner of the house and the grounds.⁵ Under the transfer agreement concluded between Prussia and the Reichsführer SS and Head of the German Police in the Reich Ministry of the Interior dated April 17, 1942 / May 1, 1942, it was used throughout the war by the Berlin police as a state hospital for the *"mildly ill"*.⁶

During the GDR-era, the Mosler villa served first as a hospital ("Albert Schweitzer" Children's Clinic) and later as a home for the disabled. The park, with a total area of 8,000 square metres, which reached all the way down to the lake, was largely destroyed in the course of the construction of the border fortifications with multiple rows of wire fencing, a wide sand strip and a road for the border troops' vehicles. The trees had already suffered badly first during the fighting at the end

3 Cf. Dieter Ziegler: Die Verdrängung der Juden aus der Dresdner Bank 1933–1938, in: Vierteljahrshefte für Zeitgeschichte, year 47, 1999, issue 2, p. 187–216, here p. 190, 191.

4 Decree of the Secret State Police Potsdam dated January 25, 1941 (journal no. 2038/40 II B.), cf. notice issued by the Regional Capital of Potsdam on December 9, 1996, Reference 12005 00103191-B22).

5 Concerning the "Properties Babelsberg, Karl-Marx-Strasse 28/29 and Rosa-Luxemburg-Strasse 27/28 (A – 1 / P 484)", Brandenburgisches Landeshauptarchiv, Rep. 401, no. 14611.

6 Notice of the Regional Capital of Potsdam dated December 9, 1996, Reference 12005 00103191-B22, p. 4.

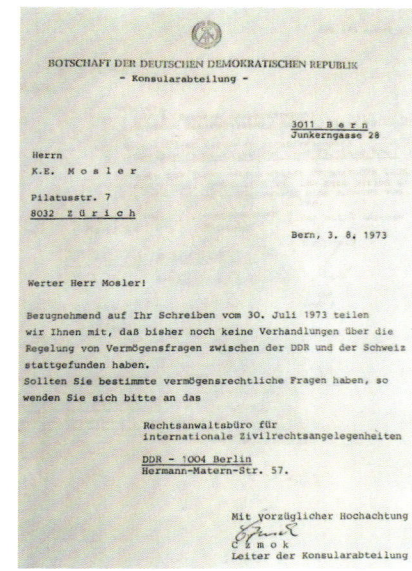

of the war and then due to logging for fuel.

The attempts undertaken by the Mosler family to win back their property over the decades that followed, were blocked with perfunctory references to bureaucratic rules by the two successor states of the German Reich. In 1957, Dora Mosler, the widow of Georg Mosler, received notice from the competent authority in the Federal Republic that the deadline for an application had already expired on June 30, 1950, and that, furthermore, the property of the Mosler family did not fall within the scope of the Act.[7] The Consular Division of the Embassy of the German Democratic Republic in Switzerland advised K. E. Mosler (this, presumably, was the son of Dora and Georg Mosler) on August 3, 1973, that there were no legally binding arrangements in place between the GDR and Switzerland concerning property issues, and, more specifically, that hitherto there had not even been any negotiations on this matter. This was in line with the East German governments' fundamental attitude towards expropriations that had been effected under the National Socialists: they evaded specific demands for restitution by not even allowing a legal basis for such claims to be established—this way, they could always evade responsibility. Amazingly, however, the GDR did not dare to complete the expropriation in the Land Register. This meant that, even after the Fall of the Wall, the owner registered there was the General Financial Administration of the State of Prussia.[8]

Renovated to pieces

With reunification, the legal situation in this area also changed. At the end of 1996, the villa and the property were returned to their rightful owner, Gert Mosler, grandson of Georg Mosler. However, the heir no longer wanted to live in his grandfather's house and decided to sell it. This proved a lengthy and laborious undertaking marred by bitter disappointment.

First, Gert Mosler fell for a fraudster, who was ultimately unable to pay the purchase price. Then, in 2000, a Berlin construction company became involved. In just a short space of time, the renovation measures did what war, occupation and

left: Border fortifications along the shoreline at Griebnitzsee, in the background, the Mosler villa, around 1966

right: Letter from the Embassy of the German Democratic Republic in Switzerland to Mr K. E. Mosler, August 3, 1973

7 Decision of May 22, 1958 (142 WGK) 73 WGA 51/57 (29.58), issued/certified: judicial clerk as authenticating official of the court office at the Regional Court Berlin.

8 Notice of the Regional Capital of Potsdam (see note 6).

third-party use had not, namely destroy a huge proportion of the interior furnishings that had remained intact. The renovation work, which was disorganised, and had not been preceded by any professional preliminary inspection concerning property issues, was carried out using *"pneumatic drills and circular saws"*, as buildings researcher Claudia Mohn incredulously noted.[9] The original tiles, the parquet flooring and other parts of the furnishings ended up in a skip; the lift and the safe were ripped out. The damage report that was subsequently prepared *"was in large parts an agonising documentation of the destruction"*.[10] The construction company withdrew from the project a short time later. However, this was not the end of the malaise: In 2004, Dutch entrepreneur Hans Ensing bought the villa, but had to vacate it again just a few years later when he ran into serious financial difficulties.

Thanks to Hasso Plattner, co-founder of the software company SAP and founder of the Hasso Plattner Institute, which is affiliated with the University of Potsdam, the search for a serious buyer finally came to a happy end. He bought the villa in 2013 and his daughter moved in. Plattner evidently appreciates the residential qualities of a house built by Mies van der Rohe; he himself resides in another building designed by this architect not far from the Mosler villa, namely the Urbig villa.

Epilogue

The Mosler family, who had emigrated to Switzerland, moved to the Netherlands after the war, where Georg Mosler's grandson, Gert Mosler, became a successful lawyer whose clients included the world's largest and most important art and antiques fair, TEFAF (The European Fine Art Fair). Upon ending his active professional career, he withdrew to live a secluded life in a Bauhaus-style bungalow by the outer ring of canals in Amsterdam. His dark past was a constant presence, however, and even here in the Netherlands, he could not shake off the feeling that, as a Jew, he was under threat. His memories of the lost family home in Neubabelsberg were also very much alive and cherished. The entrance to his driveway was adorned with tiles from the stove in his grandfather's villa, some fired according to the original patterns, which are carefully kept in safe storage; a friend of Gert Mosler had recovered the tiles from the rubble piled up during the devastating renovation of the house in 2000.

Disheartened by the political developments in the Netherlands, the lawyer Gert Mosler has since returned to Switzerland. He visited the house at Griebnitzsee only once. He remembers with gratitude that Plattner's daughter welcomed him in, despite his having turned up unannounced.

Salvaged ceramic tile from the Mosler villa

9 Cf. Susanne Rost: Was aus den Häusern wurde, die der berühmte Architekt Mies van der Rohe in Brandenburg baute: Mies drauf – ein bisschen, in: Berliner Zeitung, 5.1.2002 (https://www.berliner-zeitung.de/was-aus-den-haeusern-wurde-die-der-beruehmte-architekt-mies-van-der-rohe-in-brandenburg-baute-mies-drauf-ein-bisschen-li.10206).

10 Ivo Hammer: Rohe – Restaurierung. Zur materiellen Erhaltung des Hauses Tugendhat in Brünn und anderer Denkmale des Neuen Bauens, in https://www.tugendhat.eu/data/Ivo_Hammer_Rohe_Restaurierung_2003.pdf. Also in: Mies van der Rohe. Frühe Bauten 2004 (see note 1), p. 14ff.

The Stülpnagel Villa

His world was the military: Joachim von Stülpnagel forged an illustrious career in the army of the German Empire and the Weimar Republic. It is likely that he was not afforded the most senior positions only because Kurt von Schleicher, a General and later Reich Chancellor, viewed the officer, who was as talented as he was ambitious, as a threat to his own aspirations. The villa in which Stülpnagel and his family lived until 1945 was subsequently the subject of protracted disputes with the authorities that were hugely distressing for the former owners and their heirs: the compensation promised by the GDR administration for the expropriation was never paid, and restitution of the property following reunification was delayed for years. To the present day, ownership of the property is still a matter of dispute.

Virchowstrasse 15 (before 1938: Ring/Luisenstrasse, after 1938: Ludwig-Troost-Strasse)

The career path of Joachim Fritz Constantin von Stülpnagel was pre-ordained. Born in 1880 in Glogau, Silesia, both his father and his grandfather had served as Infantry Generals in the Prussian army. His grandfather on his mother's side had also been a General and even Prussian Minister of War in the 1880s. Joachim von Stülpnagel began his military training at age twelve. He first attended cadet school in Potsdam, then the Royal Prussian Main Cadet School Gross-Lichterfelde.

left: The Stülpnagel villa, front, 2020

right: The Stülpnagel villa, garden side, 2020

Joachim von Stülpnagel as Lieutenant General (Commander of the Third Division and Commander in Chief of Wehrkreis III military district), 1931

It is worth highlighting the fact that, from 1900 to 1904, Stülpnagel was deployed in Geneva and Paris several times, where he also learned French. Having trained as a Staff Officer at the Prussian War Academy in Berlin, he was appointed to the Grand General Staff responsible for war planning and conduct in 1910. At the end of World War I, he was Chief of the Operations Department in the Supreme Army Command and thus held one of the most important planning positions.

His ascent continued unchecked during the Weimar Republic era. At the Reich Ministry of Defence, Stülpnagel worked first in the personnel department, and in 1922 was appointed head of department in the Troops Office. Next, he held the post of regimental commander in 1926 and, in 1929, having been promoted to Lieutenant General, was commander of the *"Wehrkreis III"* military district, which included the Reich capital of Berlin, the provinces of Brandenburg and Silesia, as well as part of West Prussia. When the Chief of Army Command retired at the end of 1930, many, including Stülpnagel himself, expected that he would be entrusted with the post. However, Minister of the Reichswehr Wilhelm Greener and Kurt von Schleicher, who had been head of the Reich Ministry of Defence since February 1929, prevented this. Apparently, Schleicher in particular feared that he would lose power if he appointed a strong and determined character like Stülpnagel to the post.

This defeat hit Stülpnagel, who had become accustomed to success, so hard that he responded the only way he felt was appropriate and took his leave the following year. The bitterest aspect for him was that, though he had fulfilled the mission that his family history had, so to speak, entrusted to him, recognition came too late: like his father and his two grandfathers, he was promoted to General of the Infantry, but only once he had retired from active service.

left: The Stülpnagel villa, garden side, mid-1930s

centre: Garden of the Stülpnagel villa, 1945

right: Garden of the Stülpnagel villa, 1990

Essayist and Publisher

The smoothness with which he mastered the transition to civil professional life after this career break was attributable mainly to two circumstances: Joachim von Stülpnagel had already been publishing political articles in the renowned, bourgeois right-wing conservative *Berliner Börsen-Zeitung* since 1924 and had made a name for himself as a commentator on politics and current affairs. Furthermore, the owner of this longstanding daily newspaper, Arnold Killisch von Horn, was the uncle of Stülpnagel's wife, Irmgard, née von Kracht. Stülpnagel joined the newspaper and in 1934 was appointed its director.[1]

In 1936—a year after the National Socialist regime had decided to rebuild the Wehrmacht and reintroduced compulsory military service—he established the publishing company "*Die Wehrmacht*" together with Killisch von Horn and a cousin. It published books on military topics but found particular success with the illustrated magazine by the same name, which was published twice monthly. The first issue was published in November 1936 with a circulation of 90,000 copies. Not long after, its circulation increased further.

The most important tasks of *Die Wehrmacht* were, *"to deepen the idea of national defence among the German people and thus to promote and secure the intimate bond between the people and the Wehrmacht"* as well as *"to cultivate the tradition of the glorious old army and navy"*.[2] Thus, its target audience encompassed both soldiers and the civilian population. The design was dominated by picture galleries presenting military operations and weapon systems in the most dynamic way possible and documenting the lives of the soldiers. It was a propaganda magazine with a modern technical layout intended to fill both soldiers and civilians alike with enthusiasm for the first war mission in Spain and, later, for the World War.

The Reich War Ministry published the magazine, based on an agreement between Stülpnagel and representatives of the Ministry. This arrangement had benefits for both sides: It provided the Reich War Ministry with its own propaganda medium, allowing it to reach a wide readership. In return, Stülpnagel and the publishing house were protected against the direct influence of the NSDAP on

[1] Cf. on this issue and the other descriptions of the publishing house and the magazine *Die Wehrmacht*: João Arthur Ciciliato Franzolin: "Die Wehrmacht". Die offizielle illustrierte Propagandazeitschrift der deutschen Wehrmacht für das In- und Ausland (1936–1944), Dissertation. Europa University Flensburg 2017, specifically p. 67–90 (https://www.zhb-flensburg.de/fileadmin/content/spezial-eirichtungen/zhb/dokumente/dissertationen/ciciliato-franzolin/ciciliato-franzolin-joao-2018.pdf).

[2] 390 BArch Berlin, R 3016/222, Angebote und Anschaffung von Zeitschriften, 1936, p. 254, p. 56, quoted based on: Ciciliato Franzolin 2017 (see note 1), p. 80.

Joachim und Irmgard (XIV, 232) mit ihren Kindern; v.l.n.r.: Waltraut (XV, 278), Edelgard (275), Jutta (277), Ilsabe (280), Rochus-Wilhelm (281), Sigrid (279) und Gisela (276)

The Stülpnagel family, around 1930

the contents of the magazine. This model was approved by General Field Marshall, Werner von Blomberg.

In 1939, Joachim von Stülpnagel purchased the house in Virchowstrasse 15, which afforded plenty of room for his large family—he and his wife had six daughters and a son. The spacious villa with the striking tower and the concave, curved hipped roof on the façade facing the street, led onto an elongated garden that reached all the way to the shore of Griebnitzsee. The same year, 1939, the Wehrmacht reactivated the experienced planner and organiser Stülpnagel and appointed him commander of a reserve army. However, this appointment was withdrawn again just a few days later in the wake of Stülpnagel's open and sharp criticism of Hitler's war policy.

The president of the Reich Press Chamber, Max Amman, who was responsible for the enforced conformity or 'Nazification' of the German press, intensified his efforts to subject *Die Wehrmacht* to NSDAP control after the dismissal of Field Marshal Blomberg and the incorporation of the War Ministry into the new High Command of the Wehrmacht (OKW) in 1938. In 1943, the National Socialist Press Office expropriated Stülpnagel, and the magazine was taken over by the Eher-Verlag, the central publishing company of the NSDAP. It only cancelled the magazine, which was successful from a propaganda perspective, in September 1944. For Stülpnagel, the expropriation of the publishing company marked the end of his professional career.

On April 22, 1944, his only son, Rochus-Wilhelm, fell near Aprilia in Italy. His son-in-law Maximilian von Knobelsdorff-Brenkenhoff was killed a short time later near Druzkopol, which at that time was part of the Russian Empire. On August 16, 1944, following the failed assassination attempt on Hitler of July 20, Joachim von Stülpnagel was arrested. His son-in-law Hans-Alexander von Voss and his distant relative Carl-Heinrich von Stülpnagel had been among the conspirators. In addition, Joachim von Stülpnagel's name had been found in the documents of Carl Goerdeler, who was involved in planning the attack. There were evidently plans for Stülpnagel to be given an important post in the successor state to the Nazi regime.³ On August 30, Carl-Heinrich was executed in Plötzensee and on November 8, 1944, Joachim's son-in-law von Voss took his own life in prison.

Joachim von Stülpnagel, was released from prison, so the family story goes, thanks to the efforts of his wife and his daughter.⁴ After the war ended, the Soviet military administration requisitioned the villa in Virchowstrasse in June 1945 in preparation for the Potsdam Conference. The Stülpnagels fled to Bavaria, where Joachim von Stülpnagel died in 1968, without ever having seen Neubabelsberg again.

Carl-Heinrich von Stülpnagel, January 1, 1940

3 Ciciliato Franzolin 2017 (see note 1), p. 231.

4 Karl Heinrich von Stülpnagel (ed.): Geschichte des Geschlechts von Stülpnagel, Band 2, Markkleeberg 2009, p. 203.

Villa with a View

"Our house was not an ostentatious villa, but it provided us with all the comforts we could want inside and had a wonderful view of the lake and the forest. One big advantage were the twelve individual rooms and four balconies, where we would sit for hours and enjoy our meals during the season, if we didn't do so on the lakeshore. When I later purchased the house, I had it decorated inside and out. Ever more flowers and flowering shrubs were planted in the small front garden. The appearance of the lakeside garden changed over the years.

At certain times of year, keeping the garden was a lot of work. Its real custodian was later Jutta, who, in addition to all of her work in Berlin, especially during the war years, very diligently took care of the garden and organised seeds and plants. Sigrid, Ilsabe and Rochus had often climbed the trees and gymnastic apparatus as children, and we all swam in the lake a lot and rowed on it. It brought the children great joy when my wife took them and a picnic basket and rowed our boats to the opposite shore at the edge of the forest. In the hardest weeks of the winter, the lake froze over, and the otherwise frequent steamer traffic with its homely tooting was still.

To me, it always seemed a huge advantage of Babelsberg that the people who lived there all wished for a quiet life and did not set much store by close relationships, conversations on the street and small-town gossip. One difficulty for the household that intensified during the war was that most of the shops were located in the neighbouring village of Nowawes. The bicycle became an increasingly common means of transport, especially for my wife, who at her age did not shy away from the effort and braved all weathers to do her shopping there by bicycle. I, too, occasionally did the same for sport. We had an almost friendly relationship with many of the small tradesmen and shopkeepers, for example with the old gardener Grahl."

Joachim von Stülpnagel: 75 Jahre meines Lebens. Privatdruck, Oberaudorf am Inn 1955, p. 318. [translation: author's own]

A hard fight for rights

Having been unlawfully evicted from their home, the Stülpnagels had to wait decades for the return of their villa. The GDR's first act was to establish facts: the council of the city of Potsdam expropriated the family by notice dated December 8, 1962, pursuant to Section 10 of the *Verteidigungsgesetz* (Defence Act) (*Gesetz vom 20. September 1961 zur Verteidigung der DDR*, Federal Gazette I, p. 175) in conjunction with the *Entschädigungsgesetz* (Compensation Act) (*Gesetz vom 25. April 1960 über die Entschädigung bei Inanspruchnahme nach dem Aufbaugesetz*, Federal Gazette. I, p. 250) and transferred the land and the villa to "national property". As confirmed in the notice of opposition dated May 31, 1999, the calculated compensation was never paid to the Stülpnagels: *"By notice dated 12. 12. 1962, compensation was set at the amount of DDM 3,288.00. This was offset against a claim entered in the Land Register in favour of the Stadtsparkasse Potsdam. For the residual amount, an application was submitted to the deutsche Notenbank, Debt Register Department for Potsdam, for the creation of a debt register claim with special notes. Based on a calculation of the current value, the compensation amount was increased to a total of DDM 5,067.00. The whereabouts of the money is unclear."*[5]

After reunification, the responsible authorities of the Federal Republic of Germany were not any faster to implement the restitution. While a Hamburg-based notary and granddaughter of the former owner had submitted the restitution claim on behalf of the heirs on time in September 1990, three years passed before anything happened. Even the protest of another grandchild, Rüdiger von Voss, who was employed at the Federal Ministry of Finance and was also a member of the board of the CDU, against the incredibly slow processing of the application was of no avail. Voss pointed out that the heirs of Joachim von Stülpnagel, who had been persecuted by the National Socialist regime, had the right to an expedited review pursuant to the priority catalogue of the federal state of Brandenburg.

[5] Notice of objection dated May 31, 1999, p. 4. Decision of the Regional Office for the Regulation of Unresolved Property Claims, Objections Committee VII Magdeburger Str. 51, 14770 Brandenburg a. d. Havel, concerning return transfer under the Act on the Settlement of Unresolved Property Claims (VermG). Source: Regional Capital of Potsdam.

Memories of the eviction from the villa

As to the question of when the old black-and-white photograph of the garden side of the Stülpnagel villa was taken, Rüdiger von Voss wrote:

"After speaking with my old aunt, Ilsabe Platte, née Stülpnagel, who is over ninety and herself lived in the house, the photo very probably dates from the mid-1930s. The onion dome was later demolished as it was structurally unsound […].

I myself experienced the invasion in 1945 by the Russian troops, who came into the house every night, looking for women and jewellery. Throughout the neighbourhood, crimes were committed against women in particular every day, and especially at night. We then had to leave the house with our grandparents, because all of the villas at Griebnitzsee were requisitioned for the Potsdam Conference. An officers' mess was set up in our house and the house was ransacked and its contents disposed of. Later on, the house was occupied by several 'reliable' SED officials. The border fence with a road for tanks ran directly along the waterfront and was inaccessible until reunification. The house itself was in very poor condition and had been completely renovated by the owner. The boathouse was gone."

Rüdiger von Voss: letter to the author dated February 17, 2021.

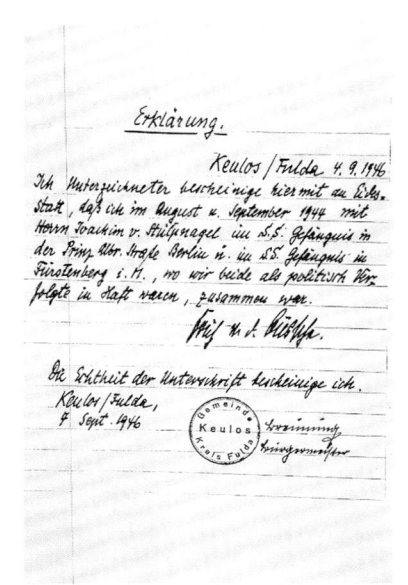

Documents acknowledging Joachim von Stülpnagel as a victim of political persecution under the National Socialist regime, 1946, 1947, 1953

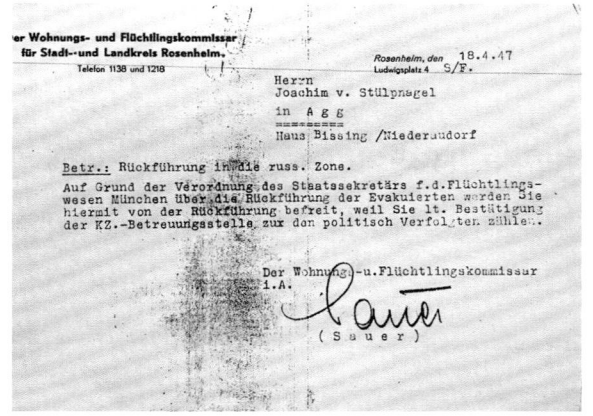

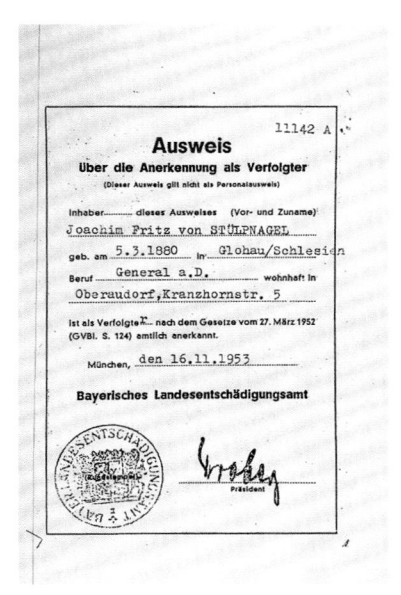

However, the municipal administration of the City of Potsdam at the time had absolutely no intentions of dealing with the restitution of the villas in Babelsberg with any particular urgency. The justification cited was the critical shortage of personnel in the responsible department:

"Pursuant to the priority catalogue of the Regional Office for the Regulation of Unresolved Property Claims of July 8, 1993, the aforementioned application falls within category II 'Applications for Reparation of Political Injustice'. This is the category to which the application has been assigned. This does not, however, mean that it can be processed immediately. Due to the lack of staff at the Office for the Regulation of Unresolved Property Claims of the City of Potsdam, the entire subject group Babelsberg is being overseen by just one clerk. Pursuant to the priority catalogue, only 20 % of working capacity is to be allocated for the processing of applications in category II.[6]

And yet, it was the City of Potsdam that had itself caused the staff shortage by reducing the number of clerks working on restitution claims to the absolute minimum. At the same time, they did everything to secure for the City of Potsdam specifically those parts of the properties upon which the Wall had been built.

Even the reference by the heirs' lawyer to the advanced age of Joachim von Stülpnagel's children—one daughter was already eighty-three—did not motivate the city employees to act with more haste. Another three years later, at the end of 1996, the Regional Capital even announced that it would be refusing the application for return transfer. In 1997, ownership of the villa was finally returned to Stülpnagel's heirs; restitution of the two Wall land properties at the lakeshore, however, was refused. The objection filed against this by the heirs in 1999 was also rejected. The explanation given was that the property had not been the subject of uncompensated expropriation:

"Accordingly, the circumstance that an obligation to pay compensation that existed under the applicable legal provisions of the GDR was not fulfilled in the specific case, for instance because the state authorities did not pay out the compensation for the property, had offset it against other claims, did not fix the compensation amount or otherwise withheld it from the

[6] Letter from the mayor E. Motzkus on behalf of the municipal administration of the City of Potsdam to Mr Brettholle dated October 8, 1993. Source: Regional Capital of Potsdam.

expropriated person's power of disposition, does not per se constitute an expropriation without compensation. [...]."[7]

Following reunification, the families of members of the resistance had done their duty for the Kohl government, their role model function for society and especially for the Bundeswehr had served its purpose. Moreover, their applications for the return of property expropriated between 1945 and 1949 were hugely inconvenient for the German treasury: state-owned land and property had already been factored into the financial planning as a considerable asset. In addition, the restitution claims also triggered discussions concerning the handling of issues of expropriation in the German Reunification Treaty. The Federal Government's portrayal of the circumstances to the effect that the Soviet Union had insisted that expropriations carried out by it in the course of the land reforms of the late 1940s could not, under any circumstances, be reversed, were rejected by the General Secretary at the time, Mikhail Gorbachev. Then-Minister of the Interior, Wolfgang Schäuble, who was leading negotiations on the 1990 Interstate Treaty on Monetary, Economic and Social Union, even made fun of the expectations of those who had been expropriated:

"Even in March, I thought it 'illusory' for those who thought that the ownership situation that had come about in the GDR since 1945 could be 'undone again', and I made fun of those, 'who are now in despair because they may not get something that, for twenty years, they never even dreamed of getting back."[8] While the Allies forcibly ensured that Schäuble's opinion did not prevail when it came to the restitution claims of those who had been racially persecuted, the basic position of the politician, who had begun his career as a financial official in Baden, conjoined perfectly with the East German elite's aversion to the restitution of real estate.

The Wall properties and the rule of law

In 1995, the federal state of Berlin prevailed upon the Bundesrat to submit a draft bill pursuant to which the 'Wall land' was to be returned within the framework of the Property Act. They argued that *"in the interests of the credibility of the state governed by the rule of law, it is not acceptable that the Federal Republic of Germany accepts these expropriations and annexes the properties to its assets as former defensive installations of the GDR"*.[9] However, the credibility of the state under the rule of law ultimately took a back seat to fiscal interests, such that draft legislation dating from February 1996 only provided for the return purchase of the property at a reduced price within the scope of the Property Act.[10] Chancellery Minister Friedrich Bohl feared a domino effect in favour of other previous owners. Thus, inclusion in the Property Act was also a step too far for the coalition parliamentary group, which is why in 1996 the Bundestag only passed the Wall Land Act (*"Gesetz über den Verkauf von Mauer- und Grenzgrundstücken an die früheren Eigentümer"*[11], Act on the Sale of Wall and Border Land to the Former Owners"). While the name of the act promised the possibility to buy back property, Section 3 of the legislation set forth far-reaching opportunities for the Bund to reject the application for purchase if it intended to use the property

7 Objection notice dated May 31, 1999, p. 6.

8 Wolfgang Schäuble: Der Vertrag. Wie ich über die deutsche Einheit verhandelte, Stuttgart 1991, p. 103.

9 Bundestag printed paper 13/120.

10 Bundestag printed paper 13/3734.

11 Bundestag printed paper 13/4589.

in question for its own urgent public purposes. This clause and the wishes of the Bund were to occupy the courts in Brandenburg for more than a decade.[12]

In 1997 Stülpnagel's heirs, demoralised by the protracted processing of their application, sold the villa property together with the claims under the Wall Land Act to the two parcels of land by the lake to Potsdam entrepreneur Wolfhard Kirsch.

However, instead of agreeing with the Bund on the creation of a lakeshore park, the regional capital of Potsdam initiated a number of proceedings against the Bund, based, among other things, on the assertion that the Wall land ought to have been allocated not to the Bund, but to Potsdam, until the Federal Administrative Court decided against the city in 2003.[13] Potsdam thereupon negotiated with the Bund, but was not prepared to pay even a token price for the waterfront properties. This made it impossible for the conscientious clerks at the Directorate General of Finance in Cottbus to sell to the City of Potsdam. At some point, the Bund no longer "wanted" to purchase the properties within the definition set forth in Section 3 of the Wall Land Act for itself or for the City of Potsdam and offered it to the former owners or their assignees. Kirsch and others at the lakeside purchased the parcels of land from the Bund. Together with the other owners Kirsch, who had organised and paid for lakeside runs and an Easter fire for everyone, then became the target of a tidal wave of administrative fines and proceedings based on the laying of lawns, the planting of sea buckthorn hedges or improvements to embankment walls.[14] Even when the owners offered a compromise, modelled on the English National Trust, to allow the public to access the lakeshore properties during the day, but to close them at night, the Regional Capital rejected this proposal. Instead, the City of Potsdam claimed that the gardens were open countryside, with respect to which there was an access right, or that the concrete patrol route where the border had been was in fact intended for the public and passed a building plan that was to form the basis for a renewed expropriation of the properties. In 2009, the courts rejected the arguments put forward by the City of Potsdam, that the area at the lakeside constituted open countryside[15] or had been earmarked under public roads legislation[16], and declared the building plan invalid[17] because the city had failed to take account of the interests of the private owners when drawing up the plans. The owners took back possession of their land. On the same day the court announced its decision, the city councillors passed a new building plan and the senior mayor even threatened expropriation. Only the then-Minister of the Interior of the Land Brandenburg, Jörg Schönbohm, argued against expropriation. The first attempt at mediation then made by former Minister of Justice for Brandenburg, Hans Otto Bräutigam, and the former premier of the GDR, Lothar de Maizière, ended in a fiasco when they offered the owners the option of deciding on the colour of the fence leading to the new lakeside promenade. Politicians, neighbours and the press talked of "obstructors" and accused the owners of being egotistical. In 2019, the Higher Administrative Court of Berlin-Brandenburg declared the new building plan invalid as it, too, failed to give due consideration to the interests of the private owners.[18] The city councillors of the regional capital of Potsdam have in the meantime decided to commission a third

12 Cf. Christoph Partsch: Aktuelle Entwicklungen der Rechtsprechung zum Mauergrundstücksgesetz, Landes- und Kommunalverwaltung 2008, p. 306ff.

13 Federal Administrative Court (BVerwG), Decision of December 16, 2003 – 3 C 50/02, VIZ 2004, 221ff.

14 Administrative Court (VG) Berlin, decision of April 24, 2006 – 4 L 26/07.

15 Higher Administrative Court (OVG) Berlin-Brandenburg, Decision of April 2, 2009 – 11 B 10.08.

16 Administrative Court (VG) Potsdam, Decision of February 5, 2009 – 10 K 3724/04.

17 Higher Administrative Court (OVG) Berlin-Brandenburg, Decision of May 28, 2009 – 2 A 11.08.

18 Higher Administrative Court (OVG) Berlin-Brandenburg, Decision of December 11, 2019 – 2 A 25.18, appeal not allowed by the Federal Administrative Court, Order of November 26, 2020 – 2 A 25.18.

building plan. 83 km of riverside walkways are publicly accessible on Potsdam city territory. On Berlin city territory, the lakeshore trails at Griebnitzsee total 3 km, all of which are publicly accessible; on Potsdam city territory, there are 3.1 km, of which 1.4 km are accessible.[19] To date, the dispute concerning just 1.7 km of historic lakeside real estate has cost the city over one million Euros in legal advice—with no end in sight.

[19] Printed paper 20/SVV/0385 of the meeting of the city councillors (*Stadtverordnetenversammlung*) of the Regional Capital of Potsdam, response to questions 10 and 11.

The Schade van Westrum Villa

The owners and residents of this house changed frequently in the turbulent 1930s and 1940s. Some left of their own accord, while others were forced out, including probably the most important among them, Berlin lawyer Udo Rukser, who has been unjustly forgotten today. Some stood in the glare of the public eye, such as British Secretary of State Anthony Eden, who resided here while on official business, or the popular motorcar racing driver, Hans Stuck and his no less famous wife, Paula Stuck von Reznicek. By contrast, this was also where a wonderful German author hid himself away. This was the well-known and much-loved Erich Kästner, whose books had been banned in Germany and who lived in fear that the Gestapo would come and arrest him at any moment.

Virchowstrasse 19/21 (before 1938: Ring/Luisenstrasse, after 1938: Ludwig-Troost-Strasse)

T he architect of the house carries another famous name: the plans were drawn up by Ernst L. Freud, one of the sons of Vienna physician, psychiatrist and founder of psychoanalysis, Sigmund Freud. After studying architecture in Vienna, where he spent time studying under Adolf Loos, and in Munich, Ernst Freud went to Berlin in 1920. He built residential properties in the city and in the area surrounding the capital, primarily for well-to-do doctors and psychiatrists. He also designed interiors and consulting rooms for their practices, as well as warehouse and production buildings for the Berlin cigarette factory which manufactured the very popular brand at the time, "Problem Cigarettes". The construction of his most famous building project, the weekend house for banker Theodor Frank in

left: Ernst Freud with his wife Lucie, probably on Hiddensee in the early 1920s

right: The Schade van Westrum villa, garden side

The garden side of the Schade van Westrum villa with the reconstructed belvedere, 2020

Geltow by Schwielowsee, is clearly influenced by Mies van der Rohe; it builds on and features different variations of the basic shape of a cube.

In 1933, Freud headed to London, where he continued to build more residential buildings in the "International Style", most of them in Hampstead, an affluent district in the north of London. The villa that Sigmund Freud moved to with his family when he emigrated to England at the end of September 1938 was also in Hampstead. Ernst Freud designed it to meet the needs of his seriously ill father, so that he could continue to receive patients.

A new villa built on old foundations

The project for which Hermine Schade van Westrum, from Hamburg, commissioned Ernst Freud in 1927, was also a renovation, but with an entirely new dimension.

Van Westrum and her architect had to take account of almost 40 years of history. In 1890, privy councillor Anton Heyroth had commissioned Berlin architect Johannes Lange to build two wooden houses on the property in Luisenstrasse, as it was called at the time. The larger of the two had steep, slate-covered hipped roofs, little towers, gables, dormers, and was decorated with lots of carving and embellishments. Hermine Schade van Westrum had purchased this magnificent multifaceted specimen from Heyroth together with a large part of the land in 1921; Heyroth kept the smaller house.

The new brick building was constructed on the foundation walls of the wooden villa and many of the wooden interior walls were left intact and merely encased in masonry work, leaving the layout unchanged. The exterior design, however, bears no resemblance to the previous building: The shapes are greatly simplified, the main body of the building with the high mansard roof is for the most part closed, while the façade on the street side has a quite emphatic simplicity.

On the side facing the lake, by contrast, the straightened façade was given an elegant touch.

Ernst Freud had several floor-length windows inserted and added a terrace that spanned the entire length of the villa; at its centre, it extends out in a semicircle. The architect added another special touch in the form of a belvedere atop four tall columns, placed directly above the semi-circle so that it traces the same curve in the air. A two-sided staircase leads from the porch into the garden, which gently slopes down towards the lake.

Hermine Schade van Westrum was not able to enjoy her new surroundings for long. For reasons unknown, she sold the house and the land in 1930 to Berlin lawyer Arno Wittgensteiner, who also acquired a pre-emptive right to buy the smaller part of the property. Wittgensteiner had close professional and family ties with large department stores, most of them in Berlin and Potsdam; he was a member of the supervisory boards at Rudolf Karstadt AG, Hamburg, Kaufhaus Grand AG, Spandau, as well as Lindemann & Co. Akt. Ges. previously F. Schwarz in Potsdam, which, according to its advertising, ran the *"largest and most refined department store"* in the city. He, too, lived in the villa for only a brief time and two years later, in 1932, the property changed hands again.

Udo Rukser—a German exile's fate

Udo Rukser, who moved into the house, was also a lawyer. He made use of the pre-emptive purchase right and also purchased the abutting strip of land on which the smaller wooden house dating from 1890 still stood. That he was able to afford this prime location property together with the lavishly converted villa bears testament to how successful Udo Rukser was in his profession. He had only studied law at his father's insistence, since his personal interests lay more in the artistic and literary realms. During his studies, he had already intensively explored international law and after the first world war, the horrors of which he had experienced first-hand as a soldier on the front from 1916, he specialised in Eastern European law. Following the conclusion of the Treaty of Versailles, signed on June 28, 1919, he found a highly fruitful field of work. West Prussia and the majority of the province of Posen were to be assigned to Poland, and the many Germans who lost property in these areas as a result, brought actions for financial compensation. Rukser, himself originally from Poland, quickly made a name for himself as the lawyer for these aggrieved parties (the *"Polengeschädigte"*, as they were known) and an expert for the newly emerging legal issues. In 1922, he was invited by the government of the German Reich to take part as a legal expert in the negotiations in Geneva with the Republic of Poland concerning Upper Silesia, which were concerned among other things with the protection of the German minority.[1]

The busy lawyer was also active as a journalist: in addition to articles in specialist legal publications, in 1921 he published the book *The Legal Position of the Germans in Poland*, in which he examined not only the rights of Germans in Poland, but also—which was quite unusual for the time—wrote objectively and

1 Cf. Martin Schumacher: "Wir wollten als Deutsche nicht abseits stehen" – Die Herausgeber der "Deutschen Blätter" in Santiago de Chile Udo Rukser (1892–1971) und Albert Theile (1904–1986), in: Bastian Hein, Manfred Kittel, Horst Möller (eds.): Gesichter der Demokratie. Porträts zur deutschen Zeitgeschichte, Munich/Berlin 2012, p. 89–107, here p. 89, 90. On Udo Rukser's life in general cf. the informative presentation by Hubert Sontheim: Udo Rukser, der Oberbühlhof und die "Deutschen Blätter". Lecture held at Oberbühlhof on August 4, 2017, on the von Magnis' estate in Schienen), http://www.forum-allmende.de/downloads/udo_rukser.pdf.

on a well-informed basis on legal issues relating to Polish citizens. He outlined, for example, how comparably simple it was under Polish law for Polish women following the dissolution of their marriage to reclaim the citizenship of their home country that they had lost by marrying a foreigner. Even dual citizenship was allowed—in Germany, this continued to be an act of sacrilege for many decades to come.[2]

In 1925, he established a new legal journal on Eastern European law together with his colleagues Erwin Loewenfelder and Heinrich Freund. It was called *Ostrecht. Die Monatsschrift für das Recht der osteuropäischen Staaten* and was financed by the German Foreign Office. In 1927, it merged with the *Zeitschrift für Osteuropäisches Recht*, which was published in Breslau, after which it became *Zeitschrift für Ostrecht (Magazine for East European Law)*.

When the Reichstag passed a law in 1930 governing the issue of compensation for property lost in Poland anew, Rukser became an extremely popular lawyer thanks to his specialised knowledge and experience in this area. He won many cases and since the value in dispute was generally very high, this work also proved highly lucrative. The fortune that Rukser accumulated in just a short space of time enabled him to pursue his real interests on a completely different scale than he had been able to in the past: he invested in works of art and made new contacts with artists, including sculptor Ewald Mataré, the expressionist painters Ludwig Meidner and Richard Janthur as well as painter, writer and film artist, Hans Richter, who had joined the Dadaist movement. His sister, Dora Richter-Rothschild, married Rukser in 1922, as his second wife.

Rukser and his wife were not, however, able to enjoy their carefree life at the Schade van Westrum villa, which Rukser had bought in 1932, for long. After the National Socialists seized power in 1933, the Prussian Ministry of Culture urged him to part ways with his Jewish co-publishers at the renowned *Zeitschrift für Ostrecht*. Rukser, who was not himself Jewish, refused to implement such "Aryanisation" of his editorial team, and ceased publication without further ado. It was evidently clear to him that this demand marked only the beginning of the reprisals.

Thus, he also disbanded the law firm that he ran together with Otto Blumenthal, the brother of his first wife, and in the winter of 1933/34 purchased the Oberbühlhof estate near Lake Constance, not far from the Swiss border. He proceeded to acquire agricultural knowledge with the same zeal as he had previously pursued his legal career and became a successful fruit farmer, even winning a gold medal for his fruit and berry juices at an international trade fair for food and beverages in Luxembourg in 1938.[3] Blumenthal, Rukser's former colleague was at high risk in Berlin as a Jew and also moved to Lake Constance where he worked on the estate as cellarman.

Their hopes of being able to wait peacefully and undisturbed far away in the countryside until the spectre of National Socialism had dissipated proved mistaken, however. In November 1938, an SS commando searched Oberbühlhof, arrested Otto Blumenthal and imprisoned him for several weeks at the Dachau concentration

Title page of Udo Rukser's at the time highly salient publication *Die Rechtsstellung der Deutschen in Polen*, 1921

2 Cf. Udo Rukser: Die Rechtsstellung der Deutschen in Polen, Berlin/Leipzig 1921, p. 33.

3 Cf. Sontheim 2017 (see note 1).

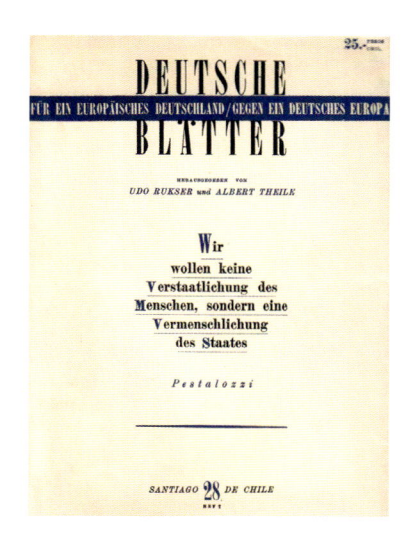

camp. For Udo Rukser, this was an unequivocal warning: together with his Jewish wife Dora, he emigrated to Chile via Switzerland in March 1939.

"For a European Germany / Against a German Europe"

Following some initial difficulties, they succeeded in finding their feet in South America and built a new life. On a former hacienda not far from the capital of Santiago, they grew fruit and vegetables. It was laborious work, but work they were able to live from after some time. Admittedly, this work did not fulfil Udo Rukser's intellectual and political ambitions. Though he was thousands of kilometres away from Germany, as far as possible he became involved in what was going on in his homeland; he had lengthy correspondence with literary figures, artists, and writers, he was keen to state his position, as well as exert influence. In 1943, when the Allies had achieved their first successes against Hitler's Germany, together with writer Albert Theile and two additional supporters, he launched the magazine

left: Udo and Dora Rukser, probably on the Oberbühlhof property, between 1934 and 1938

right: Cover of Udo Rukser and Albert Theile's exile publication *Deutsche Blätter*, issue 28, published in Santiago de Chile

A fresh start in Chile

"So, on May 8, we stepped foot in this country, full of fear, curiosity, hope and with the best will to rebuild and make a home for ourselves here. Of course, that was far more difficult than we imagined, the language for starters—Udo was and continues to be most proficient. We travelled across the country, but it took almost two years until we found something that suited both our wishes and our budget. Until then, we lived in Santiago, it was especially challenging for Udo, who suffered greatly from not earning any money. I really enjoyed being frugal, and especially cooking with the wonderful vegetables etc. etc. […] Today, my dears, that is, since January '41, we've been sitting here in Chile's best region, between Santiago and Valparaiso, in the Aconcagua valley on a small piece of land, 14 hectares of the most heavenly earth in an old house, colonial style, built around a patio with a front gallery and a gallery (a covered walkway around the patio like in a monastery, large and with electric light, mains water, telephone anything but rainforest!!!) and cultivating, still no babies, unfortunately, but wonderful citrus, avocados and cherimoya fruit, as well as vegetables. Udo is working like crazy, and one could live off the yield."

Letter from Dora Rukser to Walter Trier, quoted from: Hubert Sontheim: Udo Rukser, der Oberbühlhof und die "Deutschen Blätter". Lecture held at Oberbühlhof on August 4, 2017, on the von Magnis' estate in Schienen, http://www.forumallmende.de/downloads/udo_rukser.pdf
[translation: author's own].

Deutsche Blätter. Its politico-cultural stance is unequivocally stated in the subtitle "For a European Germany / Against a German Europe': The Nazis aggressive claim to power over Europe had to be resisted. Instead, Germany ought to seek its place in a cooperative Europe—an extremely forward-looking concept.

For a second time, Udo Rukser was able to achieve his goal—within just a few months, *Deutsche Blätter* had become one of the most important German exile periodicals. Authors such as Hermann Broch, Carl Zuckmayer, Oskar Maria Graf, and Hermann Hesse wrote pieces, as did Carl Gustav Jung and educationalist Georg Kerschensteiner; even the great author Thomas Mann provided his work, assuring the readership that this periodical was *"more necessary than ever these days"* and utterly *"indispensable"*.[4] However, Rukser also strived to bring Latin American literature, which at that time was barely known, closer to German readers by printing poems by Pablo Neruda and texts by Jorge Luis Borges. Rukser himself also wrote for the publication—book reviews, articles, essays about art, literature, philosophy, and political issues that would become important in the future. He published some of his contributions under various pseudonyms, including Friedrich Ballhausen, Friedrich v. Hove, Eduard Sinn.[5] *Deutsche Blätter* was also one of the first publications to report on the genocide of the Jews in Europe:

"According to official Swedish sources, the number of Jews who have died (read: who have been murdered) in Europe since the war broke out is estimated at 3.4 million."[6]

With the Allied victory and the end of the Nazi regime, the situation for Germans in exile also changed. Without doubt, the publisher of *Deutsche Blätter* continued to voice many concerns about the future of his homeland and Europe; by that time, however, he garnered less attention, since efforts were more focused on rebuilding Germany.

Due to the fact that the financial support for the periodical, in the form of donations, had decreased and his own financial means had been almost exhausted, Rukser stopped publication of *Deutsche Blätter* at the end of 1946 after four years. While he considered returning to Germany, following protracted but ultimately successful negotiations concerning the return of the Oberbühlhof, he decided against this. The early Adenauer Republic opposed the return of innocent Germans, and Rukser no longer had any friends at the Foreign Office. Many former Nazis secured themselves positions in the administration with high pensions. Rukser therefore focused instead over the next few decades first and foremost on cultural exchange between South America and Germany and published various articles and books about the image of German authors like Goethe, Heine and Nietzsche in the Hispanic world. Forgotten in Germany, awarded the highest accolades in Chile, Udo Rukser died in his new home in 1971.

The Golden Couple of German Sport

The world kept on turning and new actors entered the stage to perform new dramas. When Udo Rukser retreated to southern Germany in 1933 to wait for better days, he rented out the villa to a couple for whom times could not have been

4 Deutsche Blätter, year 3, issue 28, November-December 1945, p. 3.

5 Cf. Deutsches Literaturarchiv Marbach. Catalogue, library, entry Rukser, Udo (https://www.dla-marbach.de/index.php?id=448&ADISDB=PE&WEB=JA&ADISOI=00050081).

6 Deutsche Blätter, year 1, issue 6, June 1943, p. 36 [translation: author's own].

sunnier. Accordingly, the scenes that came to pass here over the ensuing period were more of a light entertainment nature.

Both of the new residents were the kind of people one would describe as successful. Hans Stuck was a racing car driver; he was friendly and charming and good looking to boot. In the second half of the 1920s and the beginning of the 1930s he won numerous hill-climb races, including the European Mountain Championship in 1932, earning him the nickname *"Bergkönig"* or "King of the Mountains". In 1936, he set a new world speed record of 286,496 km/h on a stretch of motorway between Frankfurt and Heidelberg. Of course, this suited the tastes of the regime and its ideology of German supremacy, not least in the technical sphere. A year prior, the *Hamburger Fremdenblatt* had published a series entitled *"How Hans Stuck became a Racing Driver"*, lending almost mythical proportions to his fascinating control of his racing car:

"Everyone knows the blond, always cheerful Hans Stuck, be it from countless photographs, from the weekly newsreels, or from their own experience by the racetrack. At breakneck speed, a man, fused with his machine, hurtles past us—a symbol of an age that is developing maximum power from both man and motor."[7]

Hans Stuck's wife, Paula Stuck von Reznicek, was every bit as popular. She had kept her second surname from her first marriage to sport journalist Burghard Freiherr von Reznicek. For around a decade, from the end of the 1920s to the end of the 1930s, she was one of Germany's best tennis players, winning more than twenty national and international tournaments. In 1929, following her victory at the International Tennis Championship in Berlin, she was ranked eighth in the world. However, she was successful not only as a sportswoman, but also as a writer and journalist, who worked, among others, for the sophisticated liberal-progressive magazine *Die Dame* during the time of the Weimar Republic. She wrote about tennis and other sports, though the majority of the books she published belonged to the "society" category: *Die perfekte Dame (The Perfect Lady)*, which provided contemporary advice on manners and etiquette was published in 1928 and supplemented by *Der vollendete Adam (The consummate Adam)*, a book of a similar ilk that she had written together with her first husband. Countless further publications

left: Portrait of Udo Rukser, date unknown

right: Portrait of tennis player and writer Paula Stuck von Reznicek with her husband, race driver Hans Stuck, published in *Die Dame*, issue 16, 1933

7 Wie Hans Stuck Rennfahrer wurde, in: *Harburger Fremdenblatt* no. 86, March 27, 1935. [translation: author's own].

followed, such as *Frauen sind komisch (Women are Funny)* (1938) and, after the war had ended, *1:0 für ihn? (1:0 for him?)* (1947), as well as *Auch Du bist schön. Ein Handbuch für die gepflegte Dame (You, too, are beautiful. A Handbook for the Well-Groomed Lady)* (1953). The contents were not as sedate and stale as some of these titles might suggest, however. Paula Stuck von Reznicek was considered to be an extremely witty and confident woman. As the obituary in the *Frankfurter Allgemeine Zeitung* puts it: *"Paula was an irreverent individual with a quick wit and a sharp tongue."*[8]

The daring racing driver and the tennis player who played a significant role in high society—the pair were one of the most famous couples of the 1930s. Of course, they were the press darlings: When they set off for South America at the end of December 1935 to take part in several races and tennis tournaments there, the newspapers reported in detail, keen to highlight the important of these appearances for the South American audience: *"Two such prominent German sportspeople, that is quite an event!"* and because all of a sudden, things had to be done very quickly following the final confirmation by the countries involved, they praised the decisiveness of *"Stuck and Paula"*. They said, *"how strange to leave overnight for the land of dreams, the country millions long to visit. A trip across America, like other people take a summer trip to the Baltic Sea. The way they approach life, they're unbeatable, these two."*[9]

But there was another side, well-hidden below the radiant surface which, at times, perhaps, seemed too cheerful. One of Paula Stuck von Reznicek's grandfathers was Jewish, meaning that, according to the 1935 *Gesetz zum Schutze des deutschen Blutes und der deutschen Ehre* ("Law for the Protection of German Blood and German Honour") she was a *"Jewish half-breed of the second degree"*. Even under the "Nuremberg Laws", her marriage to Hans Stuck, who was of *"German blood"* in 1932 would have been permitted though any other configuration would have been prohibited. Thus, her marriage to Hans Stuck also afforded her protection in the National Socialist state.

A banned author is forced to write

Following the emigration of Udo Rukser and his wife Dora to Chile in 1939, the publisher of the *Spandauer Zeitung*, Erich Stückrath, became the owner of the property. He had the wooden villa dating from 1890, which still stood on the smaller part of the property, removed and redesigned the garden. The landscape gardener tasked with the redesign was Heinrich Wiepking-Jürgensmann, one of the most influential garden designers of the Nazi era, whom Heinrich Himmler appointed as Special Representative of the "Reich Commissioner for the Consolidation of German Nationality" in 1941.

At the beginning of the 1940s, Erich Kästner was a frequent visitor to the villa of Erich and Edith Stückrath, and sometimes even spent the night. The writer led a restless life at that time, ever mindful of avoiding the surveillance and stalking of the Gestapo. He had stood and watched on May 10, 1933, in Berlin, in the square between the Opera House and the University, today Bebelplatz, as his books had

8 *Frankfurter Allgemeine Zeitung*, October 14, 1976, p. 19 [translation: author's own].

9 *Hamburger Fremdenblatt*, no. 91, April 1, 1935 [translation: author's own].

Erich Kästner at his desk, 1969

been among those the Nazis threw into the fire, but he had decided not to emigrate. Like many others, he didn't believe the regime would last for long. A strict ban on the publication of his works was imposed. He was arrested and interrogated twice by the Gestapo and the NS-propaganda reviled him as a "cultural Bolshevist"—but still, Kästner stayed.

All of the rights in his books were now held by the publishing company founded in Basel by Kurt Maschler, Atrium Verlag, which sent him the royalties from the sale of his books, so that he had the financial means to survive. Hugely welcome additional income came when his books were made into films overseas; in 1935, American film company Metro Goldwyn Mayer purchased the film rights for the crime thriller *The Missing Miniature*, which had been published the same year.[10]

In 1942, life dealt the increasingly isolated Erich Kästner a special last hand. The regime that had banned him from publishing commissioned him to write the screenplay for the largest and most lavish film production of its time—*Münchhausen*, a costume film with splendid, indeed luxurious sets, startling special effects and the leading actors and actresses of the day: Hans Albers in the title role, with Brigitte Horney, Ilse Werner, Käthe Haack, Hans Brausewetter, Hubert von Meyerinck, Leo Slezak, Eduard von Winterstein and many more. The film was first screened to mark the Ufa's twenty-five-year anniversary on March 5, 1943,

10 Cf. Helga Bemmann: Erich Kästner. Leben und Wek, Berlin 1999 (2nd ed.), p. 239. Also, on Kästner's stay in Neubabelsberg Karim Saab: Was trieb und dachte Erich Kästner im "Dritten Reich"? Interview with Sven Hanuschek, in: *Dresdner Neueste Nachrichten*, March 27, 2018 (www.dnn.de/Nachrichten/Kultur/Kultur-Weltweit/-Was-trieb-und-dachte-Erich-Kaestner_im_Dritten-Reich).

Time for epigrams

During this period of growing isolation, Erich Kästner dedicated himself to the lyrical form of the epigram, a brief, memorable statement. That such statements could often, while not directly, nevertheless contain clear references to current events can be seen in this epigram, which was published in 1948 in the collection *Kurz und Bündig:*

A word of advice to Damocles
Look up to the ceiling with care!
The proximity of imminent danger
lies not in the keenness of the blade,
but in the thinness of the thread
[Translation: Author's own]

but was intended first and foremost, to boost morale in the fourth year of the war and to suggest to the public that there were still plentiful resources to draw on, despite the fact that the reality proved more barren by the day. The striking irony of this endeavour is that Ufa attempted to do this by means of a film in which the main character, Baron Münchhausen, tries to impress people with his tall tales and lies.

Evidently, both Reich Film Director Fritz Hippler and Joseph Goebbels were of the opinion that there was no better person to write the screenplay than "cultural Bolshevik" Kästner. He agreed to the deal, if only because he had not received any royalty payments from abroad since the beginning of the war in 1939 and urgently needed the money. Of course, no one could know that the officially banned author was secretly involved, and in a decisive role (and that he did an excellent job of it!). Thus, the program states a pseudonym—Berthold Bürger next to "Screenplay", while other official announcements did not state even that.

At that time, Kästner was often at the Ufa site in Babelsberg, to oversee the filming, and, as his correspondence with his mother states, spent a lot of time with Hans Albers and also often met Heinz Rühmann.[11] It cannot be assumed that he was working on the screenplay for *Münchhausen* when he stayed with the Stückraths at the Schade van Westrum villa; it is known that he wrote part of it at the home of Ufa-actress Brigitte Horney, with whom he was good friends. During his visits to the Stückraths, it is likely that he dedicated his time to the *Blaue Buch* (lit. *The Blue Book*), his "secret diary of the war", which he kept with him at all times. In it, he commented critically on the situation in Germany and the propagandist representation thereof by the regime. He made his entries in Gabelsberger shorthand, though this would not have saved him either, had the diary fallen into the hands of the Gestapo, since there were still lots of people in the 1940s who were able to read this form of shorthand which had been used frequently at the beginning of the twentieth century. Atrium Verlag, which is now based in Zurich did not publish Kästner's transcribed *"The Blue Book"* until 2018.

After the war ended

Erich und Edith Stückrath's villa was among those requisitioned by the Soviet military administration in Germany in the early summer of 1945 for the planned Potsdam Conference. British foreign minister Anthony Eden, like Churchill a member of the Conservative Party and an experienced diplomat who had served as foreign minister for three cabinets and himself led the government as prime minister from 1955 to 1957, moved in in mid-July.

Although the foreign ministers—alongside Eden, James F. Byrnes for the USA and Vyacheslav Mikhailovich Molotov for the USSR—may not have been in the spotlight at the Potsdam Conference in the same way as heads of state Truman, Stalin und Churchill were, they may ultimately have played an even more important role. Together with their staff, it was they who spent the mornings preparing the resolutions that were discussed, amended if necessary and passed by the heads of state in the afternoon. After the last votes had been counted in the British

11 Cf. Bemmann 1999 (see note 10), p. 268.

parliamentary elections on July 5, 1945, and the Labour Party's landslide victory had been officially confirmed, Anthony Eden returned to Britain; his successor Ernest Bevin arrived in Potsdam together with the new British Prime Minister, Clement Attlee, on July 28. The Conference at Cecilienhof Palace, which had been interrupted for two days, was resumed and on August 2, shortly after midnight, came to a close with the signature of the protocol of the negotiations.

The subsequent fate of the Schade van Westrum villa is similar to that of the other buildings at Griebnitzsee: the glow lent by the Potsdamer Conference quickly faded to be replaced with dreary routine. First, the Soviet occupying forces used the house and gardens, followed by the GDR border control guards and, later, members of the state security service. The balcony atop the semi-circular veranda on the side facing the lake was removed and part of the garden fell victim to the construction of the Berlin Wall.

After reunification, ownership of the property was restituted to the heirs of Erich und Edith Stückrath, who then sold the property to its present owners.

left: Anthony Eden (right) together with his foreign minister colleagues, V. M. Molotov (USSR, left) and J. F. Byrnes (USA) during a break at the Potsdam Conference, Cecilienhof Palace, July/August 1945

right: Border fortifications at the shore of Griebnitzsee, in the background the Schade van Westrum villa (second from left), around 1966

The Urbig Villa

A veteran of the banking trade, an outstanding expert in the international world of finance, with a great deal of overseas experience, who spoke both English and French perfectly and had a pronounced skill for negotiating attributable not least to his impressive eloquence—it may be surprising to hear that the man who garnered such lofty praise came from a very modest background indeed and left school early. Franz Urbig quickly climbed the ranks in the Wilhelmine Empire and in the Weimar Republic. His villa at Griebnitzsee was designed by a young architect who was only at the very beginning of his career at the time: Ludwig Mies van der Rohe.

Virchowstrasse 23 (before 1938: Ring/Luisenstrasse, after 1938: Ludwig-Troost-Strasse)

Franz Urbig was born in 1864 in Luckenwalde, Brandenburg. He was forced to leave school and fend for himself aged just fourteen, following the early death of his father. In 1878, he took on a post as a clerk at the Local Court in Luckenwalde and stayed there for around six years, though he was unhappy in the post that offered him nothing in the way of prospects.

"Urbig chose the path of achievement ..."

In 1884, he moved to Berlin, where he found a job with the Disconto-Gesellschaft, one of the largest German banking companies. At first, he performed only undemanding tasks, but his ambition, tremendous diligence and great discipline soon opened the door to new challenges. In 1889, in large measure due to his language skills (he had learned English and French in his free time) he took over the records office of the Board Secretariat, in which he worked directly under the bank's board of directors. This executive position provided a good starting point for further career advancement: in 1894, he was appointed authorised signatory of the Deutsch-Asiatische Bank (DAB), which had been established by Disconto-Gesellschaft and a number of other banks in order to encourage trade been Germany and East Asia. The following year, in 1895, he went to Tientsin (China) where he took over the management of the DAB branch there. He was appointed to the DAB board in 1896 and in 1898, he led negotiations in China concerning the establishment of a German-Chinese railway company. This was followed in 1900 by a stay in London, where he worked as deputy director of the London branch of Disconto-Gesellschaft. In 1902, he became an "owner", i.e., a shareholder in the bank and, consequently, a member of the board of directors of Disconto-Gesellschaft. His involvement in the bank's foreign trade expanded to include Africa and, through this, the financial support of the German Empire's colonial activities there. This encompassed in particular German South West Africa, today Namibia, as well as East Africa. Urbig was instrumental in the establishment of the German East Africa Company that operated there.[1]

Later eulogies repeatedly emphasised the fact that Urbig was himself responsible for his career advancement. According to one newspaper marking his fiftieth year in service, his vita was *"a particularly fine example of how a small, 'untrained' young man without a diploma or title to his name, can become a great financial figure, how diligence, open-mindedness and the retention of good common sense is able to withstand competition from those with the advantage of being born into the aristocracy or money. Urbig chose the path of achievement; in this time of healthy individualism in financial life, there was hardly any other choice."*[2] Another put it more pointedly: *"Moreover, Urbig was also an example illustrating that a bank director does not need to be born with a silver spoon in his mouth in order to achieve this position, contrary to what many people often assume."*[3]

The banker Franz Urbig, 1900

The Seefried House

The bank director and *"great financial figure"* had a summer house built outside Berlin, in the villa settlement at Griebnitzsee. Over time, this became his preferred abode and main residence. For Franz Urbig and his wife Dorothea, the question of which architect was right for the job was quickly answered: they were keen on the home of their friends, the Riehls, and so it came to pass that Ludwig Mies van der Rohe won his second contract in the 'celebrity district' of Neubabelsberg.

The young architect who, in the meantime had set up his own firm, was confronted with clear ideas from his clients, far more so than had been the case with the Riehl property: it was to be an imposing house in the neoclassical style, inspired by Friedrich Schinkel's construction methods, with some sprinklings of Baroque, especially in the interior. Mies van der Rohe, who had initially submitted drafts depicting a one-storey villa with a flat roof,[4] complied with the wishes of his clients. The result is a surprise to those who find out that this is, in fact, a design by Mies van der Rohe: an elegant, two-storey, highly symmetrical front façade with full-length windows on the ground floor and pilasters protruding only slightly from the wall (in the draft, these had been fluted) and a hipped roof with five hipped roof dormer windows. Due to the slope of the land down to the lake, like the Riehl House, the back of the building has a very different look. To the rear, the building has three storeys, with access from the living area to a large terrace bordered on the side by a sizeable annex with magnificent views over the lake. From here, steps lead into the garden, which stretches right down to the lakeshore. A bourgeois lakeside villa ensemble would not be complete without a gardener's house and a jetty, and these also feature here.

The villa was built in 1915 to 1917, in the middle of World War I. This was not without consequence for the progress of construction work. Difficulties in procuring materials led to delays, as a letter dating from December 1916 states, in which Urbig advised the land registry office of Klein Glienicke that the planned date upon which a *"condition of inhabitability"* was to be attained, could not be met.[5]

1 Cf. on Franz Urbig's biography the details in: Historische Gesellschaft der Deutschen Bank e. V. Personen A–Z, in: www.bankgeschichte.de/de/content/849.html.

2 Franz Urbig. 50 Jahre in der DD-Bank, in: Deutsche Allgemeine Zeitung (Berlin), no. 324 of July 14, 1934.

3 Reinhold Sellien: Briefe eines Bankdirektors an seinen Sohn, Wiesbaden 1955, p. 106.

4 Cf. Jörg Limberg: Potsdam. Die Villen- und Landshauskolonie Neubabelsberg, in: Brandenburgische Denkmalpflege, year 2, Berlin 1993, issue 1, p. 46.

5 Letter from Franz Urbig of December 9/10, 1916, to the Land Registry Office Klein Glienicke, Potsdam City Archives, shelf number: 1-13/0752, Film-no. 2932, page 0228.

Mies van der Rohe was called up for military service in 1915 and only returned to Berlin at the beginning of 1919. During this time, at Franz and Dorothea Urbig's request, the architect Werner von Walthausen performed several construction and furnishing measures, which Mies had not planned. These included a square window in the dining room facing the terrace[6] and presumably also the bay window in the drawing room on the south-east-facing short side of the house, which juts out of the otherwise closed main body. The allegorical murals in the reception area, painted by Frankfurt artist Fritz Rumpf, who lived in Potsdam, are also likely to have been created at the behest of the lady of the house.

The spacious villa, which even had its own gymnasium, was completed and habitable in 1917. The residence, called "Haus Seefried" by its owners, soon after the war became a centre for societal exchange. The Urbigs had many contacts among their neighbours. As mentioned earlier, they became friends with the Riehls and with the artist Carl Saltzmann. Furthermore, the younger generation ensured lively interaction between the residents of the villa settlement—Franz and Dorothea Urbig's daughters, Marie Louise and Elisabeth, were of ages with the children of Friedrich and Maria Sarre.

A photograph that appeared in illustrated fashion magazine *Die Dame* in 1932 shows that they also had in common a desire to present their communal entertainment in a sophisticated manner commensurate to their status. Ladies and gentlemen in high spirits, among them Elisabeth Urbig, dressed in riding attire prepare for a paperchase either on horseback or in a chic cabriolet. The general public, always keen to bathe in the reflected glamour of the rich and the beautiful, in 1935 even had the opportunity to take a look inside this elegant world, though this, too, was arranged and cheerfully staged—the Urbig villa served as the film set for Ufa comedy film *Fresh Wind from Canada*. In addition to Paul Hörbiger, the film also

left: The Urbig villa, front 2018

right: Letter from Franz Urbig to the Land Registry Office of Klein Glienicke with the notice that the completion of the construction work would be delayed, December 9/10, 1916

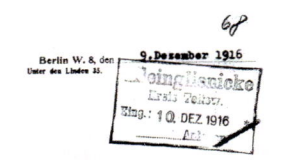

6 See the note in Limberg 1993 (see note 4), p. 46.

starred cabaret artist and author Werner Finck, who was arrested later in 1935, interned at a concentration camp and thereafter prohibited from working for one year.

An International Reputation as a Financial Expert

Following the end of World War I, in the course of which Germany's foreign trading links had largely disintegrated, a man like Franz Urbig, who over many decades had gathered experience in the international world of finance and had many connections, was in high demand. As an expert for trade and finance, he was part of the German delegation that was permitted, though at a very late stage—to take part in the peace talks in Versailles. His warnings that the high reparation payments to the victors demanded by France and set down in the treaty would completely overwhelm the German economy went unheeded.

In the following years, he succeeded in part in reactivating his dealings with his overseas business partners. In Germany, in the meantime he attempted in various capacities to stabilise the economy. For instance, as a member of the administrative board of the Deutsche Rentenbank, he played a key role in the introduction of the Rentenmark (later called Reichsmark) in November 1923, which brought an end to hyperinflation. A year later, he was appointed to the newly established General Council of the Reichsbank; this executive body, which comprised seven German and seven foreign financial experts, selected the new president of the Reichsbank. After Disconto-Gesellschaft merged with the Deutsche Bank in 1929, Urbig withdrew from operational business, though he continued to oversee the fate of the banking institution as chairman of the Supervisory Board until 1942.

Opinion in historical research is divided as to the role Urbig played at the bank during National Socialism. It is acknowledged that he did not foster any sympathy for Hitler's regime. To what extent, however, he protected Jewish employees or was, in fact, involved to some extent in removing them from the bank, has not been established. In January 1934, he wrote to the deputy chairman of the supervisory board of Deutsche Bank: *"Different times may come again and in the interests of the bank it is imperative that we cannot at any point be faced with accusations that the most senior*

Meeting for a paper-chase. From right to left: Gerhard Freese, Heddy Weiss, Elisabeth Urbig (daughter of banker Franz Urbig), name unknown. Photographer: Argusfot, published in the magazine Die Dame, issue 4, 1932

*administrative body of the bank, through its representatives, contributed to the non-Aryan members of the board having to leave the bank."*⁷ Admittedly, this wording is so convoluted in its cautious conjecture that one has the impression that Urbig's main priority was to protect the bank's reputation. Furthermore, this letter was written at a later date, after the two Jewish board members Oscar Wassermann and Theodor Frank had either already been dismissed or were about to lose their jobs.⁸

Another member of the board, Georg Solmssen, who was born Jewish and later converted to Christianity, transferred to the supervisory board of the Deutsche Bank in 1934 but was forced out in 1936. From the outset, he had not been under any illusion as to what Hitler's seizure of power would mean and stated this in much clearer and forward-looking terms than Urbig: *"I fear we are only at the beginning of a development purposefully aimed, on the basis of well-considered plans, at the financial and moral destruction of all members of the Jewish race living in Germany, without exception. [...] the absence of any feeling of solidarity on the part of those who to date have worked side by side with Jewish colleagues in those establishments, the ever more evident desire to draw benefit from posts being vacated [...]—all of this indicates such a hopeless situation that it would be wrong not to view these things straight on, without any attempt to gloss over the issues."*⁹

Franz Urbig died in Babelsberg on September 28, 1944. When Potsdam also fell victim to the Allied bombs, part of the family headed for Bavaria. Only Urbig's daughter Elisabeth and her step-niece Marie Louise Gericke remained at the villa. However, they, too were only able to enjoy their familiar surroundings for a few weeks. They were forced to leave their home in early June 1945.

Churchill moves into the Urbig villa

Discussions were to be held at Cecilienhof Palace in Potsdam on how to deal with the defeated Germany and to establish an order for lasting world peace. Suitable accommodation needed to be found for the heads of government of the United States, the Soviet Union and Great Britain, along with their delegations, in the vicinity of the negotiation venue—which the Soviet troops then requisitioned without further ado. The Urbig villa was intended for the British prime minister.

7 Letter from Franz Urbig to Ernst Enno Russel of January 18, 1934, quoted based on: Die Commerzbank und die Juden 1933–1945, published by Ludolf Herbst and Thomas Weihe, Munich 2004, p. 330 (note 68).

8 Cf. on this: Großbürger und Unternehmer. Die deutsche Wirtschaftselite im 20. Jahrhundert, published by Dieter Ziegler, Göttingen 2000, p. 50.

9 Georg Solmssen to Franz Urbig, April 9, 1933, in Georg Solmssen—ein deutscher Bankier. Briefe aus einem halben Jahrhundert 1900–1956, published by Harold James and Martin L. Müller, Munich 2012, p. 43.

10 Letter from Alexander Cadogan to his wife Theodosia, July 18, 1945, in: The Diaries of Sir Alexander Cadogan, 1938–1945, edited by David Dilks, London 1971, p. 765.

Villas for the Victors

In the summer of 2015, Franz Urbig's step-granddaughter, Marie Louise Gericke, who was eighty years old by that time, reported on her last days in the Urbig villa. The piece in the *Märkische Allgemeine* newspaper reads:
"On May 30, at half-past eleven at night, around twenty Soviet officers forced their way into the house. They were led by a General that Marie Louise Gericke believes must have been Nikolai Berzarin, the first commander of the Soviet occupying forces in Berlin. They are very polite, shining their torches around the villa—there has been no electricity since the bombing of Potsdam on April 24. They are looking for houses with large rooms. They ask if there are other suitable villas in the neighbourhood. They say the victors are going to hold a conference.
This is the first rumour that Marie Louise Gericke hears. The next day, Soviet officers return once more and two days later, a delegation led by Potsdam's High Commander officially orders the evacuation of the premises."
Jan Sternberg: Churchill und die lila Plüschmöbel, in: *Märkische Allgemeine* of July 13, 2015 (cited based on: www.maz-online.de/Thema/Specials/P/Potsdamer-Konferenz/Villa-Urbig-am-Griebnitzsee).

When the Potsdam Conference began on July 17, 1945, this post was held by Winston Churchill, who arrived at the villa with his youngest daughter, Mary, the day before. Following a landslide victory for the Labour Party under Clement Attlee in the parliamentary elections on July 5, however, Churchill's time as prime minister soon came to an end. Churchill's attendance of the conference as one of the "Big Three"— and his presence next to Truman and Stalin in nearly all of the photographs as the representative for Britain, was due only to the fact that the counting of the votes took longer than expected. After eleven days, the defeated prime minister returned to London and left his successor both his place at the negotiating table in Cecilienhof Palace and in the Urbig villa.

It is safe to assume that not everyone on the British delegation was sorry to see Churchill go. Experienced diplomat Alexander Cadogan, who became Great Britain's first permanent representative in the United Nations in 1946, wrote in a letter to his wife on July 28 that since his arrival, the Prime Minister had refused to work or to read anything. This was fine, Cadogan continued, but Churchill ought then, if he knew nothing of the current topic of conversation, remain silent or ask his foreign minister to speak on his behalf. *"Instead of that, he butts in on every occasion and talks the most irrelevant rubbish, and risks giving away our case at every point."*[10]

The conference in Potsdam, which was codenamed "Terminal" by the British, had been prepared in minute detail. This was especially true in the arrangements for the care and provisioning for the members of the delegation. One month before the conference began, a list was made of what was considered necessary, in order to properly support the Prime Minister and his entourage during the difficult negotiations. In terms of staff, there were employees for various menial tasks, such as heating the boilers, and other heavy work, as well as catering officers, cooks and waitresses. Furnishings from mattresses to carpets and even flower vases were to be provided, as well as pots, dishes, glasses and additional utensils for cooking and dining such as tablecloths and napkins. They were evidently steadfastly determined to prevent any shortage of alcoholic beverages. The list records three hundred bottles of red wine, just as many of white wine, as well as five hundred bottles of

left: Meeting of the General Council of the new Reichsbank in Berlin. Seated, from left: Charles Sergent (F), Franz Urbig, Hjalmar Schacht, G. Bachmann (CH), Hans Remshard, Emile Francqui (B); standing from left: Louis Hagen, G. W. Bruins (NL), Charles Addis (GB), Carlo Feltrinelli (I), Oscar Wassermann, Gates McGarrah (USA), 1924

right: The "Big Three" in front of the Urbig villa, photo opportunity to mark the departure of Winston Churchill to London for the announcement of the results of the British parliamentary elections. From left to right: Prime Minister Winston Churchill, the American President Harry S. Truman, Soviet head of state Joseph Stalin; behind Churchill on the right, his interpreter Major Arthur Birse, July 25, 1945

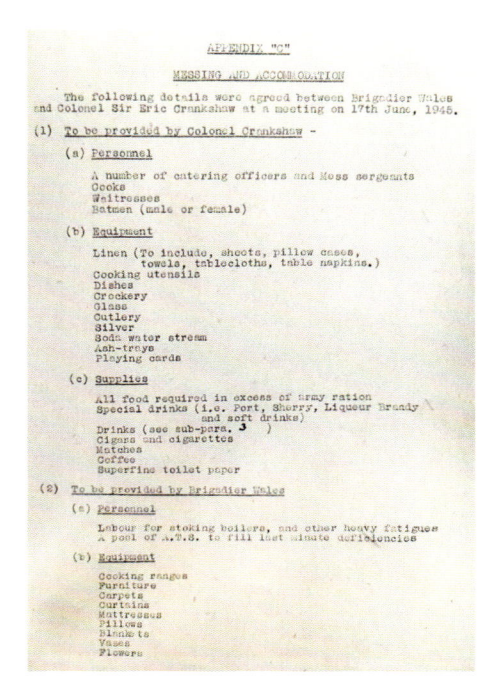

List of staff, equipment, food supplies and alcohol for the British delegation during the Potsdam Conference, approved during a meeting on June 17, 1945

Champagne, in addition to one hundred bottles each of whiskey and gin. Requirements for 'bitters', meanwhile, was comparatively low at only ten bottles. In addition, for the more relaxed moments, playing cards were to be made available, as well as, of course, cigars, cigarettes and coffee. Last but not least, as noted directly below that, "Superfine toilet paper".

The Potsdam Conference ended on August 2, 1945. Its outcome was published in a communiqué often referred to as the "Potsdam Treaty". When the delegations departed, the city of Potsdam and the villa settlement by Griebnitzsee returned to its place on the side-lines of world events.

Back in Private Hands

Following the establishment of the German Democratic Republic, the bourgeois Urbig villa was used as a state guesthouse for the Academy of Legal Studies and Political Science. As was the case for the other residences in the neighbourhood, the Wall, constructed in 1961, blocked access to the lake and the boathouse that belonged to the grounds was demolished.

left: The Urbig villa, used as the guest house of the German Academy of Legal Studies and Political Science of the GDR

right: The Urbig villa (left) and the Althoff villa. The East German border fortifications blocked access to the lake, around 1966

Until the reunification of Germany, the villa remained in state administration before being transferred back to Franz Urbig's heirs relatively swiftly and without complication in 1991. They sold the house in 2005 to a real estate entrepreneur, who had it comprehensively and expertly renovated.

Hasso Plattner, co-founder of successful IT-company SAP and a philanthropist active in many fields, has owned this prestigious villa since 2009. With the Museum Barberini in the reconstructed city palace at the centre of Potsdam, Plattner has created one of the most well-appointed private museums in Germany. The works of art on display there include Claude Monet's 1908 masterpiece, *The Doge's* Palace, which Plattner bought from Goldschmidt's heirs at an auction in New York in 2015. It is the only painting from Jakob Goldschmidt's collection to be returned to Potsdam.

The Saltzmann Villa

The life story of Carl Saltzmann, the owner of this villa, is a tale of quite spectacular success. The vital momentum behind the painter's almost fairy-tale-like ascent from a poor background came from the highest echelons of society, namely from members of the Prussian monarchy. Saltzmann enjoyed the beneficence of Wilhelm II., whom he accompanied on countless sea voyages over many decades. The approval of this patron from the heights of aristocracy not only brought an enormous boost to his societal reputation, but also led to the kind of financial success that was rare for an artist. From the proceeds of the sale of his works he was able to build his own villa in the 'celebrity district' by Griebnitzsee.

Virchowstrasse 27 (before 1938: Ring/Luisenstrasse, after 1938: Ludwig-Troost-Strasse)

This was despite the fact that the Hohenzollerns' appreciation of art was not particularly developed. In this context, Wilhelm II. can be seen as a praiseworthy exception—as a young man, he took painting and drawing lessons with Anton von Werner and Carl Saltzmann and as a result developed a certain understanding of the art of paining and for architecture. This interest, which was unusual for the Prussian royals, was fostered by his mother. Princess Royal and later German Empress Victoria, was not born a Hohenzollern—she was the daughter of British queen Victoria, of the Sachsen-Coburg and Gotha dynasty. In a conversation with the diplomat Richard von Kühlmann, Wilhelm II. commented: *"Everything I know about art, I know from my mother, who was an enthusiastic lover of all things of beauty and truly engaged with art in depth and at length."*[1]

Acquittal for the Arts

It was also the Princess Royal who had come across the painter Carl Saltzmann after purchasing a small marine painting in 1878 and lending his career a powerful boost in the process. His having contact with royalty was by no means to have been expected. Carl, who was born in Berlin on September 23, 1847, came from a poor family, his father having been a master shoemaker. On completing elementary school, he began an apprenticeship with a goldsmith at age fourteen and took his journeyman's examination in 1866. As he wrote in a brief biography for the Royal Academy of the Arts, this was the equivalent of an *"acquittal"* for him, enabling him finally to do that which, as he went on to explain, *"I had ached to do since my school years"*[2], namely, to devote himself entirely to painting. Following a brief period at the Academy of the Arts in Berlin, he trained at the atelier of marine and landscape painter Hermann Eschke from 1868 to 1871, after which he went to Düsseldorf,

[1] Walter Kiaulehn: Berlin. Schicksal einer Weltstadt, Munich 1997, p. 369.

where he continued to learn *"at my own initiative"*³ through his *"contacts with the most important painters"*, who studied at the academy there. From Berlin, to which he had returned in 1875, he undertook several study trips, for the most part only to North or Southern Germany *"due to my lack of funds, which has become chronic"*⁴, but also to Holland and Scandinavia and even Northern Italy.

Then, in 1878, came the major turning point in his life: the Princess Royal not only bought a painting from him, but soon thereafter recruited him as a companion for her son Heinrich, the younger brother of Wilhelm II., who in the same year set off on a two-year sea voyage around the world. The route took them across the Atlantic and around South America to Hawaii, Japan, China and past the Cape of Good Hope, then back to Europe. Highlights of the trip included a reception with the King of Hawaii and especially their time in Japan, where they spent several months, during which Prince Heinrich and his entourage received invitations from the Tennō—the emperor. Saltzmann was tasked with documenting the various stops on their trip in drawings and paintings, which he did in great detail and to the complete satisfaction of his high-born client.

After the round-the-world voyage, the painter compiled his studies and the paintings based thereon in an exhibition that toured several German cities and made a significant contribution to his prominence beyond the bounds of the Prussian capital. It is curious, not to say strange, that Saltzmann's participation in the voyage nearly fell through because he not only had to finance his own equipment, but also had to pay eight hundred Thaler up front to cover private expenses. Neither Saltzmann nor his friends had the means to pay such a considerable sum; in the end, Crown Prince Wilhelm helped him out of his predicament by purchasing a painting for precisely this amount.⁵

An Emperor and his Painter

It proved to be a worthwhile investment for both of them. Saltzmann proved his worth during the long voyage, putting himself forward for additional tasks. Wilhelm not only found a teacher who taught him and his brother Heinrich

left: The Saltzmann villa, street-facing side, 2007

right: Carl Saltzmann, 1908

2 Carl Saltzmann, letter dated October 10, 1892 to the Royal Academy of the Arts. Preußische Akademie der Künste, shelf number: PrAdK Pers. BK 432.

3 Ibid.

4 Ibid.

5 Carl Saltzmann (1847–1923). Potsdamer Landschafts- und Marinemaler. Gemälde – Gouachen – Grafiken – Zeichnungen. Published by Christina Mahnkopf. Including a contribution by Martin J. Ottma, Berlin 2000, p. 14–15. Much of the additional information about Carl Saltzmann's biography originates from this catalogue.

drawing and painting in 1884 and 1885, but also an experienced passenger who assumed the role of artistic reporter for future maritime expeditions. In July 1888, just four weeks after taking the throne, Emperor Wilhelm II. invited Saltzmann to accompany him on a voyage to Russia, Sweden and Denmark. Between then and 1914, Saltzmann took part in twenty-two of a total of twenty-six Nordic tours by Wilhelm II., which on several occasions took them as far as the North Cape. Saltzmann was also part of the crew during a voyage to Italy and onwards to Greece in 1889.

It seems there were several reasons why the emperor set great store by this painter from the humblest of backgrounds being in attendance. Saltzmann was sociable and funny and evidently always contributed to the good atmosphere on board, especially at the entertainment evenings when he recited poems in thick Berlin dialect or jumped into action as a speed painter. The diplomat Philipp Fürst zu Eulenburg und Hertefeld said of Saltzmann that he was "very talented" and *"incredibly funny"*, while also being *"very natural and so tactful in his dealings that he is friends with everybody"*[6]. Wilhelm II. himself, looking back on his lessons with Saltzmann, emphasised that these had been particularly inspiring when the painter *"allowed his delectable Berlin humour free rein"*.[7]

Another reason is likely to have been that Carl Saltzmann had demonstrated his virtuosity in all subjects and aspects of marine painting: he was equally capable of depicting wild coastal landscapes as ports and cities, he could capture the churning waves of a stormy sea, but also tense calm waters, he had a feeling for the dramatic interplay of ocean and sky, light and atmosphere under various weather conditions, as well as for the insignificance of humans in the vastness of the ocean. He was also able to portray ships as elegant heralds of technical advancement and as imposing instruments of power and dominance. The latter was particularly important for Wilhelm II. whose enthusiasm for the navy led after the turn of the century to a huge expansion of the German fleet—*"Our future lies on the water"* was the well-known approach of the emperor, whose declared aim was to make the German Empire a world power.

Last but not least, the Emperor's fondness for Saltzmann was expressed in their

left: S.M.S. "Prinz Adalbert". Weltreise Prinz Heinrich von Preußen, 1879, oil on canvas, 47.5 × 74.5 cm. Berlinische Galerie—donated by the Dr. Jörg Thiede-Stiftung, 2014

right: Japan, Binnlandsee mit erleuchtetem Tempel am Ufer und Vulkanberg, 1879, oil on canvas, 37 × 54 cm, Berlinische Galerie—donated by the Dr. Jörg Thiede-Stiftung, 2014

6 Ibid, p. 28.

7 Ibid, p. 18.

left: Emperor Wilhelm II. at the helm. Drawing by Carl Saltzmann, 1890

right: Aboard the "Hohenzollern" during a Nordic voyage: Emperor Wilhelm II. (to the right of the centre in uniform, carrying a sabre) and his attendants; fifth from the left, Carl Saltzmann

personal dealings. He and the Empress became the godparents of Saltzmann's son Wilhelm August in 1891. This was also down to the fact that he saw in the painter a dependable ally in his fight against a modern age that no longer wanted to live by the guiding principle that the arts were entrusted with, namely maintaining and upholding traditional values and serving the true, the good and the beautiful. Wilhelm II polemicised against the French Impressionist movement and the Berlin Secession art movement founded by Max Liebermann and others; he ranted about contemporary opera—Richard Strauss' Salome was *"perverse"* and *Der Rosenkavalier* immoral; following the performance of Gerhart Hauptmann's naturalistic Drama *Die Weber* at the *Deutsche Theater*, he refused ever to set foot in the theatre again. His criticism that modern art had lowered itself *"into the gutter"*, raised in his speech on December 18, 1901, in Berlin to mark the inauguration of the Siegesallee, has gained both fame and infamy.

In fact, Carl Saltzmann could not have been expected to participate in the activities of the avantgarde arts scene—he was conventional, and his seascapes echoed the great Dutch and British marine artists of the eighteenth and nineteenth century. However, it would not do him justice to view him only as a representative

Art is meant to elevate …

"Art should assist in educating the public. By way of its ideals, it should also offer [the members of] the lower classes the opportunity—after a day of strenuous work and effort—to refresh and strengthen themselves. […] If art, now, does no more than portray misery—as happens so often today—in an even more dreadful light than that in which it is already cast, then it sins against the German people. The nurturing of ideals is at the same time the greatest task of culture. And if we want to be and remain a model to other peoples, we [the German people] must all work at this together. And if culture is to truly fulfil its duty, it must penetrate the lowest levels of society. Art can only do this [however] when it offers its hand, when it elevates, when it does not lower itself into the gutter instead."

Wilhelm II. Speech on "True Art" on December 18, 1901, English version accessible at https://ghdi.ghi-dc.org/docpage.cfm?docpage_id=1184

of a backward-looking academic perception of art; as a seascape painter always concerned with the effects of light and depiction of atmosphere, he followed with interest the attempts of the Impressionists to explore the perception of colour and shape in various lighting conditions. In the midst of the scandal surrounding an exhibition of works by Norwegian painter Edvard Munch at the Verein Berliner Künstler in November 1892, which closed after just a week following fierce protests by traditionalists like Anton von Werner and Hermann Eschke, Saltzmann's teacher, Carl Saltzmann was among those who spoke out in favour of the continuation of the exhibition.

The artistic spoils of the Nordic voyages were vast and Saltzmann used the sketches that he had made during the journey to create numerous paintings, some of them large-scale, several of which were purchased by the Royal Court. Two of these monumental seascapes were exhibited in one of the great halls of the Berlin Palace, while others were presented as gifts to foreign heads of state. One of Saltzmann's paintings, depicting whaling, was exhibited at the World's Columbian Exposition in Chicago in 1893. He contributed more than 150 illustrations to a comprehensive travelogue about the trips to Scandinavia by Wilhelm II., written by geographer Paul Güßfeldt, who had previously undertaken extensive expeditions to central Africa and the Andes.[8] The artist won many accolades for his paintings at art exhibitions, and was amply endowed with medals, including the Knight's Cross of the House of Hohenzollern and a First-Class Knight of the Swedish Order of Vasa.[9]

A villa in a well-known location

All of this not only boosted Saltzmann's reputation but was also highly conducive to business. The income that he earned from the sale of his paintings meant he was able to settle in the villa district of Neubabelsberg—this, too, impressive proof of his remarkable social ascent. In 1889, he commissioned the architects Ende & Böckmann, who had already constructed a villa for theatre director Adolphe L'Arronge in 1881, which was then redesigned by Alfred Breslauer at the beginning of the 1920s for banker Jakob Goldschmidt. In 1890, Carl Saltzmann moved into his new home at Luisenstrasse 10 with his wife Clara Auguste, née Schulz, their two daughters, a sister-in-law and his mother-in-law. His son Wilhelm August was born a year later.

8 Paul Güßfeldt. Kaiser Wilhelm's Reisen nach Norwegen in den Jahren 1889 bis 1892, Berlin 1892.

9 Cf. on this Carl Saltzmann (1847–1923). Potsdamer Landschafts- und Marinemaler (see note 5), p. 11.

Decorations for a man of order

"The last honour I received was my appointment as a full member of the Royal Academy of Arts in Berlin. I am a knight of four different orders, though I rarely enter into battle, except when I am greatly irritated. I am also otherwise a rather orderly person and have the honour of recommending myself to you most obediently."

Carl Saltzmann: Letter of October 10, 1892, to the Royal Academy of the Arts. Archiv Preußische Akademie der Künste, shelf number: PrAdK Pers. BK 432.

The villa with the steep pitched roofs, the large terrace and the striking tower crowned with an onion dome was expanded with an extension in which the artist set up his atelier. There, he worked on his own pieces and gave painting and drawing lessons. In the years that followed, the house was not only a cherished family retreat for the master of the house, who was often away on trips, but also became a popular meeting place, especially for Berlin artists and colleagues from the Berlin Academy of Arts. Saltzmann was appointed head of Marine Painting there in 1894—a post created especially for him, and in 1896 the Academy made him a professor. From 1904 to 1912, he also held the office of Chairman of the Berlin Artists' Exhibition Association and was a member of several associations. The extent to which Carl Saltzmann communed with his successful neighbours from the world of politics, finance and banks, has not been established. It is known only that he had closer contact with banker Franz Urbig, who also lived in Luisenstrasse and, significantly, also came from a poor background.

Following the death of his wife in 1912, Carl Saltzmann sold the villa by Griebnitzsee and moved to Schillerstrasse in Berlin-Charlottenburg. Twice more he accompanied Emperor Wilhelm II. on sea voyages to the North of Europe. The painter died in January 1923 and was buried at the cemetery in Klein Glienicke.

Different Times, Different Owners

Hans Wolff, the director of life insurance company Berlinische Lebensversicherungsgesellschaft purchased the Saltzmann villa. He immediately had the spacious atelier renovated; the work was completed in April 1913, as a letter from the construction company commissioned to do the work to the competent police administration in Klein Glienicke states. Further structural changes, again in the area of

Illustrations by Carl Saltzmann for: Paul Güßfeldt: Kaiser Wilhelm's Reisen nach Norwegen in den Jahren 1889 bis 1890, Berlin 1892 (top left: "Insel, Torgatten"; below left: "Fuglö", above right: "Auf der Walstatt"; below right: "Schlussvignette")

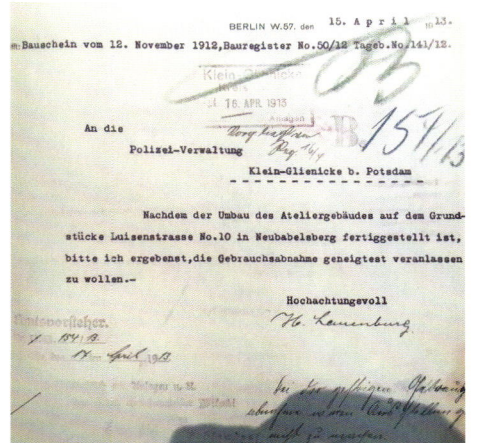

top: Carl Saltzmann in his atelier. On the easel, the sketch for the painting *Eine Manöverfahrt* (A Manoeuvre), 1896

top: The Saltzmann family in the garden at their villa, 1911

bottom: Carl and Clara Auguste Saltzmann's daughters, Elisabeth and Katharina, posing in the garden, 1897

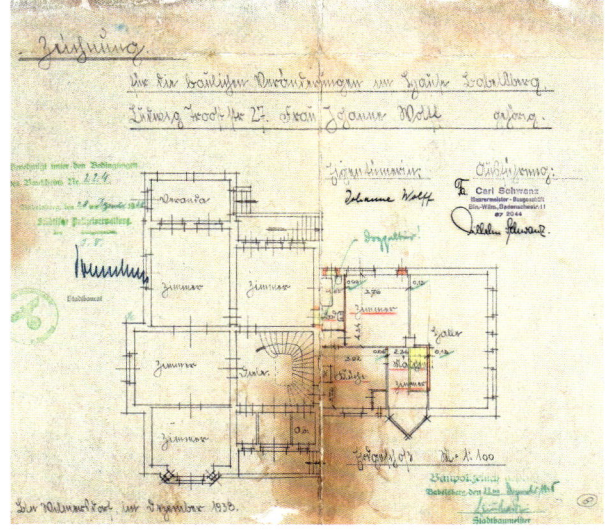

centre right: Application for approval of the renovated atelier, 1913

bottom: "Plans for the structural changes" in the house at Ludwig-Troost-Strasse 27, December 1938

what had once been the atelier, were implemented at the beginning of 1939, with Johanne Wolff, presumably the widow of Hans Wolff, named on the building plans as the owner and client.

The villa evidently survived World War II without major damage. Part of the garden, including the jetty for motor and rowboats—like those at many of the other villas at the lakeside, fell victim to the construction of the border fortifications in 1961, blocking access to the lake. In 1990, the heirs of the Wolff family applied for the restitution of the villa and the land. When this was granted, they sold the property.

The new owner, economic scientist and entrepreneur Professor Jörg Thiede, brought new life to the property. Following the thorough restoration of the house and garden, Jörg and Traute Thiede ensured through a series of events and exhibitions that this location once again became a societal meeting place for Berlin and Potsdam. Professor Thiede had the resolve to focus on the builder and namesake of the villa. In early summer of 2000, the Thiedes organised an exhibition featuring selected works by Carl Saltzmann in what was once his atelier—a late homage to the painter who has today been largely forgotten. The exhibition was accompanied by a book filled with images of his works and a well-researched overview of his life. Thiede himself donated the majority of his collection of Saltzmann paintings to the Berlinische Galerie. This marked a brief resurgence of the generous patronage that had distinguished many villa owners during the days of the Weimar Republic.

The Goldschmidt Villa

Virchowstrasse 43 (before 1938: Ring/Luisenstrasse, after 1938: Ludwig-Troost-Strasse)

The frontage of this grand two-storey country house has a uniform, surprisingly simple façade. The highlight of this building was to the rear, the side facing the lake: a somewhat overly-dominant portico with four thick pillars that very clearly conveys the desire to rise above mediocrity in every way. This was certainly fitting for the master of the house—Jakob Goldschmidt was one of the most influential bankers of the Weimar Republic, as well as being an art collector, philanthropist and supporter of Jewish culture. As such, he was also particularly exposed to anti-Semitic hostility. In 1933, he emigrated to Switzerland and on to the US a year later. The National Socialists expropriated the family's property and the Goldschmidt heirs' battle for restitution and compensation continued until very recently.

Jakob Goldschmidt came by the property—one of *"the most scenic spots on the lakeside at Griebnitzsee"*[1]—in 1920 to 1922 when he purchased three parcels of land[2] on either side of what was at that time Luisenstrasse and then commissioned the architect Alfred Breslauer to build a villa. Breslauer, born in 1866, was a well-known name in Berlin; he had worked for Alfred Messel and had designed both commercial buildings and a large department store, though he had made a name for himself mainly with his country houses. Wilhelm von Bode, General Director of the state art collections, declared that his *"suburban villas"* were *"the best that Germany has to offer in this field"*.[3] He particularly praised Breslauer's ability to incorporate older construction traditions in his design without simply copying them while, on the other hand, also giving due consideration to the local situation and the surrounding countryside.

Architecture and Landscape

The brief that Breslauer received from Goldschmidt was a good opportunity to demonstrate the latter skill in particular, since there was already a villa at the site that would need to be incorporated into the plans. It had been built in 1881 for playwright, theatre director and conductor Adolphe L'Arronge, who ran the Kroll Opera House in Berlin and the Lobe Theatre in Breslau among others. In 1881, he also took over the Friedrich-Wilhelmstädtische Theater in Berlin, which he

[1] Alfred Breslauer. Ausgeführte Bauten 1897–1927, Berlin 1927, p. 27.

[2] 4,930 square metres at Luisenstrasse 15, 2539 at Luisenstrasse 24 and a further 377 square metres next to the access road Ringbrücke.

[3] Alfred Breslauer 1927 (see note 1), p. 12.

left: "Landhaus Dr Jakob Goldschmidt, Potsdam-Griebnitzsee, garden side. Project period: 1921–1922"

right: Floorplan of the ground floor of the Goldschmidt villa, photograph published in 1927

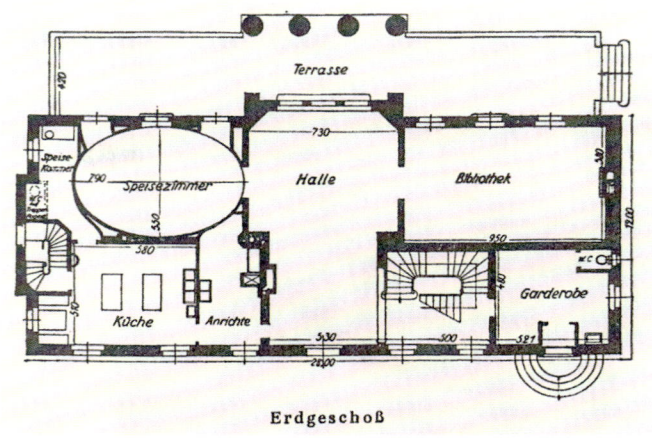

operated with great success under the name of Deutsches Theater until 1894. The programme, which went down very well with the middle-class audience, featured both dramatic literature classics and popular plays, some of which he had himself penned, in which light entertainment was peppered with pointed socio-critical remarks. His most famous works include *Mein Leopold* (*My Leopold*) (1873), of which there have been several film adaptations, most recently the one made by the GDR state television broadcaster in 1987, and *Hasemanns Töchter* (*Hasemann's Daughters*) (1877). L'Arronge was succeeded in the post of director of the Deutsche Theater by Otto Brahm and, from 1905, Max Reinhardt.

Due to the scarcity of materials at the time construction began in 1921, Breslauer had to use part of the existing building in his plans for the new villa. This influenced both the floor plan and to some extent also the interior design. However, the architect was highly skilled in cleverly integrating the old into the new: *"For the interior design of the oval dining room, old Dutch painted wood panels were incorporated and, in some instances, supplemented where appropriate. It was possible to use a painted Italian wooden ceiling dating from the seventeenth century in the study, which was designed to be furnished with old Renaissance items."*[4]

When it came to the outdoor area, Breslauer had free rein. On the garden side, he placed *"A loggia created with wide sandstone pillars crowned with a gabled roof"* at an axis to the country house, and installed an elongated terrace, *"from where the beholder can enjoy a wonderful view to the south of the green areas of the park sloping down towards*

4 Ibid., p. 28.

Finer Home Décor

"Breslauer also shares with his teacher Messel that ability, so rare and yet so vital for the builder of a grand detached house, of being able to empathise with the special tendencies, the habits and the individual tastes of his client. This ability, which can be fostered only through an inherent feeling for the demands of finer home décor, developed through favourable conditions, also enables Breslauer to utilise the existing or collected inventory of old works of art in the rooms, in line with the owner's tastes, to harmonious effect."

Wilhelm von Bode: Der Architekt Alfred Breslauer, in: Alfred Breslauer. Ausgeführte Bauten 1897–1927, Berlin 1927, p. 7–14, here p. 13–14 [translation: author's own].

*the lake and shore".*⁵ The attention the architect devoted to providing the residents of the villa with the best opportunities to enjoy the wonderful countryside can be seen in the boathouse that he had constructed at the south-eastern edge of the property: its flat roof was extended to provide an elegant seating area directly by the lakeshore.

Naturally, the house and garden also provided a popular stage for social gatherings and celebrations. A lively cultural life that provided an opportunity to maintain good relationships with the neighbours, as well as to present one's accomplishments, was among the societal conventions in the villa settlement in Neubabelsberg. Every year, Jakob Goldschmidt threw a huge party to celebrate his son's birthday, which ended with a spectacular firework display that could be seen from far around.⁶ Following the death of the lady of the house in 1922, the actress Käthe Dorsch often appeared as the hostess. She had come to Berlin in 1911 and her engagements included acting at the Deutsche Theater for some time. The events at the Goldschmidt's residence were, as banker Carl Fürstenberg once commented, *"never very large, but always very select."*⁷

A Stellar Career despite the Global Economic Crisis

The gatherings at the villa were not all of a private nature. Jakob Goldschmidt was regularly in contact with politicians, representatives of the economy and the financial world—and there was much to discuss at that time. The economic situation in Germany at the beginning of the 1920s was disastrous: in addition to the damage caused directly by the war, came hyperinflation, the decline of the currency and not least the claims for the payment of reparations set down in the Treaty of Versailles in 1919, which exceeded the capacities of the German economy for many years. Not until the mid-1920s did the economic situation stabilise temporarily, only to become more critical as a result of the global economic crisis which began in 1929. This led to countless bankruptcies, renewed dramatic rates of hyperinflation, mass unemployment, the impoverishment of large swathes of the

left: The Goldschmidt villa, hall and staircase, photograph published in 1927

centre: The Goldschmidt villa, dining room, photograph published in 1927

right: The Goldschmidt villa, Garden terrace and portico from the side, photograph published in 1927

5 Ibid.

6 Cf. Joachim Vogler: Villenkolonie Neubabelsberg, Virchowstr. 43, TU-Berlin, Fb. 14 Landschaftsplanung, p. 10.

7 Michael Jurk: Jakob Goldschmidt. Zum Leben und Wirken eines jüdischen Bankiers, 1882–1955, Master's Thesis, Mainz 1984, p. 99.

Landfront des Bootshauses

population and political radicalisation, in particular on the national and right-wing spectrum.

As one of the leading bankers of the time, Jakob Goldschmidt—together with his colleagues from the banking world, as well as industrialists like Walther Rathenau and politicians including Gustav Stresemann—faced the task, under the most challenging of circumstances, of ensuring the continued functioning of the financial structures. His ability to take inspired action and not to shy away from risk had provided him with an impressive career. In 1909, aged just twenty-seven, he founded the banking house Schwarz, Goldschmidt & Co. in Berlin; in 1918, he was appointed to the board of directors of the Nationalbank für Deutschland, which, contrary to what the name suggests, was a private bank. After merging with the Darmstädter Bank für Handel und Industrie in 1922, it became Darmstädter und Nationalbank, known as Danat-Bank. Under the leadership of Goldschmidt, who was a personally liable shareholder and, as such, the *de facto* owner of the bank, it grew into Germany's second-largest bank by 1931.

The exceptionally industrious Goldschmidt was also one of the co-founders of the Internationale Bank Amsterdam, founded in 1924, and was a member of the supervisory boards of numerous important companies, including Ufa (Universum-Film Aktiengesellschaft), which was established in Neubabelsberg in 1917. It was originally intended to be a production company for propaganda films under the supervision of the Ministry of War—Chief of Staff Erich Ludendorff wrote to the Ministry of War in Berlin on July 7, 1917: *"For a happy end to the war it is absolutely vital that the film is shown with the utmost urgency, everywhere where German influence*

above left: The boathouse on the shore of Griebnitzsee with a small decorative temple on the terrace, drawing of the structure, published in 1927

below left: Jakob Goldschmidt (front, second from left) at the opening of the boathouse in Babelsberg, 1930

right: Jakob Goldschmidt, portrait photograph

Paul Cézanne, Still life with Apples, 1890/94

can still be exerted." [8] The effects that Ludendorff hoped to achieve did not come to pass and instead Ufa quickly developed into one of Europe's largest film companies in the early years of the Weimar Republic. With directors such as Ernst Lubitsch, Fritz Lang and Friedrich Wilhelm Murnau, it made a significant contribution to the artistic revival of German film.

In 1930 and 1931, Jakob Goldschmidt was also a member of the supervisory board of I. G. Farbenindustrie AG, the most important German company group in the chemicals industry, to which Agfa, BASF, Bayer and Hoechst also belonged. The bitter irony is that this company group, for which many prominent Jewish entrepreneurs and bankers had worked, prompting agitation by the National Socialists, just a few years later in 1941, by which time it had been fully "Aryanised", had a factory for the manufacture of synthetic rubber and fuel built in the small Polish town of Auschwitz. The factory was built by prisoners of the concentration camp of the same name. Ever since, the name I. G. Farben has been inextricably associated with the Holocaust and the National Socialists' largest extermination camp.

Art Collector and Philanthropist

Jakob Goldschmidt was just as innovative, ambitious and industrious when it came to his personal fortunes: at the beginning of 1931, he is said to have been worth around 50 million Reichsmark. Since the early 1920s, he had invested a considerable proportion of his fortune in art.[9] It is not known whether this was due more to

8 Quoted based on Antonia Meiners and Antje Taffelt: Träume Bilder. Bilder Träume. Die Geschichte der UFA von 1917 bis heute, published by UFA Film & TV-Produktion GmbH, Berlin 2007, p. 20.

9 Cf. Jurk 1984 (see note 7), p. 100.

his business acumen and his desire for standing or whether the main motivation was, in fact, his enthusiasm for art. Acquiring a collection of exquisite and expensive works, most of them from recognised artists, was at the time, as is still the case today, an established custom among certain elite echelons of society. As Max Friedländer, art historian and until 1933 Director of the Gemäldegalerie in Berlin, wrote: *"Ownership of art is practically the only decent way of presenting wealth that good taste permits. Dispelling any appearance of gaudy ostentation, it extends a sense of inherited culture. The creations of the great masters lend the owner some of their of grandeur, initially only purportedly, but, ultimately, in reality also."*[10]

Goldschmidt had a very extensive collection of French Impressionist paintings. This style had also been recognized in Germany since the turn of the century and was especially highly valued in bourgeois circles. Highlights of his collection included paintings by Édouard Manet (*Self-portrait with Palette*, 1879, *The Promenade* (Madame Gamby), around 1880, and *Road Workers, Rue de Berne*, 1878), Paul Cézanne (*Still Life with Apples*, 1890/94, *Boy in a Red Vest*, 1889/90) and Pierre-Auguste Renoir (*Thought (Young Woman Seated)*), 1877. He acquired these works through the Galerie Matthiesen which specialized in French Impressionism and had been established in Berlin in 1923 by Jewish art dealer Franz Zatzenstein-Matthiesen. In 1933, Matthiesen emigrated to Zürich and later to London. The gallery continued to operate under employees loyal to the regime, who several years later sold works to the organisation "Special Commission: Linz" for Adolf Hitler's planned "Führermuseum" in Linz.

As well as creating his own exquisite art collection, Goldschmidt was also a philanthropist. It was thanks to his generous financial support, for instance, that the Nationalgalerie Berlin was able to purchase a version of Vincent van Gogh's *Garden of Daubigny* (1890). The Dutch painter's works were already hugely popular at this time and the purchase price was 240,000 Reichsmark (the equivalent of around one million Euros in today's money).

In addition, Goldschmidt was a generous supporter of the ambitious academic project, *Encyclopaedia Judaica*. He was a member of the committee that decided to compile this encyclopaedia of the history and culture of Judaism. He himself

10 Max J Friedländer: Über das Kunstsammeln, in: Der Kunstwanderer 1 (1919), p. 1 [translation: author's own].

Generous Funding of Academia

In their acknowledgements in the first volume of Encyclopaedia Judaica, the publishers and editors of the Eschkol Verlag wrote:
"The financial security of a work of such a scale would not have been possible without generous support. To the fore was Mr Jakob Goldschmidt of Berlin, who was actively involved in the inception of this undertaking from the very beginning and whose generous and active participation supported the publication of the Encyclopaedia Judaica to a great degree. He succeeded in forming a committee of supporters for this work who donated the majority of the funds necessary. The knowledge and understanding of Judaism, which will receive a huge boost from the publication of this work will forever owe a debt of gratitude to Mr Jakob Goldschmidt."
Encyclopaedia Judaica. Das Judentum in Geschichte und Gegenwart, editor-in-chief Jakob Klatzkin, deputy editor-in-chief Ismar Elbogen, volume 1, Berlin 1928, p. XII [translation: author's own]..

provided a significant amount of funding and convinced other donors to become involved.

Many renowned Jewish academics and writers were involved in the project, which was published by Berlin publishing house, Verlag Eschkol. Of the fifteen planned volumes, however, only ten were published in the period between 1928 and 1933 (the tenth volume ends with the entry "*Lyra*"). After the National Socialists seized power, they destroyed forty-thousand printed copies of the encyclopaedia.

The Collapse of the Banks

After more than two decades of incredible success, Jakob Goldschmidt's career took a fateful turn at the beginning of the 1930s. The Great Depression led to the collapse of his bank, the Danat-Bank. Following the massive downturn in the share prices on the New York stock exchange in October 1929, many foreign investors withdrew their capital from German banks. This trend became more pronounced when the NSDAP became the second-strongest party in the elections of September 1930. In the case of Danat-Bank, the already precarious situation that all of the banks found themselves in, was exacerbated by another additional and decisive factor: The bank's largest borrower, Norddeutsche Wollkämmerei & Kammgarnspinnerei, unexpectedly filed for bankruptcy in July 1931. It transpired that the most important textiles company in Europe at the time had been falsifying accounts for several years. Though many other creditor banks were affected by the bankruptcy, Danat-Bank suffered the greatest loss at 48 million Reichsmark. The bank, which had too little capital resources as a result of a generally risky lending policy and buy-backs of its own shares, was unable to withstand this loss and it, too, became insolvent. The collapse of Germany's second-largest banking institution shattered the small investor's faith in financial institutions and led to a general banking crisis. Directly after the closure of the Danat-Bank, for example, the Dresdner Bank also had to admit that it was no longer solvent. Whether and to what extent Jakob Goldschmidt was complicit in the collapse of the Danat-Bank can scarcely be established at this point. The statements and documents are too greatly influenced by the events that followed; the attempts at deposit release made against the Dresdner Bank; the "Aryanisation" and the bitter resistance of the Dresdner Bank against Jakob Goldschmidt's compensation claims after the war had ended.[11]

For Jakob Goldschmidt, the collapse of "his" bank not only meant the loss of his career, a significant portion of his fortune and his art collection,[12] it increasingly made him the target of the antisemitic propaganda of the National Socialists. An NSDAP election poster in November 1932 denounced him as one of the "*backers*" of Franz von Papen's conservative government and as "Jewish mastermind" jointly responsible for the "*old policies in favour of the financial capital*" and "*against the working German population*". In addition, "*with his Danat-Bank collapse*" he cost "*Germany hundreds of millions.*"

It became clear in January 1933 that Adolf Hitler would be appointed Reich Chancellor and take over the government. Goldschmidt, who was under no illusions

11 Cf. Sabine Rudolph: Jakob Goldschmidt – Ewige Schuld?, in: Kunst und Recht (KUR), volume 22, issue 3–4, 2020, p. 70ff.

12 He had to transfer ownership of "the paintings, porcelain, sculptures and other works of art as well as items of period furniture located in his houses in Berlin, Matthäikirchstrasse 31 and Neubabelsberg, Luisenstrasse 15". Historisches Archiv der Commerzbank Frankfurt am Main (HAC), HAC-500/45363-2001. BE, contract for the assignment as security dated December 22, 1931.

13 Notice from the Regional Capital of Potsdam dated June 22, 1998, Ref 12005 378010 98 B20, p. 5.

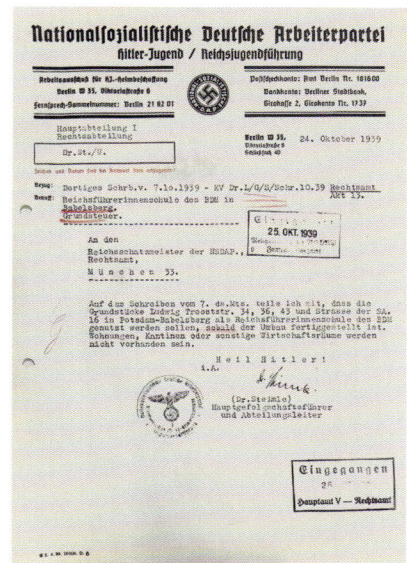

as to the consequences this would have for him as a Jew and prominent representative of the Weimar Republic, fled to Switzerland. A year later, in 1934, he went into exile in the USA.

Seizure and Auction

From his exile in America, Goldschmidt negotiated in vain for the release of his assets at the Dresdner Bank, which in April 1932 took over the Danat-Bank at the wish of Reich Chancellor Brüning. He was forced to sell his Griebnitzsee villa to the NSDAP in 1938. The deed for the sale, dated October 20, was issued by the notary Dr Rüdiger Graf von der Goltz (Deedroll-no. 388/1938). A year later, the "home procurement" working committee of the Hitler Youth announced that the villa and the grounds, together with other properties in the neighbourhood, was to be provided to the League of German Girls (BDM) as *Reichsführer* school. The subsequent renovation of the villa paid no heed to the *"sophisticated living culture"*, that Wilhelm von Bode had highlighted when describing the work of architect Alfred Breslauer: the precious interiors and furnishings including the painted Italian wooden ceilings dating from the seventeenth century and the oval dining room with the old Dutch wall panels, were all destroyed. The portico on the garden side was also removed.[13]

The Nazi regime then set about eliminating all remaining traces of the existence of Jakob Goldschmidt in Berlin. The withdrawal of his citizenship cleared the way for the seizure of his remaining assets. This applied in particular to Goldschmidt's extensive art collection, which he had been required to assign as security to the Dresdner Bank before emigrating.[14] The Dresdner Bank asserted claims against Goldschmidt based on its own calculations amounting to 769,000 Reichsmark and by letter dated June 19, 1941, requested that the Moabit-West

left: Election propaganda of the NSDAP in the run-up to the Reichstag elections of November 1932

right: Announcement by the "Working Committee for Hitler Jugend 'Heimbeschaffung'", announcing that the former property of Jakob Goldschmidt and the neighbouring properties are to be used for the "Reichsführerinnenschule of the League of German Girls"

14 Cf. Letter from the Industry Secretary I of Dresdner Bank of June 5, 1941, to the Moabit-West tax office, Berlin C 2, Münzstrasse 12: "In response to your inquiry of the 29th of last month 29 we advise that we are currently involved in compiling the extensive art collection of Mr Goldschmidt assigned to us as security for our claims against him." (BLHA, Rep. 36 A (II) Oberfinanzpräsident Berlin-Brandenburg no. 12990).

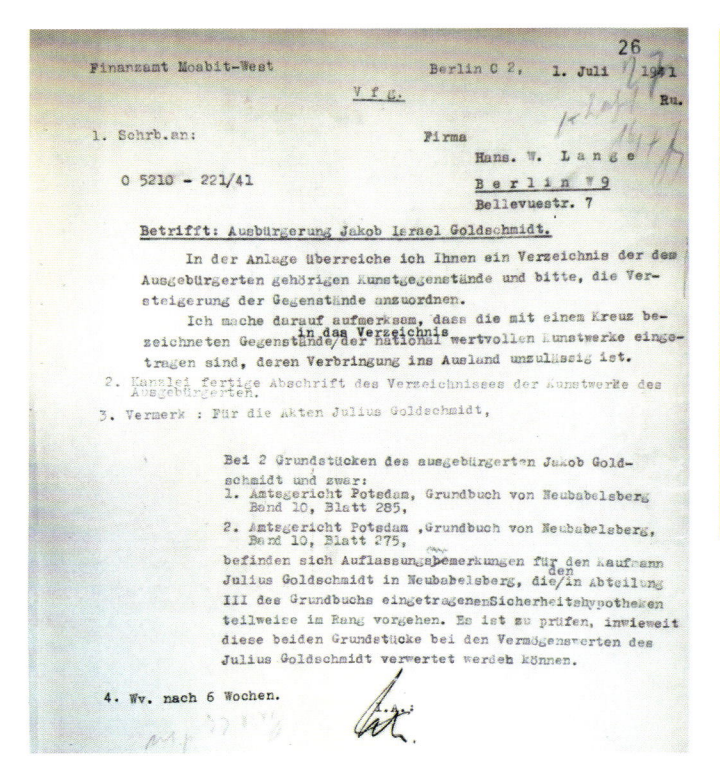

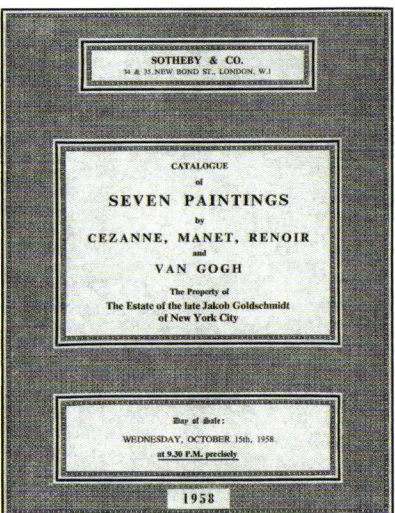

left: Order of the Moabit-West Tax Office on the auction of the art collection of Jakob Goldschmidt, July 1, 1941

right: Title page of the catalogue for the auction of seven paintings from the Goldschmidt Collection, 1958

tax office release Goldschmidt's painting collection for *"realisation"*. Once the tax office agreed, Dresdner Bank commissioned Berlin auction house Hans W. Lange in Bellevuestrasse 7 to auction the paintings. The auction entitled "Paintings and decorative art from the former collection J. G./Berlin" took place on September 25, 1941. The description "Sammlung J. G." was not sufficient to conceal the origin of the works of art; anyone who knew their way around the arts scene, knew to whom they had belonged. The auction was a resounding success with proceeds totalling 816,000 Reichsmark (RM), of which RM 199,865 were payable to Moabit-West tax office.[15]

Painfully slow reparations

In the United States, Jakob Goldschmidt succeeded in building on his career successes of the 1910s and 1920s and finding his feet in the economy of his new home. The expertise of the experienced banker was appreciated so greatly that he was appointed to the supervisory boards of several companies.

After the end of World War II, he made several attempts from New York to obtain compensation for the financial loss he had suffered. One of these attempts is documented by the letter of June 30, 1948, from tax advisor Otto Hesselbarth, who had set out on Goldschmidt's behalf to establish the whereabouts of the works of art auctioned in 1941. Hesselbarth submitted an inquiry to the President of the State Tax Office for Greater Berlin as to whether the accounts of the Moabit-West tax office concerning the auction of Goldschmidt's art collection contained any details of who had bought the artworks. Only in one instance was the search, which had already gone on for some time, successful, as the tax advisor wrote further: *"Thus far, all we know is that one item passed to the possession of the city of Frankfurt am Main."*[16]

15 Cf. The letter from Otto Hesselbarth, Berlin-Dahlem, Altensteinstrasse 48a of June 30, 1948, to Mr President Weltzien, by letter Regional Tax Office for Groß-Berlin, Berlin W.15, Kurfürstendamm 193/194 ("Re: Jacob Goldschmidt—Wiedergutmachung.") p. 1 (BLHA Rep. 36 A (II) Oberfinanzpräsident Berlin-Brandenburg no. 12990/1).

16 Ibid.

There is no evidence of whether or how the President of the State Tax Office of Greater Berlin responded to the inquiry. There are, however, countless indications that Goldschmidt continued his investigations with a number of successes. The investigators commissioned by him found out, for example, that a certain Countess von der Goltz had bought the painting *Woman seated in bed* by Henri de Toulouse-Lautrec and a watercolour by Édouard Manet entitled *Two Plums* at auction in 1941. The painting by Toulouse-Lautrec had been sold on prior to 1945, while Manet's watercolour was seized by the Soviet army in 1945 but later returned to the von Goltz family. In 1950, Jakob Goldschmidt reached an out-of-court settlement with the heir of the Countess.[17]

With respect to another watercolour by Toulouse-Lautrec, *Capucine Monk in brown habit*, following an action for restitution brought by Goldschmidt against the new owner in Baden-Baden Regional Court in 1949, the action was withdrawn in 1950, presumably also as the result of a settlement.[18]

The attempt made in 1953 to claim compensation against Dresdner Bank to the tune of DM 5.3 million was unsuccessful, as was an action for reparations brought against the Federal Republic of Germany. Berlin Regional Court argued in its rejection of the case that Goldschmidt's "*loss of assets*" had not been caused by unlawful actions by the National Socialists, since he "*had through his extremely risky investments brought about the collapse of the Danat-Bank*" and that this insolvency had, in turn, been partially responsible for the economic crisis, "*which ultimately paved the way for Hitler.*"[19] In other words: Berlin Regional Court not only refused to acknowledge that Goldschmidt, who had been forced to emigrate, had no means of challenging the excessive claims of the Dresdner Bank, but also implied that Goldschmidt was himself responsible for the loss of the majority of his fortune—indeed, that the collapse of his bank, had facilitated Hitler's rise to power. This is a scandalous judgement that the Dresdner Bank and its lawyers frequently cited thereafter, and its impact has lasted until the present day. In 1978, a lawyer by the name of Norman Schmidt wrote in similarly spiteful terms for a publication by legal publishing company, C. H. Beck:[20] "*J. G. emigrated from Germany in the spring of 1933. He later repeatedly claimed that he had had to hurriedly leave the territory of the Reich, persecuted by the SS for being a Jew, which means he probably sought to claim the status of racially persecuted already for the year 1933.*"[21]

Jakob Goldschmidt died in New York on September 23, 1955. His heirs gave the seven paintings in total that had been returned to him to Sotheby's auction house in London. In 1958 Sotheby's held the first, highly successful auction of important Impressionist works following the Second World War.

Public awareness of this issue has increased considerably since the release in December 1998 of the Washington Conference Principles on Nazi-Confiscated Art, calling for such artworks to be identified, the rightful owners or their heirs found and works returned or at least a "just and fair solution" achieved. Many museums have begun to pay far closer attention to the provenance of the works in their care and, if necessary, to research it.

17 Cf. Marius Golgath: Der Enteignungsfall Jakob Goldschmidt. Toulouse-Lautrec und Manet im Staatsarchiv Sigmaringen, https://www.leo-bw.de/web/guest/themen/wissenswertes/recht-und-konflikt/der-enteignungsfall-jakob-goldschmidt.

18 https://www.landesarchiv-bw.de/de/search?query=Jakob+Goldschmidt (Staatsarchiv Freiburg F 165/1 no. 206).

19 Regional Court Berlin, decision of April 24, 1974 – 146 WGK 100/70.

20 To the present day, the success of the C. H. Beck'sche Verlagsbuchhandlung is based on the acquisition of the publishing house of Jewish publisher Otto Liebmann, who was forced to sell his business, as well as on the Commentary on the German Civil Code published yearly under the name '*Palandt*' until 2021. Palandt was a Nazi party member from 1933 on and head of the Reich Ministry for Justice. This book, now renamed, continues to be a standard work in legal studies.

21 Norman Schmidt: Ein Fall bewußter Irreführung der Rückerstattungsjustiz, in: Rechtsprechung zum Wiedergutmachungsrecht 29 (1978), p. 81–89, here p. 83.

In recent years, this has resulted in a large number of restitutions, including the return of a painting from the Goldschmidt collection. The inventory of the art collections in Chemnitz had for many decades listed one painting as the work of an unknown artist; thanks to extensive research by the museum, it was possible to establish that the picture in question was *Am Klavier (At the Piano)* by Salzburg-born artist Fritz Schider, which had belonged to Jakob Goldschmidt's collection since 1929 at the latest. The painting was returned to his heirs in 2013.[22]

The Goldschmidt villa, Virchowstrasse 43 (left), the Heidmann villa no. 45 (centre) and the Treitel-Menckhoff villa, no. 47 (right); the GDR border fortifications at the shore of the lake, around 1966

The villa after the war

Around half a year following the end of World War II, the property that sloped down to Griebnitzsee with the garden and villa was transferred to the *"ownership of the people"* by order no. 124/126 of the Soviet Military Administration of October 30/31, 1945. In a wild sequence of transfers which served both the appearance of lawful actions and the concealment of ownership, the properties passed first, in 1951, to administration in trust by the Potsdam City Council, then to Potsdam City Council and then, in 1952, to the GDR Academy of Legal Studies and Political Science "Walter Ulbricht"; from 1959, the municipal housing authority of the city of Potsdam took over responsibility and then again in 1960 the "Walter Ulbricht" Academy. Finally, in 1964, the villa passed to the customs authorities, District Administration for Potsdam, which used the villa until the Fall of the Wall in 1989 as a residential facility and thereafter as training centre. These various entities gave no consideration to the remaining historical legacy. In May 1952, an application was filed for the demolition of the grand terrace on the side of the building facing the lake—allegedly because it was structurally unsound. In fact, the goal was probably to complete the border fortifications, for which a floodlight station was requested and installed in 1959. The construction of the border fortifications around 1961 led to the destruction of both the park and the boathouse.

When it came to the issue of the restitution of stolen Jewish property, the GDR

22 Cf. Chemnitz returns painting, Kunstmarkt.Com/Ulrich Raphael Firsching (http://www.kunstmarkt.com/pagesmag/kunst/_id290386-/news_detail.html?_q=%20); see also: Wiedergutmachung. Museum in Chemnitz gibt NS-Raubkunst zurück, in: *Hamburger Abendblatt*, 29.5.2013.

resolutely refused to accept any historic and moral responsibility whatsoever to the extent that it avoided even establishing any legal provisions for this situation. As a result, Jakob Goldschmidt's heirs resumed their efforts to have the property at Griebnitzsee returned to them only after reunification. However, it took until the end of the century until their legitimate claim was met. By notice dated June 22, 1998, the Regional Capital of Potsdam, Office for the Regulation of Unresolved Property Claims, refused to return the property. The notice cited an exception to the effect that there was no need for restitution if the buildings in question *"have through considerable construction effort been changed in their type of use or purpose and there is a public interest in this use"*. This, it was claimed, was the case here: *"At the time of the decision concerning the claim of the heirs of Jakob Goldschmidt there is a public interest in the continuation of the changed type of use or purpose [...] The customs administration performs tasks that are in the public interest."*[23] The individual responsible for issuing the notice failed to acknowledge the fact that the customs administration of the GDR no longer had any tasks at Griebnitzsee in 1998. To the present day, this individual works as a lawyer for buildings and the protection of historic monuments. The notice was later repealed, and the property returned by way of restitution to the Goldschmidt heirs.

However, even this did not end the legal dispute. The City of Potsdam had reached another decision by resolution dated May 20, 1992. In the convoluted language of GDR-officials, lord mayor Dr. Horst Gramlich announced the latest unlawful landgrab on March 25, 1992, stating:

"Based on the resolution of the meeting of the town councillors on 28.02.1990, for the lakeside areas mentioned, urban planning designs were developed [...]. In the interest of the realisation of these designs on the south shore of Griebnitzsee—creation of a public waterside walkway—it is necessary to leave in place the concrete patrol route of the former border facilities as well as to secure the embankments laid with lawn grid panels until such time as the design of the lakeshore area has been completed in order, inter alia, to maintain the accessibility of the shore area."[24] Both the urban planners and the City of Potsdam claimed in the many court proceedings that ensued that the owner at the time, the Federal Republic of Germany, represented by the finance office in Cottbus, had consented to this. This was, however, incorrect and such consent was never issued nor submitted in the course of the proceedings.

The Goldschmidt villa, façade and garden on the side facing the lake, 2018

The City of Potsdam nevertheless succeeded in gaining ownership of the shoreside property in 2020 by means of a trick. The Goldschmidt heirs, who wanted to sell the entire property following restitution, in 2007 granted the purchaser of the parcel of land upon which the villa stood, an option, limited until November 12, 2009, also to purchase the two parcels of land on the lake side.[25] This arrangement was necessary because the City of Potsdam had issued a pre-emption right regulation for the parcels of land on the lakeshore and the heirs hoped that this statute would have been revoked by 2009.

23 Notice issued by the regional Capital of Potsdam dated June 22, 1998, Reference 12005 378010 98 B20, p. 9.

24 Statement by the municipality to the effect that there are no objections from a spatial planning perspective to the retention of parts of the former border fortification installations, 25.03.1992, signed Dr Horst Gramlich.

25 Notarial Deed dated November 12, 2007. Cf. Deedroll-no. S 172/2007 of the Notary Stassen, Berlin.

In 2009 the Higher Administrative Court of Berlin-Brandenburg did in fact declare the building plan invalid, but on the evening of the hearing, the city councillors decided to draw up a new building plan in order to be able to uphold the rules on the pre-emptive right. This case was followed by additional actions by the City of Potsdam, all with similar aims. For example, it submitted an offer to the new owner of the villa, who was in financial difficulties, that he could sell the two parcels at the lakeside if, in return, he would permit the city to use part thereof as a public walkway. There was, however, one problem: these parts of the property did not actually belong to him, as he had not utilised the option to purchase them granted to him by the Goldschmidt heirs—and the option was valid only until November 2009. A solution was quickly found: ostensibly legitimated by an executive power of attorney issued to an employee of the Berlin-based notary, the notary and the seller extended the option for an additional ten years until 2019.[26] The seller then exercised this option and, as requested, granted the City of Potsdam permission to create the shoreline walkway (the "easement"[27]). The very same day, he sold the two parcels of land.[28]

Thus, without any financial consideration whatsoever, the City of Potsdam acquired the right of way on the hereditary property of the Goldschmidts by devious means. By order of June 23, 2020, the Higher Regional Court of Brandenburg rejected the appeal of the Goldschmidt heirs against this landgrab.[29] While the notarial

Villa Goldschmidt, seeseitige Fassade und Garten, 2018

26 Notarial Deed dated November 10, 2009. Deedroll-no. S 252/2009 (extension) as well as of February 27, 2019, S 93/2019 (acceptance of offer) of the Notary Stassen, Berlin.

27 Notarial Deed dated February 27, 2019, Deedroll-no. 170/2019 of the Notary Domröse, Potsdam.

28 Deedroll-no. 170/2019 of the Notary Domröse, Potsdam.

29 Higher Regional Court (OLG) Berlin-Brandenburg, decision of June 23, 2020 – 5 W 7/20, p. 10f.

employee had not been authorised in due form pursuant to Section 29 of the Land Registration Code, there was an implied authorisation since the Goldschmidts' lawyers had not objected to the draft of the extension of the offer.[29] This ruling contradicts basic principles of both the German Civil Code and the land registry laws. Once again, the dispute concerning the Goldschmidt's property—in this instance their ownership of the property in Potsdam, ended in judicial scandal.

The hillside that slopes down behind the Goldschmidt villa to the lakeshore has again been restored to a park-like arrangement. Here, all is peaceful.

The Heidmann Villa

At the western end of Griebnitzsee, the villa that sat atop the small hill once dominated the panorama, as old postcards from the 1910s and 1920s show. Today, there is barely any trace of this incredible building, and even the history of the villa and its former residents is largely unknown to the general public. And yet, nowhere else in Potsdam did contradictions clash as profoundly as here. At the beginning of the twentieth century, this building was the magnificent residence of affluent members of the upper-middle-class who were keen to demonstrate their standing. Later, it was a stopover for many Jews from the surrounding area on the way to the National Socialists' death camps.

Spitzweggasse 1 (formerly Bergstrasse 1; the building no longer exists)

left: Postcard showing the Heidmann villa and the description "Neubabelsberg Bergeshalde", around 1918 (published by: Hofphotograph E. Eichgrün, Potsdam)

right: Postcard with the description "Babelsberg. Villas in the Strasse der SA at Griebnitzsee", with the Heidmann villa on the right, around 1938 (published by: J. G. B.)

Sumptuous Scenery

This villa, crowned with an enormous dome, was striking, without doubt. The question as to whether it was as impressive in architectural and aesthetic terms is bound to be answered differently today than it was a century ago. At that time, shortly after the turn of the twentieth century, the architects of the time clearly took immense joy in a free-handed, playful approach to historical styles and designs.

The building, built for Jewish physician Dr Karl Heidmann in approximately 1905, around the same time as the Sarre villa, which is just a short distance away, comprised various different segments that did not seem to entirely fit together. The surviving basic floorplan shows that the main body of the building consisted of a square which extended in a semi-circular shape to the west. This part was broken up by two rows of large windows. The three-storey east-facing front with the two protruding dwelling towers and crenelations, by contrast, create a closed, fortress-like impression. On the narrow, north-facing side overlooking Griebnitzsee there was an annex with an entirely different architectural impact, namely a covered terrace in the style of a Greek temple. At the heart of the building was the central hall, above which was the imposing dome topped with a small lantern. The practicality and function of this theatrically showy hotchpotch of references to various architectural eras was very limited— the living space was only 289 square metres. A tax record sheet of the municipality of Klein Glienicke nevertheless described the villa as a country house with a dome and stables.[1]

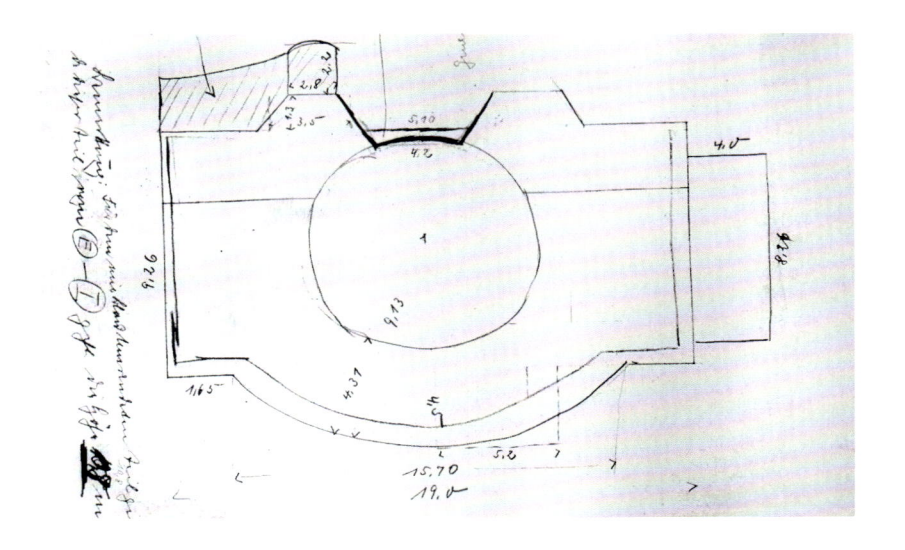

Sketch showing the floorplan of the Heidmann villa, probably around 1912

The next owner of the villa was wealthy mining engineer, Moses Abramowitsch Eisenberg, who lived in the genteel Mommsenstrasse in Berlin. When he encountered financial difficulties at the beginning of 1929, he mortgaged the property at Griebnitzsee. It was purchased in the compulsory auction just a short while later by the private bank A. E. Wassermann, which was headquartered in Bamberg. The following year, 1930, Sima Gurewitsch, the well-to-do wife of State Council member Isaak Gurewitsch, purchased the property at auction together with Mrs Marianne Wischniak. Mrs Gurewitsch's main residence was at Bleibtreustrasse 37/38. The two women are likely to have been fleeing the unsettled Baltic region. Just a few years later, they left Germany behind, too: Sima Gurewitsch emigrated to the South of France in 1935, while Marianne Wischniak went to South America, where all trace of her disappears.

"Jewish Home for the Infirm and Elderly"

The national body representing the interests of the German Jews, which had existed since September 1933, was 'Nazified' by the regime in 1939. From that point onwards, under the new name "Reich Association of German Jews" it was nothing more than an administrative body required to execute the orders of the National Socialist authorities. The Reich Association rented the Heidmann villa in April 1940, to transform it into a "Jewish Home for the Infirm and Elderly" to serve as a residence for sick and elderly Jews. The cruel truth concealed behind this official version was very different, however. The home was, in fact, a collection station from where Jews from Potsdam and the surrounding area, as well as from other parts of Europe were transported to the ghetto in Riga and to the extermination camps.

1 Property appraisal form of the municipality of Klein Glienicke no. 128 for Bergstrasse 1, Potsdam City Archives, shelf number 1-13/681.

GUREWITSCH or **BICHOWSKY** Sima of 8 Rue Guiglia Nice **France** widow died 29 December 1946 at The Belvedere Clinic 12 Boulevard Tzarevitch Nice Administration (with Will) (limited) **London** 5 April to David Bertram Levinson solicitor attorney of Tamara Lipszyc and Zerta Nacht. Effects £32204 11s. 4d. in England.

left: Notice announcing the death of Sima Gurewitsch in: The Palestine Gazette no. 1579, Thursday May 15, 1947, p. 506

right: The Heidmann villa, 1940

Among those forcibly quartered here was Samuel Guttmann, the last cantor of the Jewish synagogue in Potsdam, and his wife Rebecka. Guttmann was not only a gifted musician but was also active as an author and a committed representative of his fraternity; in 1928, for example, he was the first chair of the Association of Cantors of Greater Berlin. After 1933, the Nazis increased pressure on the Jewish community in Potsdam with ever more aggressive attacks. In 1938 they destroyed the interior of the synagogue—the fact that it was not set alight is probably because they did not want to put the post office, which was in the direct vicinity, at any risk. Guttmann himself was placed in "protective custody" from November 10, 1938, until May 3, 1939, after which he and his wife were committed to the Jewish Home for the Infirm and Elderly in the Heidmann villa, where his wife died in 1942 aged not sixty-five.[2]

How disgracefully the Nazi authorities acted can be seen not least in the fact that they plundered their victims down to the very last Reichsmark and even had them pay for their own deportation and detainment, which usually ended in a violent death. All of this was arranged and documented with "German thoroughness" in accordance with the applicable administrative rules. Shortly after the death of his wife, Samuel Guttmann was presented with a "home purchase contract" for accommodation in Theresienstadt concentration camp, which was extolled in the Nazi Propaganda as being a "model Jewish city":

Home Purchase Contract no. II 39, 42 [...]
a) Mr Samuel Guttmann hereby acknowledges the following:
As the Reich Association is responsible for furnishing the funds for the entirety of those to be accommodated together (in Theresienstadt), including those in need of assistance, it is the duty of all persons designated for community accommodation who have the available means through the purchase sum to be paid by them to the Reich Association to cover not only the costs of their own accommodation but also, to the extent possible, the costs of providing for those in need of financial assistance. [...]
Home Purchase Contract no. II 39, 42. Babelsberg, October 18, 1942

Samuel Guttmann signed the "contract" on October 18 and handed the last of his cash to the employees of the Reich Association of Jews in Germany (225 Reichsmark) as well as his savings book with the Stadtsparkasse Potsdam, with a balance of RM 1624.67. His name was already crossed off the list of Jews still resident in Potsdam on October 6, 1942. On January 16, 1943, the Gestapo closed the Jewish

2 Cf. List of Jews resident in Potsdam as per 6.10.1942, Brandenburgisches Landesarchiv Potsdam, Rep 2 A, Regierung Potsdam I Pol.

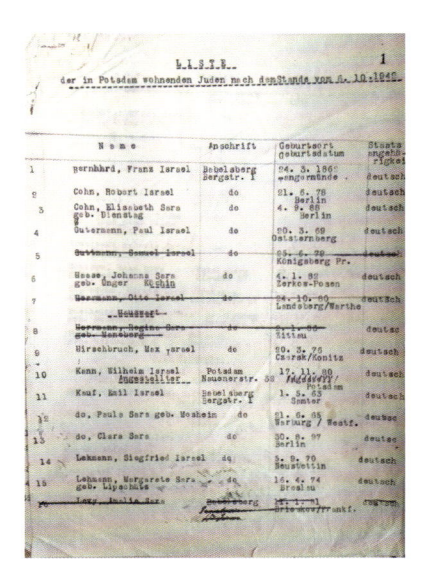

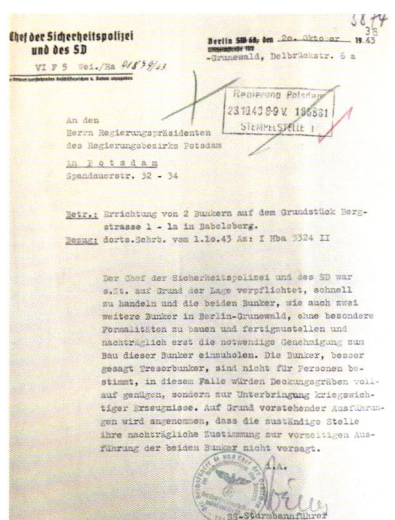

Home for the Infirm and Elderly. Together with the other remaining inmates, Samuel Guttmann was brought to Theresienstadt where he was murdered in May 1943.

The sudden evacuation of the Heidmann villa is likely to have been related to the construction of two vault bunkers there, intended not for persons, but for *"war-related products"*. As the official correspondence details, the building department of the Prussian Building and Finance Directorate in charge of constructing the bunkers advised the leadership of the local government in Potsdam, that the two bunkers had been completed *"for urgent reasons"*—this is doubtless a reference to the increasingly precarious military situation—without prior approval. The approval was to be subsequently issued. Whether it concerned the deportation of innocent people to extermination camps, or the military measures deemed necessary, it is evident that the maintenance of orderly procedures was afforded priority at every step of the official National Socialist actions.

The Secret State Police subsequently implemented the expropriation under administrative law and seized the property of Mrs Wischniak by notice dated May 3, 1944, IV 4 b 1 – W 181/44 citing the Decree of the Reich President for the Protection of People and State of February 28, 1933, in conjunction with Section 14 of the Police Administration Law of June 1, 1931, and Section 1 of the Law concerning the Secret State Police of February 10, 1936.[3]

Reticent Remembrance

Based on the entry in the Land Registry, when the war ended the land belonging to the Heidmann villa, and the building itself, which had suffered war damage, was still the property of Sima Gurewitsch and Marianne Wischniak. In the GDR, the municipal housing administration was responsible for property administration. The villa, which, following the deportation of the last inmates, had for a time served as an office for the SS, fell into disrepair. In 1963, Raoul Hurlin, the surveyor commissioned by the City of Potsdam, determined that the building could no longer be rescued. His report states *"The building is categorised as a destroyed structure (ruin)."*[4]

left: Although Samuel Guttmann only signed the "home purchase contract" on October 18, 1942, his name had already been crossed off the list of "Jews resident in Potsdam" dated "6.10.1942" (see no. "5")

centre: "… to be built without further formalities …" Request for the retroactive approval of the construction of two "vault bunkers" on the Heidmann villa property, October 1943

right: Memorial to the fate of the Jews who died in the Heidmann villa or were transported from here to Nazi extermination camps, 2010

3 Brandenburgisches Landeshauptarchiv, Rep. 105 Ga K V Pdm Neubabelsberg, volume 17, sheet 411 P 1266.

4 Current value appraisal survey of January 4, 1963, Potsdam City Archives, archive shelf number: Soz/04767.

It is likely, however, that the desire to vacate the property for GDR border troops at this strategically important site was behind this evaluation. The villa was thereupon demolished. For decades, there was no reminder of Karl Heidmann's striking domed villa, nor of the fate of the people who had lived in the Jewish Home for the Infirm and Elderly.

Following reunification, a house to home several families was built at the place where the villa once stood. It is thanks not to state or municipal authorities, but to an initiative of students from the Espengrund-Gymnasium, which has since closed, that a memorial stone with a bronze plaque in front of the new building keeps alive the memory of the history of this unique place.[5]

5 Cf. Memorial Jewish Home for the Elderly, https://potsdam-wiki.de/index.php/Gedenkstein_J%C3%BCdisches_Altenheim.

"... collected under rather brutal circumstances"

Marie Louise Sarre, the neighbour who lived in the villa at Bergstrasse 6, had attempted to help the Jews interned at the Jewish Home for the Infirm and Elderly. As she wrote in a letter to a friend, she was not afraid to go to the Gestapo:

"I did a very stupid thing in January 1943. Do you remember the big domed villa opposite our house, in Bergstr.? It looked like an observatory. In '38 or '39 it was made into a Jewish care home for the elderly. I was often over there at night, in secret, to take care of the people—I brought them food and procured false passports etc. They were very simple Jewish people from Galicia and Czechoslovakia, among them an absolutely charming young doctor with whom I established a real rapport. It's all too long to describe in full. In short: one night, the mother of the doctor had me told that they were all to be removed to Poland and asked if there was anything I could do. They were collected the next day under rather brutal circumstances. I visited them, again at night, in the Jewish camp in Auguststr. in Berlin. A terrible place (I thought at the time, though one later saw far more terrible things). Having already spoken to several important people to no avail, I could think of no other way, and next morning entered the lion's den in Prinz Albrecht Str. to speak with Wolff (who at the time was still Himmler's aide, the same person who negotiated with Gero here). I knew him a little and knew that he was somebody that one could talk to. Unfortunately, he wasn't there, but I couldn't wait because these people were to be transported onward to certain death the very next morning. So, I spoke with another high-up man, his deputy, soon realised that it was pointless, but by that time it was already too late, and I ended up having quite a set-to with him. (He later claimed that I had shouted at him). He told the whole story to the Gestapo in Potsdam, who—albeit not until four weeks later!—picked me up out of the blue in February 1943. House search etc. Seizure of contents of my desk, a pretty awful prison in Potsdam and questioning all day long. The outcome: six months in a concentration camp for aiding and abetting Jews. L. saved me from this after three days. The whole story was a blessing. After all, it meant I was "somewhat familiar" with the methods and approach of these people. When I was free again, I destroyed all written records, which later saved my life. (Without the warning, I would never have become so careful)."

Marie Louise Sarre, letter dated October 11, 1945, German Resistance Memorial Centre, Berlin [translation: author's own].

The Riehl House

This house owes its existence to a gamble, some would even say a reckless decision. The contract for the design of the building was awarded to Ludwig Mies van der Rohe in 1906. At that time, van der Rohe was just twenty years old, an as yet unknown student of the Academy of Fine Arts, without a single completed project to his name. The daring clients in question were philosopher Alois Riehl and his wife. Riehl had been awarded a professorship the year before at the Friedrich-Wilhelm University in Berlin (today's Humboldt University). Riehl evidently had the inner freedom and largesse to be impressed by the personality of the budding architect.

Spitzweggasse 3 (formerly Bergstrasse 3)

Academic Career

Alois Riehl was born in 1844 by Bozen in South-Tyrol, which at the time belonged to Austria. On completing his studies and his state examinations, he was awarded a doctorate in philosophy at the University of Innsbruck. A postdoctoral lecturing qualification at the University of Graz followed, where he taught first as a non-salaried lecturer and later as a professor. From 1882, he spent thirteen years working as a university lecturer in Freiburg, then in Kiel and, from 1898 to 1904, in Halle. By 1905, when Riehl took over the professorial chair in Berlin from Wilhelm Dilthey, one of the main proponents of the *'Lebensphilosophie'* (lit. philosophy of life) movement and the founder of hermeneutics as one of the fundamental methods in academic study, he had already enjoyed a long and successful academic career.

The Riehl House, south-east side with entry, 1940

This was in spite of the fact that he was anything but a careerist—just as he was far from being a dull academic who always toed the line. He maintained his free-thinking independence in the face of all ideology and was never afraid to speak his mind. In his early publication *Moral und Dogma* (1871) he had polemicised against the Catholic church's claim to the absolute truth of its doctrine and described dogma as an *"injustice against humanity"* and as a *"delusion, which cannot be pursued and eradicated enough"*[1]. He was so resolute in his views that he left the Catholic church. All of this exposed him to the wrath of the Archbishop in Freiburg, who prohibited the theology students at the university there from visiting Riehl's lectures—thereby emphatically confirming precisely what Riehl had so harshly criticised. Riehl was forced to retreat to Halle.

In Halle, a year after his appointment, the philosopher was selected to join the *"Spirituskreis"* (Spiritus Circle). Founded in 1890, it was a thoroughly elitist group of professors from the faculties of philosophy, theology, and law at the university. They met regularly to exchange academic ideas across the bounds of their respective disciplines, not at the university but privately, which was unusual at the time, when such discussion groups were established in many university towns[2]. The professorial circle, always composed of twelve members, existed until 1958. The circle, which upheld bourgeois traditions, was prohibited by members of the SED-regime, which suspected it of having "revisionist" ambitions.

From Kant to Nietzsche

Alois Riehl's work is considered a part of Neo-Kantianism, a movement that heavily influenced philosophy in Germany for around half a century, until the 1920s. It took Immanuel Kant's critical thinking as its starting point and attempted, taking account of more recent developments, to continue these considerations in the humanities and in the natural sciences. Kant's "transcendental philosophical"

left: Alois Riehl

right: The "Spirituskreis" in 1902. Standing from left to right: Georg Wissowa, Eduard Meyer, Alois Riehl, Johannes Conrad, Carl Robert, Rudolf Stammler, Emil Kautzsch, Max Reischle. Seated from left to right: Erich Haupt, Edgar Loening, Friedrich Loofs, Wilhelm Dittenberger. The portraits on the wall depict Benno Erdmann and Richard Pischel. The picture on the chair to the right is of Hermann Schmidt.

1 Quoted based on Hans-Ludwig Ollig: Der Neukantianismus, Stuttgart 1979, p. 26.

2 Cf. Matthias Asche, Dietmar Klenke (eds.) with the assistance of Sabrina Lausen: Von Professorenzirkeln, Studentenkneipen und akademischem Networking. Universitäre Geselligkeiten von der Aufklärung bis zur Gegenwart, Cologne/Weimar/Vienna 2017, p. 68.

approach, as developed in his *Critique of Pure Reason* aimed first to establish the conditions of knowledge independent of empirical experience. Now, one of Riehl's main goals was to answer, at least in part, one of the questions that Kant had left unanswered, namely: to what extent do the ideas of the world that we have based on our own individual form of consciousness, correspond with those of the "real" existence of things. Kant had explained that it was not possible to make any statements as to how the world is made independently from our understanding—the famous "thing-in-itself" is something that largely remains inaccessible to us.

Riehl, by contrast, argued (here, too, going against all purely subjectivist interpretations of Kant's theory) that it is, on the one hand, reasonable to rely on a reality that references our knowledge and that, secondly, there are ways of directly perceiving these *per se* existing realities, namely by using our senses, which do not create things but only respond thereto; or by using our altruistic feelings, upon which we stake our social relationships; and finally through the experience that our will continually reaches its limits, thereby confirming a resistant reality beyond the bounds of our consciousness.[3]

In addition to these considerations relating to epistemological realism, as developed in his main work, which spans three volumes, *Philosophy of Criticism and its Significance for Positive Science*, Riehl also explored issues in other areas, such as the history of the natural sciences, aesthetics, as well as issues relating to poetry. His early interest in the work of Friedrich Nietzsche was unusual. Nietzsche was viewed with a degree of contempt in academic philosophical circles. His aphoristic style, his harsh polemic against Christianity and the moral ideals shaped by it, his deconstruction of the traditional definition of truth, his concept of *"Will to Power"*— most professors of philosophy found the radical nature of these views and concepts off-putting.

Riehl, whose essay *Friedrich Nietzsche. Der Künstler und der Denker (Friedrich Nietzsche. The Artist and the Thinker)* was published in 1897, is likely to have been one of the first people to recognise the importance of Nietzsche's work. However, Riehl made

[3] Cf. Hans-Ludwig Ollig: Riehl, Alois, in. Metzler Philosophen-Lexikon. Von den Vorsokratikern bis zu den Neuen Philosophen, published by Bernd Lutz, third updated and revised edition, Stuttgart 2015, p. 606f.

The exclusive Spiritus Circle

"Soon after knowledge of its existence spread, the professorial circle at Halle University was given the nickname 'Spirituskreis', which was originally intended as an insult. Scientists who would have liked to have been a part of this decidedly exclusive academic circle had to acknowledge with disappointment that their presence was not welcome. In response, inspired by the "Spirituskartell" (lit. the alcohol cartel), they settled on the name "Spirituskreis". The members targeted by the insult simply turned the tables. They applied the term "Spiritus" in the medieval sense, meaning 'spirit' and from then on self-deprecatingly referred to themselves as the "Spirit Circle". Even colleagues from the faculty of philosophy who as academics proposed positions that were alien and untenable to them, were not tolerated and were instead vehemently challenged as foes."

Matthias Asche, Dietmar Klenke (eds.) with the assistance of Sabrina Lausen: Von Professorenzirkeln, Studentenkneipen und akademischem Networking. Universitäre Geselligkeiten von der Aufklärung bis zur Gegenwart, Cologne/Weimar/Vienna 2017, p. 67 [translation: author's own].

a surprising mistake when he suggested, together with colleagues, that Elisabeth Förster-Nietzsche, the sister and executor of the philosopher's estate, be awarded the Nobel prize for Literature in 1908. Elisabeth Förster-Nietzsche did not herself have any great understanding of philosophy, nor had she demonstrated any notable literary accomplishments. Incidentally, the many forgeries and manipulations she had made in her brother's letters following his death had not yet come to light at this time.

Riehl had the opportunity to enjoy late academic recognition of his efforts to have Nietzsche's philosophy appropriately interpreted when he retired. In a speech presented on April 26, 1924, which again underlines the explosive nature of Nietzsche's thinking, the rector of Friedrich-Wilhelm University attested to his departing colleague: *"You placed fundamental and problematic philosophical figures in their historical context, but also based on their personal core, you appreciated Nietzsche's dangerous and yet so infinitely fruitful prophesying in a profound understanding of its symptomatic significance for the power of struggling living souls, and fought for a new understanding of Kant's outstanding personality, which continues to determine all of our philosophical thinking."*[4] The disconcerting, almost militant pathos with which the philosophers are here elevated to the status of intellectual heroes, who see themselves as fighting for what is right, struggling for truth, was very much in keeping with the mood of the time; indeed, it was none other than Nietzsche who had pushed this tendency to its limits when he said of himself: *"I am not a man, I am dynamite."*[5] As professors at the universities, philosophers like Riehl were something of the popstars of their time. Hundreds, sometimes thousands of students came to their lectures and worshipped them like heroes. Riehl wrote of his profession: *"Being able to see what is so obvious that it is overlooked by most people is the true mark of scientific genius."*

The Riehl House—Mies van der Rohe's architectural debut

The way the decision as to who should build his house was reached was every bit as unconventional as Alois Riehl's choice of architect. In a conversation with his grandson Dirk Lohan, Ludwig Mies van der Rohe described his first exchanges concerning the project with Sophie Riehl, the wife of the philosopher:

"... I had a conversation with Mrs Riehl, who asked me: 'Well, what have you built to date?' 'Nothing', I said, to which she responded: 'We can't have that—we don't want to be guinea pigs.' 'Yes', I said, 'I can build a house. I just haven't done it on my own yet. I've done it though. Imagine if people were to ask me: 'Have you done this before?' until I'm sixty or so.' She had to laugh and wanted to introduce me to her husband. That very evening she would be having company, a dinner party at her house ..."

Mies van der Rohe, who at the time was employed as an assistant at the offices of renowned Berlin-based architect Bruno Paul while also attending lectures at the School of Arts and Crafts and the Academy of Fine Arts, appeared at the Riehls' that evening and paid the master of the house a visit dressed in a frockcoat he had hurriedly bought on credit: *"After the meal, the privy councillor then invited me into his library. We went there and he asked me questions, about all kinds of things,*

4 The Rector of Friedrich-Wilhelms-Universität, speech of April 26, 1924, Humboldt University Archives HU UA, UK Personalia, no. R141, volume 1.

5 Friedrich Nietzsche: Ecce Homo. How One Becomes What One Is (Section "Why I Am a Destiny", I), in: Friedrich Nietzsche: Werke III, published by Karl Schlechta, Frankfurt am Main/Berlin/Vienna 1976, p. 598.

Alois Riehl on the essence of genius in science: "Being able to see what is so obvious that it is overlooked by most people is the true mark of scientific genius. This is how Newton saw the moon falling earthwards, which had provided him insights into the mechanics of the heavens." June 24, 1882 [translation: author's own]

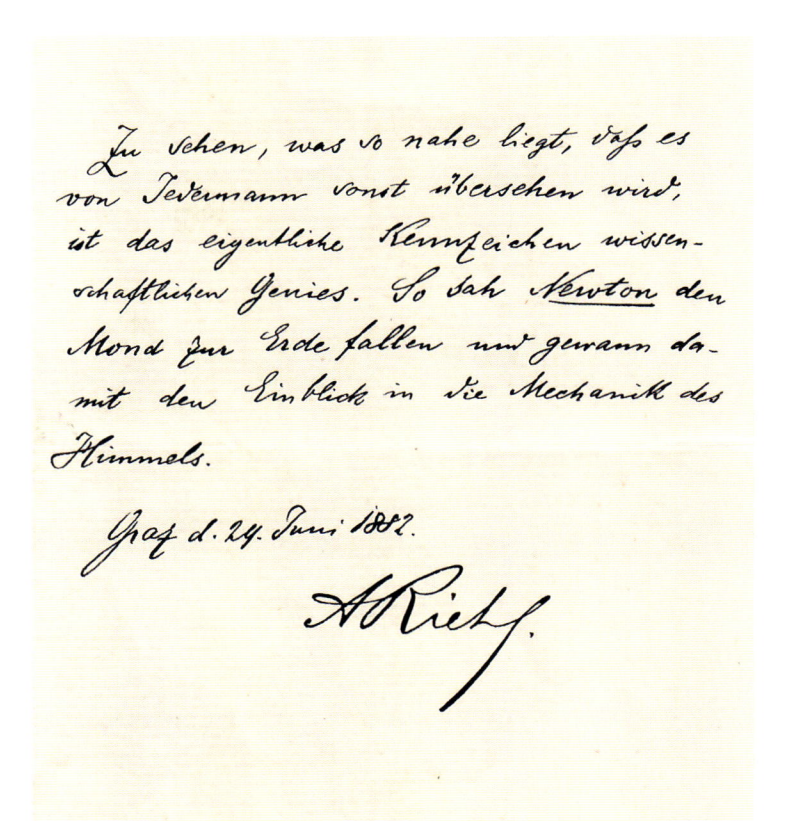

none of which I can remember any more. Then he said: 'We mustn't keep the other guests waiting', and we returned to the dining room. To his wife, he said: 'He is going to build our house.'[6]

And so it came to pass. Construction work began in 1907 following the approval of the draft submitted by Mies. Whether the building was completed the same year or in 1908 is the subject of debate. The question of whether the six-week trip to Italy that Mies undertook at the suggestion of the Riehls and with their financial support took place before he finished the draft and had served as preparation or whether it took place after the completion of the house, as a reward so to speak, has not been conclusively ascertained either.[7]

According to Mies, the house is *"not a villa"*, but *"rather, its character resembled the houses in the Märkische region, like those in Werder which have a simple pitched roof, a gable and a pair of dormers, usually of the eyebrow kind."*[8] While this is indisputably true, it is not the whole truth. The short side facing Bergstrasse (today Spitzweggasse) in particular has a pronounced simple style with its smooth façade—one could almost call it bare, were it not for the central balcony. The opposite side facing Griebnitzsee, however, provides an entirely different picture. Mies made clever use of the slope of the land by constructing a wide supporting wall, which served as the base for a small garden, but first and foremost as a plinth for the loggia and the gable above. The result is that this part of the house rises high above the park area in front of it, which slopes down to the lakeshore, lending a whole new perspective to the loggia with its four pillars. From this angle, the simple Märkisch-style house looked like an antique temple that dominated the landscape above the lake.

6 Fritz Neumeyer, Mies van der Rohe. Das kunstlose Wort: Gedanken zur Baukunst, Berlin 1986, p. 65f.

7 Cf. Jörg Limberg: Haus Riehl, Neubabelsberg. Sanierung und denkmalpflegerische Begleitung, in: Mies van der Rohe. Frühe Bauten, Probleme der Erhaltung, Probleme der Bewertung, published by Johannes Cramer and Dorothée Sack, Petersberg 2004 (Berliner Beiträge zur Bauforschung und Denkmalpflege 1), p. 27–41, especially the section "Gedanken zur Neudatierung des Hauses", p. 36–38.

8 Ludwig Mies van der Rohe in conversation in the documentary film Mies van der Rohe by Georgia van der Rohe, 1986, quoted based on: Carsten Krohn: Mies van der Rohe, Das gebaute Werk, Basel 2014, p. 16.

121

It was presumably in the 1930s that the loggia, which until that point had been open, was fully glazed and enclosed. As a result, the original temple-like feel no longer exists, though the observer can still enjoy an impressive view of the building.

The architecture designed by Mies van der Rohe is characterised by its clarity and simplicity, as well as by calculability and rationality. This applies both to the exterior of the building, the façade, and to the interior. How precisely considered the rooms inside the Riehl House are became clear during the course of the comprehensive renovation work conducted between 1998 and 2001: an inspection of various elements of the interior showed that Mies had calculated a basic dimension that recurs frequently in various modified forms and in this way determined a large proportion of the room components like a variable grid. The tiles on the fireplace, for example, are fifteen centimetres squared, the wall panels in the central hall have precisely double the area, namely thirty centimetres × thirty centimetres; the staircase has a ratio of thirty centimetres (stair width) to fifteen centimetres (stair height). While this strict geometric design is not upheld throughout, the principle is evident and is echoed again on the façade in the form of the forty-five-centimetre-wide pilasters.[9]

These efforts to build the architectural design on a rational concept likely reflects the influence of Peter Behrens, who also used a universal organisation system as the basis for his building and to whose offices Mies transferred in 1908. Even more, however, Mies is likely to have oriented his work towards his teacher, Bruno Paul, as Mies biographer Franz Schulze surmises: *"Although the Riehl House represents a respectable attempt, it was nevertheless an educational piece that, through its mixture of ideas from different provenances, shows how much its builder was still searching for his own style. Even if some things point compellingly in this direction, most of the house points to the influence of Bruno Paul."*[10]

The meeting place of the intellectual world

It is important also to mention the Arts-and-Crafts movement. Some of its ideas may have inspired the layout and design of the interiors, such as the large hall at the

left: The Riehl House with open loggia shortly after completion, between 1908 and 1910

right: The Riehl House with fully-glazed loggia, 2006

9 Cf. Limberg 2004 (see note 7), p. 39.

10 Franz Schulze: Mies van der Rohe. Leben und Werk, Berlin 1986, p. 31 [translation: author's own].

centre of the ground floor, which led on the side facing the street to the living room and study and, on the side facing the lake, to the loggia with views of Griebnitzsee. This was an ideal place for socialising—while Alois Riehl did not entertain an elite academic crowd at his home in Neubabelsberg like the 'Spirituskränzchen' in Halle, many colleagues and friends visited, including Walther Rathenau and the great art historian, Heinrich Wölfflin. Wölfflin made a key contribution to the systematisation of terminology with his main work on the fundamentals of art history, first published in 1915. The young Mies van der Rohe was also part of the Riehl's inner circle for many years. He met lots of people at the house, some of whom helped to advance his career and others who enriched his private life. It was during a visit to the Riehls that he met dancer Ada Bruhn, who at the time was living with her friend Mary Wigman, founder of modern expressive dance, in the garden city of Hellerau near Dresden. From then on, Mies van der Rohe visited Hellerau frequently. He married Ada Bruhn in April 1913.

In 1916, Riehl welcomed educationalist Eduard Spranger, a student of Wilhelm Dilthey, as a permanent guest. Spranger became seriously ill that year and had requested a year's release from his duties as professor of philosophy and pedagogy at the University of Leipzig. In 1919 he was appointed to Friedrich-Wilhelms University Berlin, where Riehl also taught. Spranger soon attained cult status and his lectures are said to have been attended by more than one-thousand-three-hundred students. His work provides important insights into cultural philosophy and psychology in the humanities and was a driving force behind the recognition of pedagogy as a distinct academic subject.

New splendour following renovation work

Alois Riehl died in November 1924 aged eighty, and it was Eduard Spranger who gave the eulogy at his graveside. Heinrich Maier, a professor of philosophy in Berlin since 1922 and, like Riehl, a Neo-Kantian, reported: *"Again we experienced all the magic*

Max Liebermann awarded the title of Dr. phil. Honoris causa

In March 1912, Friedrich-Wilhelm University Berlin awarded Max Liebermann an honorary doctorate. The corresponding application to the Dean of the Philosophy Faculty, which states that Liebermann had been "over three decades the most powerful force in Berlin's arts scene" features Alois Riehl's signature alongside many others. The application dated February 25, 1912, further explains: "Even if Impressionism is no longer the art form par excellence of our times, this name nevertheless describes one of the most German and most glorious phases in the development of modern art and is inextricably linked with Liebermann personally." The surprising use of the superlative of "German" in conjunction with Impressionism especially is likely not to have best pleased the Emperor, Wilhelm II., a fierce critic of modern art. The professor of philosophy and privy councillor Alois Riehl was also a member of the three-strong delegation of the University who presented Liebermann with *"the diploma attesting his new honour"* on March 20, 1912, at his home on Pariser Platz.

Quotes in: Max Liebermann: Briefe. volume 5, 1911–1915, compiled, commended and published by Ernst Braun, Baden-Baden 2015, p. 501 and 502 [translation: author's own].

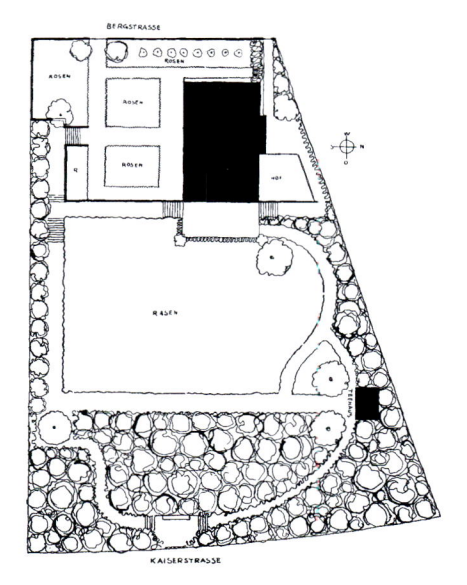

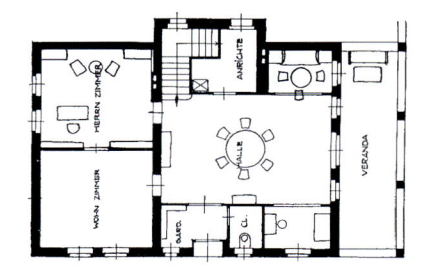

left: The Riehl House, south-east side, following repairs, reconstruction and interior work by Folkerts Architekten (1998–2000), 2001

right: The Riehl House, site plan and floor plans

The Riehl House following comprehensive restoration, 2020 (left: the street side, right: north-west side)

that he, the kind, warm-hearted person and astute, profound and far-sighted philosopher once exuded."[11] Alois Riehl's gravestone was designed by Mies van der Rohe.[12]

Following the death of his widow, Sophie Riehl, presumably towards the end of the 1920s, the house changed hands several times in the space of just a few years. Pursuant to the entry in the Land Register, however, the property continued to be owned by the Riehl family. Directly after the end of World War II, at the order of the Red Army, the Riehl House was cleared, along with the other villas in the area.

Until 1962, it served as the central office for the Border Patrol department of the People's Police in the GDR. Next, the administration of the "Konrad Wolf" Hochschule für Film und Fernsehen took up residence in the house and remained there until 1997.[13]

After the sale of the house in 1998 and the careful architectural-historical investigation that brought to light many new findings about the building, the new owner developed a comprehensive redevelopment concept in cooperation with the department for historic monuments. Ultimately, the overall condition of the house *"on account of the significant loss of original features both in the interior and on the exterior, can be categorised as under threat"*[14]. A clearly visible sign of this was the absence of the balcony on the street-facing gabled end. In the course of the meticulous restoration, the original floor plans and many details of the interior design were restored. Some changes remained in line with the wishes of the owner, like the loggia, which was originally open and was developed into more of a living space.[15] Following various different uses in the post-war period and decades of neglect, the first house ever built by Mies van der Rohe is today again that which it was intended to be, namely a simple but sophisticated, truly unique home that, together with the garden, provides a spacious and comfortable setting for its residents. Unfortunately, the Griebnitzsee is now no longer visible from the house.

---

11 Heinrich Maier: Alois Riehl. Memorial speech, held on January 24, 1925, in Kant-Studien, volume 31, issue 1-3, January 1, 1926, p. 563–579, here p. 563 [translation: author's own].

12 Neumeyer 1986 (see note 6), p. 68.

13 Cf. Limberg 2004 (see note 7), p. 27f.

14 Ibid., p. 32.

15 Cf. Ibid., p. 33.

The Sarre Villa

The splendid villa in the Italian Early-Renaissance style that Friedrich Sarre, affluent collector and the founder of Islamic art history, had built up high, overlooking Griebnitzsee, was a truly cosmopolitan place. Members of the Prussian aristocracy were frequent guests, as were representatives of the financial world, alongside scholars, museum directors and diplomats from the Ottoman Empire. For several years, the villa was home to an unusual guest—a war criminal wanted internationally. A little-known fact, however, is that the villa was also a hotbed of resistance against the Nazi regime.

Spitzweggasse 6 (formerly Bergstrasse 6)

A photograph dating from 1899 shows the owner of the villa, Friedrich Sarre, wearing oriental robes and sitting cross-legged (a position also known in Germany at the time as "sitting Turkish style") on a carpet. His outfit is complete with a 'Kufiyah', the traditional Arab headscarf and an 'Agal', the cord used to fasten the scarf. Behind Sarre, several pieces from his extensive collection of antique Islamic works of art are visible. Dressing *au style oriental* appears to have been popular among members of the Sarre family: another photograph, taken in around 1913, shows his four children, all elaborately dressed, with artfully wrapped turbans

Garden side of the Sarre villa with the three-arched loggia, 2019

instead of the Kufiyah. These unusual arrangements say a great deal about Friedrich Sarre, his life path, his academic interests and probably also about the way he saw himself.

In fact, these enactments, obviously celebrated with great gravity, were not all that unusual during that era. Over the course of the nineteenth century, Orientalism had become an established fixture in literature, art, and architecture. The paintings of classical French artists such as Jean-Auguste- Dominique Ingres and Jean-Léon Gérôme depicting Turkish baths and harem chambers were also popular among the German art audience. At the centre of Potsdam, Ludwig Persius had built his steam engine house, which could be seen for miles around, in the form of a mosque with a minaret-shaped chimney. Prussia's official contribution to the International Exposition in Paris in 1867 was a "Moorish" kiosk, designed by Berlin architect Carl von Diebitsch.

The self-portrayals of some explorers, authors and others with a vivid imagination demonstratively revealed a fascination with the Orient. There is, for instance, a photograph dating from 1880 of highly successful French travel writer Pierre Loti, who had a mihrab (an Islamic prayer niche) installed at his home; in the photograph, like Friedrich Sarre, he is wearing an ankle-length robe, a Kufiyah and Agal. Shortly before the turn of the century, the writer Karl May was photographed as his alter ego 'Kara ben Nemsi' wearing a sash and a Fez.[1] There are even reports that patriotic Bavarian king, Ludwig II., enjoyed "oriental" pastimes like drinking Arak and smoking a waterpipe, seated on carpets and appropriately costumed, of course, in the Turkish room of his hunting lodge in the Alps. The Bavarian king purchased the aforementioned Moorish kiosk designed by Prussian architect Carl von Diebitsch some years after the exposition and had the magnificent ornamental building placed in the park of his Linderhof Palace.

left: Friedrich Sarre wearing oriental robes

right: The Sarre children dressed in oriental costumes: Friedrich-Carl, Hans, Marie Louise, Irene (from left to right), Neubabelsberg around 1913 [?]

1 Cf. For example, Alfred Marquart: Aus Ardistan nach Dschinnistan, in: Exotische Welten. Europäische Phantasien, published by the Institut für Auslandsbeziehungen and the Württembergische Kunstverein, Stuttgart 1987, p. 78–81.

Friedrich Sarre

Friedrich Sarre

It is likely that, for Friedrich Sarre too, a longing for a different—perhaps more exciting—life contributed to his enjoyment of dressing in Oriental costume and having his photograph taken. However, it can be assumed that his enthusiasm for the Orient was not influenced by the caricatures of the culture that were common in Europe and the sometimes obscure projections of superficial exoticism. Rather, ideally prepared by his academic qualifications, it is likely that he was driven by scientific and political interests.

An Explorer and Collector

Friedrich Sarre came from a Huguenot family that had fled from Metz to Prussia in 1685 after Louis XIV prohibited Protestantism in France. Sarre's father Théodore André Sarre worked as a merchant at the Berlin copper and iron processing undertaking of industrial magnate and philanthropist, Carl-Justus Heckmann, whose daughter Mathilde Théodore married. Her sister, Elise Wentzel-Heckmann took Sarre in following the early death of his parents and it was also she who throughout his life financed his research expeditions as well as the construction of his splendid villa in Babelsberg.

From 1885 to 1890, Friedrich Sarre studied art history in Leipzig, where he was also awarded a PhD. Back in Berlin, he became an academic assistant at the royal museums of Berlin and published books on Berlin's goldsmiths' guild and on German silver craftsmanship of the eighteenth century. He was also involved in the catalogue detailing the Empress Victoria's extensive collection published in 1896 by Wilhelm von Bode, the director of the art gallery and the sculpture department[2]. The wife of Emperor Friedrich III, who had a keen interest in art, had been *"very pleased"* with the catalogue and *"did not know how to thank me enough"*[3]. It is thought that his work on this publication was what ignited Sarre's enthusiasm for ancient

2 "Certain parts of this work were completed by former assistants of my department, including Fr. Sarre, R. Graul and others [...]". Wilhelm von Bode: Mein Leben, volume 2, Berlin 1930, p. 104 [translation: author's own].

3 Ibid. p. 111.

128

Islamic art. His enthusiasm was evidently so great that he was not content to academically record, and document works of art in Berlin, but instead wanted to travel to the Orient and carry out his own research there and, possibly, even to discover something new.

Following various failed attempts to obtain the consent of the Ottoman authorities for a dig in the Hittite capital of Hattuša (approx. 1550–1200 B.C.), Sarre decided in 1895 to study the architecture of the Seljuks and Ottomans in the southern Turkish city of Konya. Konya had been the capital of the Seljuk Sultanate of Rum In the twelfth century. On his way there, he visited the archaeologist Carl Humann in Smyrna (today Izmir), who had overseen the archaeological excavations in Pergamon and brought the famous Pergamon altar to Berlin. At that time, Humann, who held the post of foreign director of the royal museums, lived in the harbour town by the Aegean. It was here that Sarre met Humann's daughter, Maria, whom he went on to marry in 1900.

This first excursion was followed by a number of extensive research expeditions to Asia Minor, Persia, and Turkistan between 1895 and 1908. The numerous photographs of Islamic buildings taken by Sarre in these regions still have great documentary value. The last archaeological expedition before World War I, from 1911 to 1913, took Sarre to Samarra, which had once been the seat of the Abbasid Caliphate. In addition to the funding he received from his aunt, Elise Wentzel-Heckmann, the Kaiser Wilhelm Society for the Advancement of Science, a fund set up by Emperor Wilhelm II, Sarre's nephew Georg Heckmann and the Deutsche Bank co-financed the trip. The expedition, together with archaeologist Ernst Herzfeld, was Sarre's greatest archaeological success.

Sarre soon became a sought-after expert on Iranian and Islamic art, not least on account of the many experiences he had gained in the course of his research expeditions. He realised with delight that, following the example of Paris, London, and New York, with the dawn of the new century, interest in the "Islamic Orient" was slowly growing in Berlin, too. In addition to the state institutions, he wrote, now *"the Berlin art trade is also beginning to concern itself with valuable older pieces of Mohammedan art; the R. Wagner company, for instance, was recently in possession of very attractively coloured medieval faience vessels of Persian and Caucasian origin, while Ludwig Glenk is currently presenting an exhibition of Persian art that is well worth seeing."*[4]

Over the years, he, too, had purchased antiques, primarily ceramics, metalwork, and carpets during his visits to the Islamic countries and was one of the first to compile his own impressive private collection. When asked how he had been able to secure the best pieces from the outset, he replied: *"It was not so, only, I have eliminated my earlier mistakes."*[5] Furthermore, he added, he had discovered far more in Paris than in the Middle East.

Sarre's excellent knowledge and his skill as a purchaser benefited not only his own interests as a collector, but also made a significant contribution to the collection of the Museum of Islamic Art in Berlin. In 1912, for example, he purchased the splendid wooden panels from a house in Aleppo, Syria, with fine ornamental

4 Friedrich Sarre: Indisch-Islamische Miniaturen, in: Kunst und Künstler 6, 1907/08, p. 472.

5 Ernst Herzfeld: Friedrich Sarre, in: Ars Islamica, volume 11/12, 1946, p. 211f.

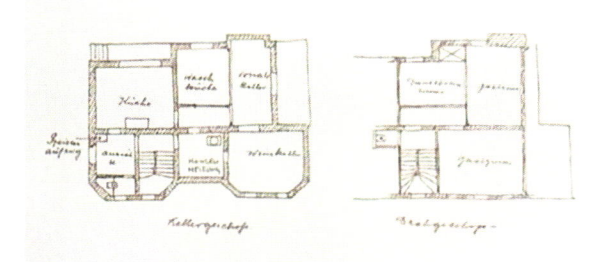

and in places figurative painting and arranged for them to be transported to the Prussian capital. To the present day, the 'Aleppo Room' is the centre piece of the Museum's collection.

Italian Renaissance by Griebnitzsee

When it came to planning his villa in Babelsberg, Friedrich Sarre looked to an entirely different artistic tradition, namely the architecture of the Renaissance. At first, however, things did not go as Sarre had envisaged. He had originally commissioned Darmstadt architect Joseph Maria Olbrich to draw up the plans for a villa. Olbrich, a devotee of art nouveau, submitted his sketches in 1903: an ingeniously transformed half-timbered house clad with blue tiles on the ground floor. Sarre, it would appear, had something more conservative in mind and found the plans too modern, too bold, and perhaps also not prestigious enough—whatever the reason, he rejected the plans.

He thereupon commissioned the official government architect for Berlin, the today largely unknown Otto Konrad Sior to prepare a new draft. It stands to reason that, by selecting a reliable and presumably less experimental architect, Sarre saw considerably more scope for himself to influence the project and to incorporate the ideas he had gathered on his many trips to Italy. Sior evidently did not disappoint. He designed a country house with a style that clearly references the Tuscan architecture of the fifteenth century and combines harmoniously with the tradition of Potsdam villa architecture established by Karl Friedrich Schinkel, which had also been inspired by the Italian archetype. The new Sarre family home was completed in 1905.

Like in a Tuscan villa, a rusticated basement, intended to be reminiscent of the fortified character of the Italian models, formed the base of the house. The Piano

left: Draft for a villa. Watercolour sketch and floorplans by the architect Joseph Maria Olbrich, 1903

right: Draft for a villa. Watercolour sketch by the architect Joseph Maria Olbrich, 1903

Nobile and the first storey above it are plastered and set off by cornices. The first level is also adorned with a portico beneath the roof, divided by pillars and corner posts. The portico and the large, three-arched loggia facing the garden break up the largely enclosed façade and add a certain lightness to the building. The portico and the arched window of the Piano Nobile reference Leon Battista Alberti's Palazzo Rucellai in Florence[6]—one of the most important buildings of the Early Renaissance, in which the influence of the architecture of Roman antiquity is particularly obvious.

    The heaviness of the main body of the villa is further diffused by the tall tower that houses a staircase leading to a tower room. Another portico crowns the tower, which provides fantastic views across Griebnitzsee and all the way to Berlin.

    Like the architects of the Renaissance, Sarre expressed his enthusiasm for antiquity with a multitude of spolia that he integrated into the façade of the

Postcard, written by Friedrich Sarre, with a photo of the Sarre villa, November 8, 1908

6 And not the villas of the Medici, as suggested by Jörg Limberg, in: Friedrich Sarre. Wohnen und Leben in der Villenkolonie Neubabelsberg, in: Wie die islamische Kunst nach Berlin kam: der Sammler und Museumsdirektor Friedrich Sarre (1865–1945), edited by Julia Gonnella and Jens Kröger, Berlin 2015, p. 61–78, here p. 65.

The Renaissance Cult

The only work on architecture passed down from antiquity, Roman author and architect Vitruvius' *The Ten Books on Architecture* had never disappeared but gained renewed popularity during the Early Renaissance. Leon Battista Alberti, who also made a name for himself as a sculptor, poet, musician, and mathematician, in his plans for Palazzo Rucellai closely observed the rules formulated by Vitruvius. However, the theoretical considerations set forth in Alberti's book *(On Architecture)*, which he completed in 1452, went far beyond Vitruvius' rules and in so doing dominated the discussion of architecture and architectural aesthetics until well into the eighteenth century.

Interest in the Italian Renaissance in Germany increased enormously as the nineteenth century drew to a conclusion. At times, it took on somewhat of a cult character. Swiss art and cultural historian Jacob Burckhardt's treatise The Civilization of the Renaissance in Italy, published in 1860, played a key role in this development and soon became part of the canon of the educated German bourgeoisie.

The lion frieze beneath the roof of the tower, 2019

building. The south side features a tombstone relief from Palmyra, a fragment of a sima (the upturned edge of a roof, which acted as a gutter on ancient buildings), and a Satyr relief. Sarre had brought these relics back from his archaeological expeditions. The other spolia were lost to plunderers during the war.

However, the showpiece, the real surprise, is the relievo made from glazed tiles with the strikingly beautiful depictions of lions against a blue background, which adorns the gallery below the roof of the tower. These are replicas of the enamelled tiles with animal motifs discovered in Babylon by Berlin archaeologist Robert Koldewey (a frequent visitor to the Sarres) several of which he brought back to Berlin. Reproductions of Babylonian relief art crowning the reproduction of a Renaissance villa—this marked Friedrich Sarre's most unique memorial to his fascination with ancient Oriental culture in his prestigious new residence. The excavations sponsored by Berlin's royal museums continued into the 1920s. The reconstruction from the many fragments discovered in Babylon of the Ishtar Gate and part of the Processional Way was not completed at the Pergamon Museum until 1930.

From Bergstrasse (today Spitzweggasse) a small bridge at ground level leads to the Piano Nobile. When it came to the floor plan and interiors, Sarre stuck to the contemporary preference for the *"hallway as the crowning glory"*[7] and placed a hall complete with a stairwell at the centre of the building. To the left of the hall, a corridor led to the "small library"—the "large library" was situated to the right of the hall. Unfortunately, directly after World War II, the entire interior furnishings, including all books and paintings, were lost to plunderers and destruction. Only one painting from the Tintoretto workshop, depicting a scene from the Battle of Lepanto, which hung in the stairwell, reappeared on the art market after the war.[8] The dining room and lounge faced north to the garden slightly below. The dining room led into the large loggia at the back of the house and from there into the garden, which sloped down towards the lake.

7 Wolfgang Brönner: Die bürgerliche Villa in Deutschland 1830 bis 1900, Worms 2009, p. 336f.

8 Jens Kröger: Friedrich Sarre, Kunsthistoriker, Sammler und Connaisseur, in: Julia Gonella und Jens Kröger 2015 (see note 6), p. 43, footnote 29.

The garden, with an area of 8,000 square metres, which also included a tennis court (modern "lawn tennis" experienced a rapid upswing in popularity in Germany around the turn of the century) was laid out like a park and led down the hill to Kaiserstrasse. Between the properties at Kaiserstrasse 27 and 28/29, a small plot of land on the opposite side of the road leads down right to the lake. Today, it still belongs to the grounds of the Sarre villa, but ends just before reaching the lake, since the return of these parcels of land was not requested following reunification. In 1911, Sarre had planned to build a boathouse with a terrace above, but the city building authorities refused to grant approval. Instead, he later had a jetty built, which was removed only when the Berlin Wall was built in 1961.

International Hospitality

The villa of Friedrich Sarre and his wife Maria in imperial Neubabelsberg had an open door and an international flair. It was, as the archaeologist and ancient-Orientalist Ernst Herzfeld wrote, *"a centre of hospitality known and admired by many people from Europe, America, and Asia"*[9]. One of the elements considered to be a matter of course for genteel bourgeois prestige was furnishing the parlour where guests were received with art treasures or other valuable possessions, to demonstrate the owners' high cultural standards. A preserved photograph of a generous living room at the Sarre villa provides an insight into the opulent interiors that were customary in upper-middle-class circles at the time. Works of art by esteemed contemporary artists also served to enhance the standing of their owners: the painter Max Liebermann, who was friends with the Sarres, painted a portrait of their son; there was a bust of Maria Sarre by sculptor Georg Kolbe. However, according to Herzfeld, in all of this Friedrich Sarre displayed a great *"modesty that never allowed him to assume an attitude of superiority"*[10].

Frequent guests included colleagues of Friedrich Sarre, such as the aforementioned archaeologists Robert Koldewey and Ernst Herzfeld, art historian Heinrich Wölfflin and museum director Wilhelm Bode. Neighbours from the Babelsberg villa colony, such as influential banker Jakob Goldschmidt, not to mention members of Berlin's social elite such as writer, diplomat, and patron of the arts Count Harry Kessler, were also guests at the villa. Kessler's diaries provide a unique insight into the Berlin of the 1920s and early 1930s, by day and by night. Maria Sarre is mentioned several times. Kessler describes conversations with her over breakfast concerning the issues of the time and reports having met her in the company of the former crown prince Wilhelm of Prussia and his wife, crown princess Cecilie, at a performance of Hofmannsthal's *The Difficult Man*: "In the first row of stalls sat the former Crown Prince and his wife along with Mrs Sarre (née Humann)." Incidentally, the sharp-tongued diarist did not pass up the opportunity after this entry to note his estimation of the crown prince. He had, despite the fact that in the meantime his hair had turned *"quite grey, almost white"*, retained all his *"junior officer mannerisms"*, and was still *"the youthful prince, who, in his character of a hussar, longed for a 'brisk, gay war'* and then *"lugged along his French whores on campaign"*. The diary entry

9 Ernst Herzfeld (see note 5), p. 211.

10 Ibid., p. 220.

closes with the malevolent summary: *"The hereditary Hohenzollern lack of taste reaches in him almost monumental proportions."*[11]

Oriental Connections

Maria Sarre grew up with her parents in Smyrna and spoke fluent French, English, and modern Greek. She shone not only as a charming hostess in the villa by Griebnitzsee but was also able to help her husband to realise his excavation projects in Turkey. All she had to do was get back in touch with old family contacts: as a little girl, she had often visited the home of Carl Humann's friend, painter and archaeologist Osman Hamdi Bey in Constantinople. He was the director of the first Ottoman museum of archaeology, as well as the general curator and, in that capacity, was responsible for approving excavations. In addition, the Sarres, as well as Maria's brother, Hans Humann also had a close friendship with Ottoman military man and politician, Enver Pasha, who had been a permanent guest of the family during his time as military attaché of the Ottoman Embassy in Berlin from 1909 to 1912. Before World War I, Enver Pasha advocated the strengthening of German-Turkish cooperation; a military alliance was intended to help prevent an Italian attack on Libya and the British attempts to expand their rule in Palestine and Syria. Later, Enver Pasha led his country into war alongside Germany and Austro-Hungary as war minister and repelled the Czarist Russian troops in the north and the British invasion by Gallipoli to the south. At the same time, he deployed brutal force against his political enemies and the Armenian population in his home country. In addition to Cemal Pasha and Talaat Pasha, he is considered one of the main persons responsible for the Armenian genocide.

For the German Empire, which under Wilhelm II. avowedly pursued the goal of advancing to become a world power, the alliance with the Ottoman Empire

left: A richly furnished living room in the Sarre Villa

right: A portrait photograph of Maria Sarre

11 Berlin, October 10, 1930. Friday, in Harry Graf Kessler. Tagebücher 1926–1937, edited by Sabine Gruber and Ulrich Ott, volume 9, Stuttgart 2010, p. 384; translated in Berlin in Lights, the diaries of Count Harry Kessler, 1918–1937". Grove Press New York 2000, p. 398/399 leaving out Mrs. Sarre; author´s own translation.

Breakfast chats

Diary entry of writer Count Harry Kessler following a visit to the German Academy for Physical Education in Grunewald:

"It is true what Mrs Sarre (née Humann) said to me later over breakfast. In many ways, especially in Germany, we are returning, unconsciously and naturally, to the habits of the Greeks. Nudity, light, fresh air, sunshine, worship of living, bodily perfection, sensuousness without either false shame or prudishness. But it is astonishing how much finer young peoples' bodies are today than before the war."

Berlin, July 14, 1930. Monday, in: Harry Graf Kessler, Tagebücher 1926–1937, edited by Sabine Gruber and Ulrich Ott, volume 9, Stuttgart 2010, p. 369; Berlin in Lights, the diaries of Count Harry Kessler, 1918–1937, Grove Press New York 2000, p. 395 leaving out Mrs. Sarre; author´s own translation

---

forged in 1914 served another important strategic function: through the territory of the new ally, it would be possible to advance directly into the Middle East and Central Asia—areas that had hitherto been under the influence of the great powers of Russia, France, and Great Britain. Friedrich Sarre, who was a cavalry captain of the reserve and a committed patriot, did not hesitate to dedicate his intimate knowledge of the geography and culture of Persia to a German-Ottoman military operation when the war broke out. The goal of the mission was, from Persia, to prevent British troops from attacking Iraq and its oil reserves, which belonged to the Ottoman Empire, and to weaken Russia's strong influence in Persia. To this end, the plan was to incite an insurgency against the government in Teheran, and ultimately, from Turkey's perspective, to have a holy war, a 'Jihad', declared against the Russians and the British. The intervention failed miserably. Sarre, who for a time was consul of a Persian counter-government in the West Persian city of Kermanshah, which was occupied by Ottoman troops, explained in a confidential report to the marine attaché in Constantinople, why the mission had been unsuccessful. His assessment was blunt: due to the lack of unified leadership of the operation, a damaging tussle for competence had ensued. The over-ambitious goals had not been attainable with the meagre means provided. In addition, both the Turks and the Persians had been dealt with wrongly. Sarre sharply criticised above all, the presumptuous, ignorant attitude of those in political and military positions of responsibility:

"Only those who were reasonably familiar with the situation never entertained the hope that it would take only the mere appearance of German officers to revolutionise the whole of Persia within a short time and, with promises of money and the prospect of the supply of arms, to mobilise the greater part of the tribes and the settled population against Russia and England. It was also to be expected that the holy war declared by the Caliph, whom the Persians did not recognise, would have no effect in a Shiite country." [12]

Sarre retreated to Constantinople where, as he had done in Palmyra, he pursued his archaeological studies further. He finally returned to Germany in 1918.

Talaat Pasha, Cemal Pasha and Enver Pasha, all three of whom by that time stood accused of war crimes in Istanbul, made their way to Berlin and Potsdam.

[12] Typewritten report by Friedrich Sarre. Copy. Neubabelsberg, July 4, 1916. 13 pages, quote from page 3. Federal Archives Freiburg, BA-MA RM 40/214, 100: F. Sarre, Report (June 1916).

Friedrich and Maria Sarre stood by their old friend and took in Enver Pasha at their villa by Griebnitzsee. He lived there until January 1921. For Maria Sarre in particular, who had also maintained confidential correspondence with him during the war years, this is sure to have posed a precarious situation. Maria, who in the past had taken care of members of his family in Potsdam and during the war had arranged for a bridge over the Teltow canal between Neubabelsberg and Klein Glienicke to be named "Enver-Pascha-Brücke", could not turn a blind eye to the suffering inflicted on the Armenian people. She had, for example, intervened directly with the Ottoman government on behalf of Armenian children who were to be deported. Her brother Hans Humann evidently had no such scruples: He had agreed with the actions taken by Enver Pasha, whom he attested, full of admiration, had not been swayed by any *"inhibitions of a moral or international law nature"*[13].

There is no known statement from Sarre himself concerning these events, despite the fact that the intra-Turkish conflict soon also reached Berlin. A young Armenian by the name of Soghomon Tehlirian assassinated Talaat Pasha in Charlottenburg in 1921. Enver Pasha fell in 1922 in battle against the Red Army near Dushanbe.

Friedrich Sarre, whose aunt had died in 1914 and who had lost a large part of his fortune in war bonds, in 1922 took on paid employment as director of the department for ancient Islamic art, a post he remained in until he retired in 1931. Wilhelm von Bode expressed his delight: *"The expansion of the Islamic Department was in the best of hands under the leadership of Professor Sarre, who took over voluntarily without joining the civil service machinery."*[14]

Sarre steadfastly continued to publish work, such as the standard reference guide *Die Kunst des alten Persien.* (The Art of Ancient Persia) in 1922. In order to tap into new sources to finance his expeditions, in 1923, together with the industrialist's son, Edmund Stinnes and banker and private collector James Loeb, he established the company Gesellschaft zur Förderung von Ausgrabungen und Forschungsreisen GmbH. Though he continued to remain faithful to the Emperor, Sarre was close friends with Walther Rathenau and other representatives of the Weimar Republic.

Dangerous Times

When the National Socialist's seized power, Sarre lost most of his friends and colleagues. Following his dismissal from his post as professor, Ernst Herzfeld, who had deciphered all of the ancient writings for Sarre, went directly from Persia into exile in London and from there to the USA. Art historians Max Friedländer and Adolph Goldschmidt, as well as orientalist Eugen Mittwoch, also fled Germany. Sarre himself was reserved with his political statements and only guarded gestures are known. In 1935, he was among the small number of former friends to attend Max Liebermann's funeral; in 1938, after Kaiserstrasse was renamed Strasse der SA, Sarre changed the address of the villa from Kaiserstrasse 39 to Bergstrasse 6. When he was appointed honorary professor at the faculty of philosophy of Friedrich-Wilhelm University and head of the department of Near Eastern studies

13 Hans Humann to Ernst Jäckh, Constantinople, mid-January 1914, in: Yale University Library New Haven, estate of Ernst Jäckh, K 1, A 1, quoted based on Malte Fuhrmann: Friedrich Sarre, der zeitgenössische ‚Orient' und der Weltkrieg, in: Julia Gonella and Jens Kröger 2015 (see note 6), p. 53.

14 Wilhelm von Bode (see note 2), p. 176.

"Confidential!" Letter to the naval staff of the Mediterranean Division, in which the marine attaché in Constantinople announces the enclosed report from Major of the Reserve, Friedrich Sarre, and submits it "respectfully for your attention".

and archaeology, he did not take on the post which had previously been held by his friend Herzfeld. In 1935, Sarre took a leave of absence on health grounds. He also succeeded in moving part of his collection to safety in Switzerland.

Marie Louise Sarre

Sarre's children were more fervent in their resistance against the regime. His son Friedrich Carl, together with his brother-in-law Eduard Wätjen, ran a law firm in Berlin, in which Helmuth James von Moltke was also a partner. Moltke, who, like Wätjen, was a member of the resistance group Kreisauer Kreis, was a frequent guest at the Sarre villa. Wätjen, the husband of Irene Sarre, during the war worked for the 'Abwehr', the German military intelligence service, under the later executed Admiral Wilhelm Canaris and met with Allen Dulles, head of the US-secret service OSS (Office of Strategic Services), in Switzerland. When Wätjen found out in 1944 that there was a warrant out for his arrest in Germany, he and his wife Irene stayed in Switzerland.

Sarre's daughter, Marie Louise, a sculptor, was also active in the resistance and was involved in the Solf Circle's tea parties. She caught the attention of the Gestapo

Marie-Louise Sarre

in Potsdam because she helped and brought food to the residents of the Jewish Home for the Infirm and Elderly in Bergstrasse 1.

On the return journey from Switzerland with the lawyer Carl Langbehn, also an opponent of the regime, both were arrested. Langbehn was executed on October 12, 1944, while Marie Louise was imprisoned for a total of 20 months, initially in Berlin, before being transferred as a protective custody prisoner to a prison directly next to the concentration camp in Ravensbrück. Following the transfer, she was able to flee to a field hospital and in April 1945 reached her parents' house in Potsdam directly before the invasion of the Russian troops. Maria Sarre described the unexpected reunion with her daughter (lovingly referred to in the family as "Puppi", lit. little doll) in a letter: *"On April 21, we had at least the unspeakable joy of suddenly seeing Puppi standing on the veranda—when I say 'joy', that is not entirely true—we were simply overwhelmed to see the child walking back in so matter-of-factly after two long, tortuous years —we did not have enough strength for joy"*[15].

Friedrich Sarre died after a short illness in the night from May 31 to June 1, 1945. As all of the bridges across Griebnitzsee had been destroyed, Sarre had to be trans-

15 Maria Sarre: typewritten letter (carbon paper). "Excerpt from the letter from Mrs Sarre (from Ascona). November 1945". German Resistance Memorial Centre, Berlin. 11 pages, here page 2 [translation: author's own].

A political prisoner in Ravensbrück

"I was helped a great deal by the serendipitous fact that Helmuth Moltke was in the cell next to mine for six months, and we were sometimes able to communicate by knocking on each other's doors and, though very rarely, talking out of the window at night. What it means to know that there is a person on the other side of a wall, who feels the same as you, who is alive and warm and thinks the same way you do—it is so endlessly comforting, and words achieve the kind of importance that they would never have 'on the outside'."

Marie Louise Sarre, Memories of her time as a political prisoner in solitary confinement in Ravensbrück, in: typewritten letter (carbon paper) of October 11, 1945, German Resistance Memorial Centre, Berlin, p. 3 [translation: author's own].

ported by boat to Klein Glienicke, where he lies buried in the cemetery. Just a day after his burial, members of the Red Army forced Maria Sarre and her daughter to leave the house within the hour. In preparation for the Potsdam Conference, the Sarre villa was cleared and most of the contents brought to a dumpsite; plunderers then removed the remaining paintings and carpets. The conqueror of Berlin, Soviet General Georgy Zhukov, moved into the villa. He had signed the Instrument of Surrender on behalf of the Soviets on May 9 and would be assisting Stalin during the Potsdam Conference.

As a former member of the Solf Circle, Marie Louise Sarre was of such importance to the US military government that in mid-August the Americans flew her, her mother Maria, and the nanny out of the Soviet zone to Frankfurt, which probably saved their lives. The Sarres emigrated to Switzerland. They were able to finance their life there with the sale of the carpet collection that Friedrich Sarre had previously deposited there. German-Swiss banker and collector Baron Eduard von der

A melancholy remembrance

"So, measured against the horrors of what had gone before, the second half of May was a pleasant respite—while the plundering continued, indeed it continued to be carried out most maliciously and thoroughly by the scum of foreign workers, Ukrainians, Poles, etc., but we had become progressively indifferent to possessions, left doors and cupboards open, and, since we personally were for the most part left undisturbed and they were interested not in our living room, but in boxes and suitcases, linens, dresses etc., we let them steal (and how they stole!) and lived out our life in the old living room, which you are well familiar with, where our beloved Papi sat by the little stove and in the evening told us tales from his rich treasure trove of memories, or read aloud Goethe.

He already seemed so calm and serene and enjoyed these quiet hours, as if he knew that they were numbered—anyhow, he had it nice and was able to enjoy some warm, sunny spring days by the pond in his little garden before his poor, tired heart stopped beating. Though I always knew that he (though not visible to others) was the centre of my life and that 'our' world would be gone forever when he left me, I knew and know it more with every passing day, that he was one of the noblest, most humble and upstanding people—a German the likes of which there were oh too few of. With him, the best part of the Sarres has passed away, and yet I am thankful that he didn't have to witness being forced out of his beloved house and left on the street like a beggar.

He died the night before Corpus Christi, June 1. Puppi spent two days trying to get a coffin (the dead were buried only in sacks). At last, a soldier's coffin was "allotted" to us—but we would need to dig the graves ourselves; we found four kind orderlies who said they would gladly take care of everything in return for a suit each (civilian suits were in high demand). On a calm, peaceful Sunday afternoon, Friedrich Sarre was transported as modestly as he may have wished for across the Griebnitzsee in an old boat (the bridges had all been bombed) and then laid to rest in the Märkisch soil of Klein Glienicke that he had held so dear. Only a few Babelsberg residents were there—there was no longer any way of letting other people know. How empty the house was without him when we returned from the cemetery, and the children and I sat together for a long time in the evening, making plans as to how to organise his estate (he had worked so much in that last period, recorded so much of his unique knowledge in outlines of essays and started essays)—early the next morning, we were ordered by Russian troops to leave the house in just one hour."

Maria Sarre: typewritten letter (carbon paper). "Excerpt from the letter from Mrs Sarre (from Ascona). November 1945". German Resistance Memorial Centre, Berlin. 11 pages, here page 6/7 [translation: author's own].

Heydt, whom the Sarres were friends with, ensured that they were able to move into an apartment in Ascona.

What remained

During the GDR era, the Sarre villa was used by the Academy of Film and Television, which saved it from dilapidation. After the fall of the Wall in 1989, the villa was extensively and expertly restored and was for many years home to a Swiss family with a great appreciation for art.

Today, the fate of the former residents of the villa is under threat of being forgotten. There is no plaque to remind people of the founder of the academic field of Oriental studies, Friedrich Sarre, nor is there any memorial detailing the courageous acts of his daughter, Marie Louise. The GDR for the most part ignored the German resistance against Hitler if those involved had been "aristocrats". Today, it seems the city of Potsdam has no interest in commemorating courageous upper-middle-class citizens either. And yet, Marie Louise's words could vindicate Germany:

"The reproach, that a change of government in Germany was only attempted when the fate of the country seemed decided, is incorrect. There were many circles of people who foresaw the inevitable long before the war began. The activists among them prepared for the removal of the regime, the theoreticians made plans for the shape of Germany after the collapse. Almost all of them had to pay with their lives for these efforts. They could not put their plans into effect. But I firmly believe that their death was not in vain. They are witnesses for the struggle of individuals against a tyranny of a brutality and recklessness without comparison in history."[16]

16 Marie Louise Sarre, Letter to Allen W. Dulles dated January 28, 1946. Sarre, Marie Louise (Puppi) 1946–1953; Allen W. Dulles Papers; Public Policy Papers, Department of Rare Books and Special Collections, Princeton University Library.

The Schleicher Villa

This villa, which stood in Klein Glienicke at the north-western end of Griebnitzsee, rose to prominence on account of its famous resident, Kurt von Schleicher, a general, and Reich chancellor for seventy days in 1932/33. Moreover, however, it became known for the events that took place on June 30, 1934. Around lunchtime, in broad daylight, a task force of six men advanced on the villa. The housekeeper, suspecting nothing, led two of them to the General's office, where they shot him without a moment's hesitation. They also murdered his wife, Elisabeth von Schleicher.

Griebnitzstrasse 4 (the building no longer exists)

The end of the Weimar Republic that many liberal and democratic-minded powers had associated with hopes of a better Germany, was anything but laudable, and that had much to do with the most senior members of the state. As different as the two last chancellors of the Weimar Republic, Franz von Papen and Kurt von Schleicher, were in terms of personal charisma, intelligence and assertiveness, they were highly similar in two respects: they were both entrenched in the belief that the high art of politics consisted of the weaving of webs of intrigue, and they hopelessly overestimated their capacity to stand up to Adolf Hitler, to "tame" him and his party and to "integrate" them into their own governments.

The long path to a brief chancellorship

Kurt von Schleicher, who had served as an officer in the general staff during World War I, and after the war swiftly climbed the career ladder at the *Reichswehrministerium*, the Reich Ministry of Defence, from the very beginning stood out on account of his decisiveness and organisational talent. He also had clear strategic goals and, last but not least, was a politically-minded military man: he wanted to secure a strong, largely independent role in the state for the Reichswehr (the official name of the armed forces of the Weimar Republic) and was determined to influence political events in Germany—by conspiratorial means, if necessary.

He was afforded every opportunity to do so when he was appointed head of the Ministry of the Reichswehr in 1929. This office, a switch point between the *Reichswehr*, the state administration and the political parties, had been created especially for Schleicher: From here, *"Schleicher now supervised the most elaborate intelligence network in Berlin. He maintained spies in every ministry; he tapped telephones; he came to know every secret that was worth knowing. He also knew from his days as a military information officer during the war, how to manipulate the press [...]"*[1]

Schleicher mercilessly exploited the instruments of power afforded to him.

1 Otto Friedrich: Before the Deluge. A portrait of Berlin in the 1920s. Harper & Row, New York, 1st ed. 1972, p. 352.

By all accounts, he was able to do so only because he also had excellent contact to the aged Reich president, Paul von Hindenburg, at this point still the most important figure in the political arena. By removing the Social Democratic Reich chancellor Hermann Müller and on March 29, 1930, appointing Heinrich Brüning as his successor without the consent of parliament, Hindenburg had installed the system of the "presidential cabinet", which weakened the position of the parliament significantly and, in return, extended the influence of the Reich president and the government appointed by him. Moreover, it was a declared objective of Hindenburg, to afford the "national forces"—which, from his point of view, were first and foremost the German Centre Party, the German National People's Party and the Bavarian People's Party—more room for manoeuvre in politics.

Schleicher, who had contacted Hindenburg through his son, Oscar, made his mark in this position as a "scene-shifter" and "kingmaker".[2]

Having been involved in the dismissal of Hermann Müller, he proposed as his successor Brüning, whom he then also dismissed before suggesting and ultimately installing the largely unknown German Centre Party politician, Franz von Papen. On June 1, 1930, von Papen formed a cabinet of "national concentration". His way of doing politics—one ought, perhaps, instead to call it an attempt to do politics, was a complete failure. He had promised Hitler that the prohibition of the two National Socialist organisations, the SA and the SS, would be reversed. This was intended to ensure that the NSDAP, which had become ever stronger in the parliamentary elections that took place in quick succession, would tolerate his government. The decision resulted in bitter fighting in the street between the SA

[2] Helmut Heiber: Die Republik von Weimar (dtv-Weltgeschichte des 20. Jahrhunderts, volume 3), Munich 1975, p. 264 and 251.

Assessments of Kurt von Schleicher

Count Harry Kessler reports in his diary on a conversation with Wilhelm Abegg, State Secretary at the Prussian Interior Ministry:

"Abegg was very dismissive of the current government of the Reich. He said they were the worst dilettantes who had ever been in power in the Reich; amateurism and lack of character were their most prominent features. He said Schleicher was the worst of them, he couldn't open his mouth without lying. As to his comments that he wanted to stifle Hitler, the only part of this that is true is that he would not accept Hitler as Reich chancellor, though he would tolerate the SA; it would become a kind of Reich army, dressed in black." Entry of July 20, 1932, Wednesday, in: Harry Graf Kesler: Das Tagebuch. Volume 9: 1926–1937, edited by Sabine Gruber and Ulrich Ott, Stuttgart 1910, p. 466; 'Berlin in Lights: the diaries of Count Harry Kessler, 1918–1937, Grove Press, New York 200, S. 42; translation: author's own.

Journalist Bella Fromm, a columnist for the *Vossische Zeitung* and the *B.Z.,* who came from an upper-class Jewish family, described a very different side of his personality:

"Bella Fromm knew General Kurt von Schleicher from various official and private events. She felt him to be one of the few people with an almost irresistible charisma: 'A brave and far-sighted man who can, at times, be very sarcastic. His voice is mellifluous, as is his laugh. The latter is a treat for the ears and eyes to behold.' Further, which was particularly important to Bella Fromm as a Jewish journalist, von Schleicher had given orders in his office, that she should always be allowed to see him, even if she appeared unannounced. 'You have been my faithful comrade all these years' he once said to her, taking her by the arm."
Martha Schad: Frauen gegen Hitler. Schicksale im Nationa sozia lismus, Munich 2001, p. 94.

and the communists. Papen's attempt to involve Hitler in his cabinet as vice-chancellor went awry—Hitler claimed the post of head of government for himself. The economic plan that von Papen had devised to tackle mass unemployment could not be realised either as nearly all of the factions in the Reichstag refused to approve it.

Schleicher, who had been minister for the Reichswehr under Papen, seized the opportunity and, with Hindenburg's consent, himself took over the helm. He held hopes of forming a cross-party national government coalition based largely on his many contacts to camps across the political spectrum and with the support of the Reichswehr. In order to achieve this, he had sounded out the situation with the unions by announcing a social programme. He also launched a risky attempt to divide the NSDAP. In the wake of the many intense election campaigns and propaganda operations of the previous months and years, the party was almost bankrupt and was in crisis. It was against this background that Otto Braun, Prussian Minister-President, sought out Schleicher on January 6, 1933, and offered him the support of the SPD: *"We will push the election until far into the springtime and fight a vigorous unified battle against the National Socialists. They have already lost two million votes in the November election; they have passed their peak and are on the decline. We just need to strike now to deal them a crushing defeat in springtime elections."*[3]

This was the last chance for democracy and for the Weimar Republic. But Schleicher chose to put his faith in the socialist wing of the NSDAP. He offered Gregor Strasser, Reich Organisation Leader of the NSDAP and Hitler's second-in-command, the position of vice chancellor of his cabinet; he was also to be appointed Minister-President for Prussia. Strasser, who in any case was more willing to compromise than the other leaders of the party, was certainly inclined to agree to this, but was not prepared to openly break with Hitler and advised him of the plans. In an outburst of rage, Hitler accused him of treason. Strasser caved to the pres-

left: The villa of Kurt von Schleicher and his family, around 1934

right: General Kurt von Schleicher in front of the Reich president's palace in Wilhelmstrasse after his appointment as Reich chancellor, December 3, 1932, photographer Georg Pahl

3 Otto Braun: Von Weimar zu Hitler, New York 1940 (2nd ed.), p. 437.

sure, gave up all party posts and retired into private life. This brought Schleicher's carefully erected national policy house of cards crashing down. In this already awkward situation, on January 11, 1933, Schleicher also started an argument with the influential National Rural League and sharply criticised the systematic misuse of 'Osthilfe' funds (lit. Eastern Aid, a policy used to provide financial support from government funds to bankrupt estates in East Prussia). This, which, presumably had not been part of the plan, turned Reich President von Hindenburg's entire circle of friends against Schleicher.[4] This was to have serious repercussions.

At the same time, another player, whom Schleicher had no longer expected, returned to the scene, namely his former protégé, Franz von Papen. *"The chancellors of the last hour,"* wrote historian Helmut Heiber, *"certainly did not have it easy with their predecessors. And the confusing web of intrigue of the time provided a fertile ground for revenge of every kind."*[5] Franz von Papen, who just a few weeks before had made no secret of how disappointed he was in Hitler, then sought contact with him and proposed a unified government—with Hitler as Reich chancellor. He also proposed this idea to Hindenburg, again with the reckless assurance that they would be able to keep Hitler in check. The Reich president, who had once emphasised in a conversation with Schleicher that he would *"perhaps appoint this Bohemian* private *as a postman", "but not as Reich chancellor"*[6], this time consented.

Schleicher resigned on January 28 after just seventy days as chancellor. On January 30, Hindenburg appointed the "Bohemian private" as Reich Chancellor. Papen was vice-chancellor in Hitler's cabinet.

Retreat into private life

Schleicher retreated from Berlin. A close friend, the industrialist Otto Wolff, found him a villa in Griebnitzstrasse 4, where he moved to together with his wife Elisabeth, whom he had only married in 1931, as well as Lonny, her fourteen-year-old daughter from her first marriage. His aged mother and his widowed sister also made their home in the country house. Schleicher had decided to write his memoirs and began collecting material to this end.

Though the Schleicher family lived a reclusive life, it came to the attention of the observant aides and informants of the new regime that their behaviour was not in line with the National Socialist code of ethics. They continued to meet old friends, some of whom where "non-Aryan", and Elisabeth von Schleicher still shopped at Jewish stores, which was once even documented with a photograph, showing her leaving such a store, in the radically antisemitic weekly newspaper *Der Stürmer*[7]. As Kurt von Schleicher made no bones about his opinion of Hitler, many friends advised the family to take a longer trip overseas in order not to further endanger themselves.

Despite this, the regime's deadly strike came as a surprise. When on June 30, 1934, the powerful SA chief of staff Ernst Röhm, and several other senior functionaries of the SA were killed on Hitler's order on the grounds of an alleged conspiracy, he also ordered many political opponents, among them Gregor Strasser

4 Cf. Hagen Schulze: Die Deutschen und ihre Nation. Weimar. Deutschland 1917–1933, Berlin 1982, p. 403f.

5 Heiber 1975 (see note 2), p. 265–266.

6 Friedrich 1998 (see note 1) p. 388.

7 Cf. Martha Schad: Frauen gegen Hitler. Schicksale im Nationalsozialismus, Munich 2001, p. 100.

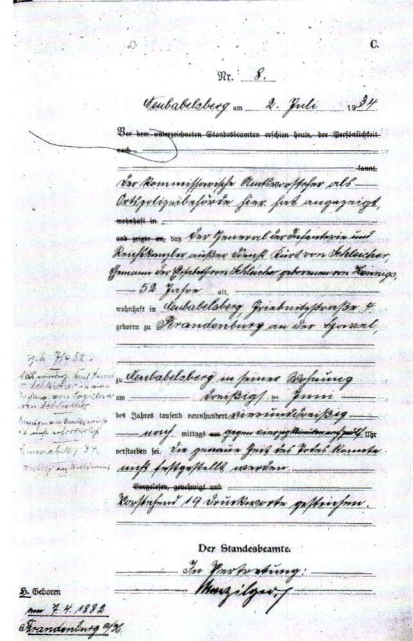

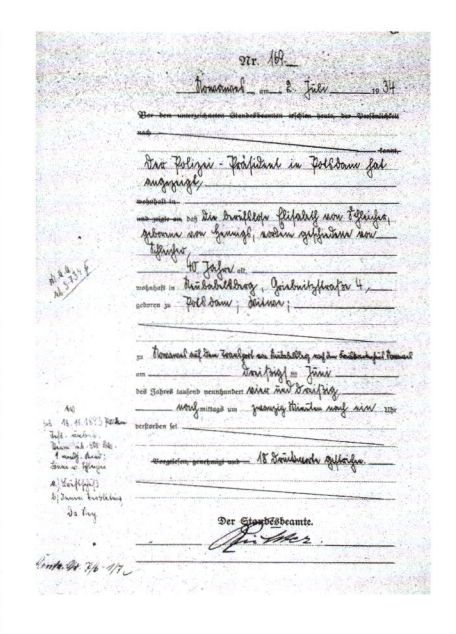

and Kurt von Schleicher, to be murdered by the SS and the Gestapo. On July 1, Joseph Goebbels laconically commented in his diary on what happened that day in the villa in Griebnitzstrasse 4, with the cynical words: *"All as planned in Berlin. No mishaps other than that Mrs Schleicher also fell. Unfortunate, but unalterable."*[8]

The arbitrary executions were retroactively legitimised on July 3 by a law governing measures of state self-defence. In any case, finer points such as these were irrelevant to the Reich Association of German Officers: In a statement issued on July 5, it congratulated *"the Führer on the forceful act"*, through which *"in a flash"* he had thwarted the coup d'état. Incidentally, Franz von Papen, whose office was sought out by agents of the regime on that day and ransacked, left the government following the "Night of the Long Knives". In August 1934, he first went to Vienna as an envoy, before acting as ambassador of the German Reich in Turkey from 1939 to 1944.

A Bitter Finale

Nowhere is any mention made of the other person seriously harmed by this attack: Lonny von Schleicher, who lost her mother and stepfather on that day. Suspecting nothing, she returned home from school at lunchtime. As she later described, June 30, had been *"a beautiful summer's day, I was looking forward to showing my good report card at home"*. At the beginning of Griebnitzstrasse, she saw police in front of the house and the road was closed off. She then learned from the housekeeper what had happened: *"Your mother was taken away in an ambulance and the General is lying shot dead in the living room."*[9] When she arrived at the hospital in Nowawes with her aunt, her mother was already dead.

The next shock came at the funeral in the park cemetery in Berlin-Lichterfelde: the coffins of Elisabeth und Kurt von Schleicher were not there. The Gestapo had already collected them in secret and burned the bodies—clearly to conceal the

left: Kurt von Schleicher and his wife Elisabeth in front of a polling station, March 5, 1933, photographer: Carl Weinrother

centre: Death certificate of the former Reich chancellor Kurt von Schleicher, issued on July 2, 1934

right: Death certificate of Elisabeth von Schleicher, issued on July 2, 1934

8   Quoted based on ibid., p. 113.

9   Katia Meyer-tien: Lonny von Schleicher verlor ihre Lieben, aber nie den Mut, in: *Mittelbayerische Zeitung*, 6.1.2010 (https://www.mittelbayerische.de/polzei/bayern/lonny-von-schleicher-verlor-ihre-lieben-aber-nie-den-mut-21759-art507773.html).

fact that the official description of events, namely that the General had resisted arrest and had been killed in the ensuing struggle while his wife had been accidentally hit by a stray bullet, could not be true.¹⁰

This did not mark the end of young Lonny von Schleicher's suffering either and, despite her youth, she was treated as an enemy of the state and monitored by the Gestapo over the following years: *"Over and over, after her class waiting for her were police officers, who took her to the police station, questioned her for hours, and accused her of planning an attack. Lonny von Schleicher's only option was small, personal resistance: she never joined the League of German Girls, she avoided raising her hand in a Hitler salute, and when her roommate at boarding school wanted to hang a picture of Hitler on the wall, she got angry—the picture remained in a drawer."*¹¹

In 1938/39, the NSDAP's Reich School of the Office of Racial Policy moved into the villa in which Kurt von Schleicher had spent the last months of his life. After the end of the Second World War, the dereliction began. When the Berlin Wall was constructed, the few families who still lived in Griebnitzstrasse had to leave their homes. The responsible GDR authorities had the former residence of the General and the vacant neighbouring villas demolished in the 1980s. The area was given a fresh start in around 2000 with the construction of five multi-family dwellings built with maximum profit in mind.

left: Declaration by the "Reichsverband Deutscher Offiziere" concerning the "Röhm affair" by its chairman, Count von der Goltz, official gazette of the RDO no. 19 of July 5, 1935

right: Lonny von Schleicher

10 Cf. Schad 2001 (see note 7), p. 117, 118.

11 Katia Meyer-tien 2010 (see note 9).

Conclusion

Anyone keen to get a feel for German history should take a walk through the wonderful deciduous woodland to the north of Griebnitzsee and look across to the southern shore of the lake. There, over a stretch of around two kilometres, stand the splendid villas built over the course of the last 120 years. Having read this book, one might pause to consider the fate of their former residents. But history was also written in the villas on the north shore of the lake.

Renowned psychologist Otto Lipmann lived with his wife Gertrude and his two children at Wannseestrasse 9, where he ran a small clinic for the treatment of psychological illnesses. Lipmann rose to fame through his use of psychology to determine career aptitude and candidate selection for specific professions, such as pilots, for example. Lipmann's development of empirical methods in career and occupational psychology, as in his *Checklist of Psychological Characteristics of Mid-level (commercial, trade and industrial) Occupations* (1918) was revolutionary. In 1932, he was awarded a chair in occupational psychology at the Berlin University. Soon after Hitler seized power, Lipmann lost the position again. In 1933, SA-officers vandalised his institute. Lipmann never recovered from the shock and died on October 7, 1933.[1] His family was able to emigrate to Egypt and Argentina.

From 1935, German-English actress Lilian Harvey lived at Griebnitzstrasse 5a. Films like *Die Drei von der Tankstelle* (*The Three from the Filling Station*) or *Der Kongress tanzt* (*Congress Dances*) had made Harvey a household name. Protected by her British passport and her popularity, she helped colleagues persecuted by the National Socialist regime, until in 1939 she, too, felt she had no choice but to emigrate.

Kurt von Schleicher lived at Griebnitzstrasse 4. As last Reich Chancellor of the Weimar Republic, von Schleicher had tried to put a stop to Hitler. He had planned a coalition of national conservative parties with the trade unions but his predecessor, Franz von Papen, plotted with the knowledge and support of Reich president Paul von Hindenburg, until von Schleicher's attempt was stymied. Schleicher retreated to a beautiful nineteenth century villa that industrialist Otto Wolff had made available for him. It was here that Kurt von Schleicher was shot in 1934.

After the Berlin Wall was built, all of the villas in Griebnitzstrasse stood empty and fell into disrepair, though they were not demolished until the 1980s. The austere apartment buildings built after the fall of the Wall and designed with profit-maximisation in mind, are the only houses on the sunny side of Griebnitzsee and to the present day enjoy unimpeded and unchallenged access to the lake.

Heading west to Waldmüllerstrasse, one comes across what was once the moat of the Glienicke Hunting Lodge. It used to separate the German Democratic Republic from West Berlin, and today marks the border between Brandenburg and Berlin. In the beautifully renovated house on the left, the residents dug a tunnel under the moat in the 1970s until they reached the "West". Around twenty people successfully fled through the tunnel. Once its existence was betrayed, the East German authorities blocked the tunnel.

1 Sven Ebisch in: Uwe Wolfradt, Elfriede Billmann-Mahecha, Armin Stock (eds.). *Deutschsprachige Psychologinnen und Psychologen 1933–1945*. Ein Personenlexikon, supplemented with a text by Erich Stern, Wiesbaden 2017 (2nd ed.), p. 282f.

Crossing the bridge towards the Babelsberg Palace, on the right-hand-side the remains of the Enver Pasha bridge are visible. Perhaps there should be a sign to explain who Enver Pasha was; he had been a frequent guest of and was later taken in as a refugee by the Sarre family, who were known for their love of art, in Bergstrasse (today Spitzweggasse). He was also, however, the orchestrator of the genocide against the Armenians in the Ottoman Empire.

To the left, Karl-Marx-Strasse leads to the villas showcased in this book. Like in a school textbook, their stories document the history of Germany from the Empire to the Weimar Republic, to the Third Reich and the German Democratic Republic. Nowadays, the Federal Republic is at pains to resolve conflicts more peaceably than its predecessors, accepting the rule of law in a democratic state. Today, Griebnitzsee, surrounded once again by charming gardens and small parks, remains a beautiful idyll that is steeped in history.

"The two bridges over the connection between Griebnitzsee (below) and Glienicker Lake (above), seen from the south", 1919

A number of people contributed to this book.

I would like to thank Mr Thomas Harding for his moving foreword. His extensive research into the house of his forebears in Groß Glienicke culminated in global bestseller *The House by the Lake* and inspired me to write this book.

Many thanks also to my co-worker Dr. Weronika Weems, who searched national and international archives for sources with a tireless energy and good cheer and extensively edited the texts.

I would also like to sincerely thank the current and former owners of the villa properties, who assisted me in my research (listed alphabetically). I owe special thanks to Mr Gert Mosler and his wife, who spontaneously welcomed me into their home in Amsterdam.

Wolfhard Kirsch
Dr. Heinrich Kruse
Tomas Pablo Lindemann
Gert Mosler and Nicole Staartjes-Mosler
Ilsabe Platte
Andreas Schlüter
Dr Alwin Scholz
John Shurman
Alexander von Stülpnagel
Prof. Jörg Thiede

Dr. phil. Rüdiger v. Voss and Monica v. Voss

Many thanks also to the following persons and institutions for their helpful assistance:
Julia Leeb, Journalist
Dr. Andrea Hohmeyer, Head of the Company Group Archive, Evonik Industries AG
Anett Schuster, Friedrich-Naumann-Stiftung, Berlin
Anne Schulte, Image research/documentation, Prussian Heritage Image Archive (Bildarchiv Preußischer Kulturbesitz, ‚bpk')
Birgit Maurer-Porat, Foundation of the Jewish Museum Berlin
Christian Tagger, Reproductions, Berlinische Galerie
Eric Heijselaar, Amsterdam City Archives (Stadsarchief Amsterdam)
Frank Schmidt, Brandenburg Main State Archive (Brandenburgisches Landeshauptarchiv, BLHA)
Franziska Pertsch, Ullstein bild
Gerhard Osterloh, Regional Capital of Potsdam, Office for the Protection of Historic Buildings and Monuments (Landeshauptstadt Potsdam, Bereich Untere Denkmalschutzbehörde)
Guido Faßbender, Curator of the Fine Arts Collection, Berlinische Galerie
Johannes Determann, Potsdam City Archives (Stadtarchiv Potsdam)
Judith Granzow, Photography Collection. Potsdam Museum – Potsdam Museum Forum für Kunst and Geschichte
Kerstin Bühring, Brandenburg Main State Archive (Brandenburgisches Landeshauptarchiv, BLHA)
Klaus Hellenthal, "GrussAusPotsdam"
Klaus Janetzki, Berlin State Archives (Landesarchiv Berlin)
Ralph Jentsch, Art Historian
Michael Jurk, Archivist
Kurt Baller, Author, Historian and Journalist
Margitta Gatzke, Zehdenick City Archives (Archiv der Stadt Zehdenick)
Martha Schad, German Historian and Author
Saskia Simons, Secret State Archives Prussian Cultural Heritage Foundation (Geheimes Staatsarchiv Preußischer Kulturbesitz)
Dr. Thomas Köhler, Director of the Berlinische Galerie
Thomas Ulbrich, Brandenburg Main State Archive (Brandenburgisches Landeshauptarchiv, BLHA)
Ulrike Fischer, Potsdam City Archive (Stadtarchiv Potsdam)

Index of Names

Albers, Hans (1891–1960) 20, 79, 80.
Amman, Max (1891–1957) 64.
Atlee, Clement (1883–1967) 15.

Baarová, Lída (1914–2000) 24.
Baruch, Robert (dates of birth and death unknown) 29.
Behrens, Peter (1868–1940) 38, 122.
Beria, Lavrentiy (1899–1953) 54.
Bevin, Ernest (1881–1951) 81.
Blomberg, Werner von (1878–1946) 63, 64.
Blumenthal, Otto (1897–1988) 74.
Böckmann, Friedrich Wilhelm (1832–1902) 11, 12, 37, 95.
Bode, Wilhelm von (1845–1929) 98, 99, 105, 128, 133, 136.
Bohl, Friedrich (born 1945) 68.
Borges, Jorge Luis (1899–1986) 76.

Brahm, Otto (1856–1912) 99.
Braun, Otto (1872–1955) 143.
Brausewetter, Hans (1899–1945) 79.
Bräutigam, Hans Otto (born 1931) 69.
Breslauer, Alfred (1866–1954) 15, 95, 98, 99, 105.
Breuer, Robert (1878–1943) 50.
Broch, Hermann (1886–1951) 76.
Bruhn, Ada (1885–1951) 123.
Brüning, Heinrich (1885–1970) 58, 105, 142.
Byrnes, James Francis (1882–1972) 44, 80, 81.

Cadogan, Alexander (1884–1968) 88.
Catherine II. (Catherine the Great) (1729–1796) 23.
Cemal Pasha (1872–1922) 135, 136.
Cézanne, Paul (1839–1906) 102, 103.
Chiang Kai-shek (1887–1975) 44.
Churchill, Winston (1874–1965) 15, 43, 44, 54, 80, 86–88.

Dietrich, Marlene (1901–1992) 7, 20.
Dilthey, Wilhelm (1833–1911) 117, 123.
Dorsch, Käthe (1890–1957) 100.
Dürer, Albrecht (1471–1528) 37.

Eden, Anthony (1897–1977) 71, 80, 81.
Eisenberg, Moses Abramowitsch (dates of birth and death unknown) 113.
Encke, Erdmann (1843–1896) 38.
Ende, Hermann (1829–1907) 11, 12, 37.
Enver Pasha (1881–1922) 135, 136, 148.
Eschke, Hermann (1823–1900) 91, 94.
Eulenburg, Philipp Fürst zu (1847–1921) 92.

Finck, Werner (1902–1978) 85.
Fontane, Theodor (1819–1898) 37.
Frank, Theodor (1871–1953) 71, 86.
Frenkel, Hermann (1850–1932) 20.

Frenssen, Gustav (1863–1945) 39.
Freud, Ernst Lucie (1892–1970) 71–73.
Freud, Sigmund (1856–1939) 71, 72.
Freund, Heinrich (1885–1948) 74.
Friedensohn, Fritz (dates of birth and death unknown) 29.
Friedländer, Max Jacob (1867–1958) 103, 137.
Fritsch, Willy (1901–1973) 13, 20, 21.
Fürstenberg, Carl (1850–1933) 100.

Gericke, Marie Louise (born 1925) 86, 87.
Goebbels, Joseph (1897–1945) 14, 24, 25, 40, 80, 145.
Goebbels, Magda (1901–1945) 24, 40.
Goerdeler, Carl Friedrich (1884–1945) 65.
Goetz, Curt (1888–1960) 21.
Gogh, Vincent van (1853–1890) 103.
Goldschmidt, Adolph (1863–1944) 137.
Goldschmidt, Jakob (1882–1955) 13, 20, 89, 95, 98, 99, 100, 98–111, 133.
Gottschalk, Joachim (1904–1941) 23.
Graf, Oskar Maria (1894–1967) 76.
Graf, Rüdiger (dates of birth and death unknown) 105.
Grenander, Alfred (1863–1931) 12, 49–51.
Groener, Karl Eduard Wilhelm (1867–1939) 62.
Großheim, Karl von (1841–1911) 25, 37.
Grosz, George (1893–1959) 30.
Guggenheim, Hans (dates of birth and death unknown) 24.
Gurewitsch, Isaak (dates of birth and death unknown) 113.
Gurewitsch, Sima (unknown–1946) 113, 114, 116.
Güßfeldt, Paul (1840–1920) 94, 95.
Gutmann, Herbert Max Magnus (1879–1942) 20, 58.
Guttmann, Samuel (1879–1943) 14, 114, 115.

Haack, Käthe (1897–1986) 79.
Hanke, Karl (1903–1945) 24.
Harvey, Lilian (1906–1968) 13, 20, 21, 23, 24, 147.
Heidmann, Karl (dates of birth and death unknown) 112–116.
Heimann, Emanuel (1854 or 1855–1910) 32.
Herpich, Julius (1876–1944) 49.
Herpich, Paul (1869–1923) 49, 53.
Hesse, Hermann (1877–1962) 76.
Hesselbarth, Otto (dates of birth and death unknown) 106, 107.
Heymann, Werner Richard (1896–1961) 20.
Heyroth, Anton (1855–1922) 72.
Himmler, Heinrich (1900–1945) 78, 116.
Hindenburg, Paul von (1847–1934) 142–144, 147.
Hippler, Fritz (1909–2002) 80.
Hörbiger, Paul (1894–1981) 85.
Horn, Arnold Killisch von (1862–1939) 62, 63.
Horney, Brigitte (1911–1988) 13, 23, 24, 79, 80.

Jacoby, Georg (1882–1964) 13, 23.
Jannings, Emil (1884–1950) 13.
Janthur, Richard (1883–1956) 74.
Jung, Carl Gustav (1875–1961) 76.

Karchow, Paul (dates of birth and death unknown) 32.
Kästner, Emil Erich (1899–1974) 71, 78–80.
Kayser, Heinrich (1842–1917) 25, 37.
Kerschensteiner, Georg (1854–1932) 76.
Kessler, Count Harry (1868–1937) 53, 134, 135, 142.
Kirsch, Wolfhard (born 1962) 69, 149.
Kleemann, Wilhelm (1885–1956) 58.
Knobelsdorff-Brenkenhoff, Maximilian von (1913–1944) 65.

Lang, Fritz (1890–1976) 20, 23, 101–102.
Lange, Johannes (dates of birth and death unknown) 72.
L'Arronge, Adolph (1838–1908) 95, 98–99.
Liebermann, Max (1847–1935) 93, 123, 133, 137.
Liebknecht, née Friedland, Elsa (dates of birth and death unknown) 31–32.
Liebknecht, Karl (1871–1919) 27.
Liebknecht, Kurt (1905–1994) 32.
Liebknecht, Otto August Wilhelm Eduard (1876–1949) 27, 30, 31, 32, 30–33.
Liebknecht, Wilhelm (1826–1900) 27.
Lipmann, Otto (1880–1933) 147.
Loewenfelder, Erwin (1888–unknown) 74.
Loos, Adolf (1870–1933) 71.
Lubitsch, Ernst (1892–1947) 20, 101.
Ludendorff, Erich (1865–1937) 19, 101.

Maier, Heinrich (1908–1945) 124.
Maizière, Lothar de (born 1940) 69.
Manet, Édouard (1832–1883) 103, 107.
Mann, Thomas (1875–1955) 76.
Martin, Paul (1899–1967) 20, 21.
Maschler, Kurt (1898–1986) 79.
Mataré, Ewald (1887–1965) 74.
Meidner, Ludwig (1884–1966) 74.
Mendelsohn, Erich (1887–1953) 52.
Messel, Alfred (1853–1909) 49, 98, 99.
Meyerinck, Hubert von (1896–1971) 52, 79.
Mies van der Rohe, Ludwig (1886–1969) 12, 56, 57, 60, 72, 82–84, 120–125.
Molotov, Vyacheslav Mikhaylovich (1890–1986) 44, 80, 81.
Mosler, née Hochsinger, Dora (1879–1968) 59.
Mosler, Georg (1872–1940) 13, 56–59.
Mosler, Gert (born 1930) 59, 60, 149.
Müller, Hermann (1876–1931) 142.
Müller-Grote, Carl (1833–1904) 25, 36–39.
Müller-Grote, née Willems, Friederike (1877–1945) 38.
Müller-Grote, Hans-Dietrich (1910–1990) 39, 40, 46.
Müller-Grote, Karl-Gustav (1867–1949) 38, 39, 41, 46.
Müller-Grote, Lore (dates of birth and death unknown) 46.
Müller-Grote, née Kolck, Ursula (born 1915–unknown) 40, 41.
Munch, Edvard (1863–1944) 94.
Murnau, Friedrich Wilhelm (1888–1931) 20, 102.
Muthesius, Hermann (1861–1927) 12, 24, 50.
Nathan, Henry (1862–1932) 58.
Negri, Pola (1897–1987) 20.

Neruda, Pablo (1904–1973) 76.
Neumann, Kurt (1884–unknown) 30.
Nietzsche, Friedrich (1844–1900) 76, 118, 120.
Nietzsche, Therese Elisabeth Alexandra (known as Förster-Nietzsche, Elisabeth) (1846–1935) 120.

Papen, Franz von (1879–1969) 141–145, 147.
Paul, Bruno (1874–1968) 121, 123.
Platte, née von Stülpnagel, Ilsabe (born 1923) 66.
Plattner, Hasso (born 1944) 60, 89.
Prussia, Friedrich Wilhelm Viktor Albert of (Wilhelm II.) (1859–1941) 90–93, 96, 123, 135.
Prussia, Victoria of (1840–1901) 90.
Prussia, Wilhelm Friedrich Ludwig of (Wilhelm I.) (1797–1888) 12, 19, 47.

Quandt, Günther (1881–1954) 40.

Raabe, Wilhelm (1831–1910) 37.
Rathenau, Walther (1867–1922) 101, 123, 137.
Redslob, Edwin (1884–1973) 38.
Reinhardt, Max (1873–1943) 99.
Renoir, Pierre-Auguste (1841–1919) 103.
Reznicek, Burghard Freiherr von (1896–1971) 77.
Richter, Hans (1888–1976) 74.
Richter-Rothschild, Dorothea Gabriele Sara (1889–1972) 74, 75, 78.
Riehl, Alois (1844–1924) 83, 84, 117–121, 123, 124.
Riehl, Sophie (dates of birth and death unknown) 83, 84, 117, 120, 121, 124.
Röhm, Ernst (1887–1934) 145.
Rökk, Marika (1913–2004) 13, 23, 24.
Roosevelt, Franklin Delano (1882–1945) 43.
Rosenheim, Arthur (1865–1942) 31.
Rühmann, Heinz (1902–1994) 13, 20, 23, 80.
Rukser, Eduard Udo Gustav (1892–1971) 71, 73–78.
Rumpf, Fritz (1856–1927) 84.

Saltzmann, Carl (1847–1923) 13, 84, 90–97.
Saltzmann, née Schulz, Clara Auguste (dates of birth and death unknown) 95, 97.
Santho, Imre von (1900–1945) 40, 41.
Sarre, Friedrich (1865–1945) 12, 14, 85, 126–133, 135–137, 139, 140, 148.
Sarre, née Humann, Maria (1875–1970) 85, 129, 133–136, 139, 140, 148.
Sarre, Marie Louise (1903–1999) 116, 127, 138, 140, 148.
Sarre, Theodor André (1816–1893) 128.
Schade van Westrum, Hermine (dates of birth and death unknown) 72, 73.
Schäuble, Wolfgang (born 1942) 68.
Schider, Fritz (1846–1907) 108.
Schinkel, Karl Friedrich (1781–1841) 83, 131.
Schleicher, Elisabeth von (1893–1934) 141, 144–146.
Schleicher, Kurt von (1882–1934) 13, 21, 61, 62, 141–147.
Schleicher, Lonny von (1919–2014) 145, 146.
Schneider, Magda (1909–1996) 18, 23.
Schulte, Alfred (dates of birth and death unknown) 30.
Schulze-Büttger, Georg (1904–1944) 30.

Slezak, Leo (1873–1946) 79.
Solmssen, Georg (1869–1957) 86.
Spranger, Eduard (1882–1963) 123, 124.
Stalin, Joseph (1878–1953) 15, 43–45, 48, 51, 54, 55, 80, 87, 140.
Stauß, Emil Georg von (1877–1942) 19.
Stern, née Vogelsdorff, Hedwig (1972–1943) 28, 30, 35.
Stern, Max (1868–1943) 14, 27–30, 35.
Sterna, Katta (née Katharina Stern) (1897–1984) 18.
Stolpe, Manfred (born 1936; died 2019) 16.
Strasser, Gregor (1892–1934) 144, 145.
Stresemann, Gustav (1878–1929) 101.
Stuck, Hans (1900–1978) 71, 77, 78.
Stuck von Reznicek, née Heimann, Paula (1895–1976) 71, 77, 78.
Stückrath, Edith (1912–unknown) 78, 80, 81.
Stückrath, Erich (1902–1955) 78, 80, 81.
Stülpnagel, Carl-Heinrich von (1886–1944) 65.
Stülpnagel, née von Kracht, Irmgard von (1883–1974) 62, 64.

Stülpnagel, Joachim Fritz Constantin von (1880–1968) 14, 15, 61–67, 70.
Stülpnagel, Rochus Wilhelm von (1925–1944) 65.

Talaat Pascha (1874–1921) 135, 136.
Theile, Albert (1904–1986) 73, 75.
Thiede, Jörg Detlef (born 1938) 92, 96, 97.
Toulouse-Lautrec, Henri de (1864–1901) 107.
Tresckow, Henning von (1901–1944) 30.
Troost, Paul Ludwig (1878–1934) 13.
Truman, Harry S. (1884–1973) 15, 36, 40–45, 54, 80, 87.
Türk, Wilhelm von (1774–1846) 11.

Urbig, née Seebeck, Dorothea Augusta Anne (1881–1968) 83, 84.
Urbig, Elisabeth (1910–1998) 85, 87.
Urbig, Franz (1864–1944) 13, 82–89, 96.

Voss, Hans-Alexander von (1907–1944) 65.
Voss, Rüdiger von (born 1939) 66, 149.
Wallot, Paul (1841–1912) 49.

Wassermann, Oscar (1869–1934) 86, 87.
Wentzel-Heckmann, Elise (1833–1914) 12, 128, 129.
Werner, Anton von (1843–1915) 90, 94.
Werner, Ilse (1921–2005) 79.
Wiepking-Jürgensmann, Heinrich (1891–1973) 78.
Wigman, Mary (1886–1973) 123.
Winterstein, Eduard von (1871–1961) 79.
Wischniak, Marianne (dates of birth and death unknown) 113, 115, 116.
Witte, Karsten (1944–1995) 21.
Wittgensteiner, Arno (1883–unknown) 73.
Wolff, Julius (1834–1910) 37.
Wolff, Otto (1881–1940) 144, 147.
Wölfflin, Heinrich (1864–1945) 123, 133.

Zatzenstein-Matthiesen, Franz (also Catzenstein, Franz) (around 1900–1963) 103.
Zeisler, Alfred (1892–1985) 23.
Zhukov, Georgy Konstantinovich (1896–1974) 45, 46, 140.
Zuckmayer, Carl (1896–1977) 76.

Picture Credits

Cover, front:
background: left: TU Berlin, Photographer: Hermann Rückwardt; right: Architekturmuseum TU Berlin, Inv. no. 40438, Erwin Albert Barth, "Villengarten am Griebnitzsee, Potsdam-Babelsberg"; front, from left to right: GrussAusPotsdam.de: card-no. 3.748; ullstein bild – Gregor Harlip; GrussAus-Potsdam.de: card-no. 3.817; Karl Heinrich von Stülpnagel für den von Stülpnagel'schen Familienverband (ed.): Geschichte des Geschlechts von Stülpnagel, volume 2, Markkleeberg 2009, p. 203

p. 2: ullstein bild – Süddeutsche Zeitung Photo / Scherl
p. 6: GrussAusPotsdam.de: card-no. 1.506
above left: Hermann Muthesius, Landhaus and Garten, p. 9, F. Bruckmann A.-G., München 1910, p. 50; above right: Architekturmuseum TU Berlin, Inv. no. F 16061; centre right: Bildarchiv Foto Marburg, image-no. KBB 2.382; below: Regional Capital of Potsdam, Office for the Protection of Historic Buildings and Monuments (Untere Denkmalschutzbehörde), collection of historic building records "Acta specialia betreffend Bausachen", Virchowstr. 27, Potsdam, volume 1, p. 33
p. 10: above: © GeoBasis-DE/LGB, dl-de/by-2-0, excerpt from the Plan of Potsdam including the surrounding area based on the original records of the topographic department of the ordnance survey of 1848", scale 1:25000; below: Architekturmuseum TU Berlin, Inv. no. 40438
p. 11: left: © GeoBasis-DE/LGB, dl-de/by-2-0, excerpt from topographic map page Potsdam issue 1877; right: © GeoBasis-DE/ LGB, dl-de/by-2-0, excerpt from topographic city map page Potsdam, scale 1:25000, issue 1989
p. 12: left: Architekturmuseum TU Berlin, Inv. no. 40440; right: Architekturmuseum TU Berlin, Inv. no. 40441
p. 13: GrussAusPotsdam.de: card-no 1.734
p. 15: left: Berlin State Archive, F Rep. 290 (02) no. 0321757, photograph: Edmund Kasperski; right: bpk / Horst E. Schulze
p. 16: nilo – Agentur für Fotografie
p. 18: left above, centre, below: from Mr Partsch's private collection; right: ullstein bild – Badekow
p. 20: left: GrussAusPotsdam.de: card-no. 719; right: GrussAusPotsdam.de: card-no. 2.361
p. 21: from Mr Partsch's private collection
p. 22: ullstein bild – Arthur Grimm
p. 24: left: Potsdam Museum – Forum für Kunst und Geschichte; right: TU Berlin, photographer: Hermann Rückwardt
p. 25: left above: nilo – Agentur für Fotografie; above right: Berlin State Archive, F Rep. 290 (02) no. 0321756, photo: Edmund Kasperski; below: Berliner S-Bahn-Museum
p. 26: nilo – Agentur für Fotografie
p. 27: nilo – Agentur für Fotografie
p. 28: Amsterdam City Archive
p. 29: private
p. 31: left: Collector: Karl Kautsky, date: approx. 1901, International Institute of Social History (Amsterdam); right: copyright-free
p. 34: Evonik Industries AG, company archive Hanau, biographical documents Liebknecht, Otto; below: Federal Archive, DVH 58 Bild-8480- GR48-055, Photographer: no information provided
p. 36: nilo – Agentur für Fotografie
p. 38: left: Bildarchiv Foto Marburg, image-No. KBB 2.382; right: Förderkreis Böhmisches Dorf

p. 39: Federal Archive, group shelf number: VBS 1013 (NS 34), archive shelf number: ZB 0199 A.04
p. 40: Federal Archive, group shelf number: R/9361/ III, archive shelf number: 136086
p. 41: ullstein bild – Imre v. Santho
p. 42: above left, above right and below left: US Army Signal Corps. Harry S. Truman Library, photographer unknown (copyright-free); below right: Bildarchiv Foto Marburg, image-no. KBB 2.3823
p. 43: US Army Signal Corps. Harry S. Truman Library, photographer unknown (copyright-free)
p. 44: US Army Signal Corps. Harry S. Truman Library, photographer unknown (copyright-free)
p. 46: Federal Archive, group shelf number: R/9361/V, archive shelf number: 148193
p. 48: nilo – Agentur für Fotografie
p. 49: left, centre left, centre right: Collection Kuhn (copyright-free); right: Collection Kuhn (copyright-free), Kürschner
p. 50: left: Berliner Architekturwelt (Public Domain), issue 14.1912 (https://digital.zlb.de/viewer/image/14192916_1912/240/); centre: "Gemeinde Neubabelsberg", panel 14; right: Berliner Architekturwelt (Public Domain), issue 14.1912 (https://digital.zlb.de/viewer/image/14192916_1912/241/)
p. 51: left: Berliner Architekturwelt (Public Domain), issue 14.1912 (https://digital.zlb.de/viewer/image/14192916_1912/242/); centre: Berliner Architekturwelt (Public Domain), issue 14.1912 (https://digital.zlb.image/14192916_1912/243/); right: Berliner Architekturwelt (Public Domain), issue 14.1912 (https://digital.zlb.de/viewer/image/14192916_1912/239/)
p. 53: left: ullstein bild – Yva; right: ullstein bild – Karl Ludwig Haenchen

p. 55: left: bpk / Herbert Hensky; right: nilo – Agentur für Fotografie

p. 57: above left: nilo – Agentur für Fotografie; above right: Martin Gaier and Claudia Mohn, TU Berlin 2000, published in: Mies van der Rohe. Frühe Bauten. Probleme der Erhaltung. Probleme der Bewertung, published by Johannes Cramer and Dorothee Sack, Petersberg 2004, p. 78; below left and below right: Regional Capital of Potsdam, Office for the Protection of Historic Buildings and Monuments (Untere Denkmalschutzbehörde), collection of historic building records, "Acta specialia betreffend Bausachen", Karl-Marx-Strasse 28/29. Published in: Martin Gaier and Claudia Mohn, in: Mies van der Rohe. Frühe Bauten. Probleme der Erhaltung. Probleme der Bewertung, published by Johannes Cramer and Dorothee Sack, Petersberg 2004, p. 77

p. 58: left and right: private

p. 59: left: Federal Archive, DVH 58 Bild-8480-GR48-076, photographer: no information provided; right: private, Gert Mosler

p. 60: private

p. 61: nilo – Agentur für Fotografie

p. 62: ullstein bild – ullstein bild

p. 63: Ilsabe Platte

p. 64: Karl Heinrich von Stülpnagel für den von Stülpnagel'schen Familienverband (ed.): Geschichte des Geschlechts von Stülpnagel, volume 2, Markkleeberg 2009, p. 203

p. 65: ullstein bild – Heinrich Hoffmann

p. 67: private

p. 71: left: Freud Museum London; right: RIBA Collections

p. 72: nilo – Agentur für Fotografie

p. 74: private

p. 75: left: collection of Marion Billo; right: private

p. 77: left: collection of Marion Billo; right: ullstein bild – Atelier Binder

p. 79: ullstein bild – AP

p. 81: left: Federal Archive Bild 183-14059-0016, photographer: no information provided; right: Federal Archive, DVH 58 Bild-8480-GR48-063, photographer: no information provided

p. 83: Library of Congress Prints & Photographs Division, author: Bain News Service, publisher, collection: George Grantham Bain Collection (copyright-free)

p. 84: left: nilo – Agentur für Fotografie; right: Potsdam City Archive, group: 1-13 – Land Registry Office, shelf number: 1-13/0752

p. 85: ullstein bild – ullstein bild, photograph by: Argusfot

p. 87: ullstein bild – ullstein bild

p. 88: The National Archives London. Sign. FO 934 Potsdam conference 1945. United Kingdom Delegates: records; below left: BEBUG mbH / Bild und Heimat, Berlin, GrussAusPotsdam.de: card no. 3328; below right: Federal Archive, DVH 58 Bild-8480- GR48-064, photographer: no information provided

p. 91: left: Photographer: Udo Unkelbach, source: https://www.joergthiede.com/baudenkmaeler/ villa-saltzmann/; right: ullstein bild – Wilhelm Fechner

p. 92: Berlinische Galerie – donation by Dr Jörg Thiede-Stiftung, 2014, photos: Kai-Annett Becker/Berlinische Galerie

p. 93: left: Secret State Archives Prussian Cultural Heritage Foundation (GStA PK), BPH, Rep. 53, no. 327; right: https://www.joergthiede.com/baudenkmaeler/villa-saltzmann/

p. 95: Secret State Archives Prussian Cultural Heritage Foundation (GStA PK), BPH, Rep. 53, no. 327

p. 96: left: photograph by Hermann Boll. https://www.joergthiede.com/baudenkmaeler/villa-saltzmann/; right: https://www.joergthiede.com/baudenkmaeler/villa-saltzmann/ below left: https://www.joergthiede.com/baudenkmaeler/villa-saltzmann/; right center: Regional Capital of Potsdam, Office for the Protection of Historic Buildings and Monuments (Untere Denkmalschutzbehörde), collection of historic building records, "Acta specialia betreffend Bausachen", Virchowstr. 27, Potsdam, volume 1, p. 26; right below: Regional Capital of Potsdam, Office for the Protection of Historic Buildings and Monuments (Untere Denkmalschutzbehörde), collection of historic building records, "Acta specialia betreffend Bausachen", Virchowstr. 27, Potsdam, volume 1, p. 33

p. 99: left: Architekturmuseum TU Berlin, Inv. no. F 16061; right: Alfred Breslauer. Ausgeführte Bauten 1897–1927, Berlin: Julius Bard Verlag 1927, p. 27

p. 100: left: Architekturmuseum TU Berlin, Inv. no. B 3634,19; centre: Architekturmuseum TU Berlin, Inv. no. B 3634,20; right: Architekturmuseum TU Berlin, Inv. no. B 3634,18 (all from: Alfred Breslauer, Ausgeführte Bauten 1897–1927, Berlin: Julius Bard Verlag 1927)

p. 101: above left: Alfred Breslauer, Ausgeführte Bauten 1897–1927, Berlin: Julius Bard Verlag 1927, p. 28; below left: ullstein bild, image number: 01092747, title: Jakob Goldschmidt; right: images relating to Jakob Goldschmidt from the image archives of "Aufbau", 1934–2004; Jewish Museum Berlin

p. 102: Catalogue of Seven Paintings by Cézanne, Manet, Renoir and van Gogh. The Property of The Estate of the late Jakob Goldschmidt of New York City, published by Sotheby & Co., 34 and 35 New Bond St., London, W 1 (Day of Sale: Wednesday, October 15, 1958)

p. 105: left: NSDAP election poster for the Reichstag election of November 6, 1932. Published in: Bernd Sösemann: Im Zwielicht bürokratischer "Arisierung", Edition Andreae, Berlin 2016, p. 28; right: Federal Archive, NS 1/1342

p. 106: left: Brandenburg Main State Archive (BLHA), Rep. 36 A (II) Oberfinanzpräsident Berlin-Brandenburg no. 12990; right: private.

p. 108: Federal Archive, DVH 58 Bild-8480-GR48-068, group: DVH 58 Bild – Stadtkommandantur der Hauptstadt der DDR Berlin – image archives. Photographer: no information provided

p. 110: nilo – Agentur für Fotografie

p. 112: left: GrussAusPotsdam.de: card-no. 2.662; right: GrussAusPotsdam.de: card-No. 4.075

p. 113: Potsdam City Archive, group: 1-13 – land registry office, shelf number: 1-13/681 F2898, sheet 0400

p. 114: left: The Palestine Gazette no. 1579, Thursday, May 15, 1947, p. 506; right: Städtische Lichtbildstelle, Potsdam Museum – Forum für Kunst and Geschichte, Inv.-no. FS 3791

p. 115: left: Brandenburg Main State Archive (BLHA), Rep. 2 A, Regierung Potsdam I Pol no. 2009; centre: BLHA, Rep. 2 A Regierung Potsdam I Hb no. 1767; right: photo: Karin Baller

p. 117: Potsdam Museum – Forum für Kunst and Geschichte/ Städtische Lichtbildstelle (FS 3793)

p. 118: left: copyright-free; right: The Picture Art Collection / Alamy stock photo, image-ID: MWYP13

p. 121: private

p. 122: left: Hermann Muthesius: Landhaus and Garten, München: F. Bruckmann A.-G. 1910, p. 51; right: Hartmann/Academic image Archive for Architecture (Wissenschaftliches Bildarchiv für Architektur)

p. 124: left: Folkerts Architekten; right: Hermann Muthesius, Landhaus and Garten, F. Bruckmann A.-G., München 1910, p. 50; below left and right: nilo – Agentur für Fotografie

p. 126: nilo – Agentur für Fotografie

p. 127: bpk / Museum für Islamische Kunst, SMB

p. 128: bpk / Kunstbibliothek, SMB, photo library Willy Römer / Willy Römer

p. 130: Architektur von Olbrich, published by Ernst Wasmuth Berlin, series III, volume 2

p. 131: Secret State Archives Prussian Cultural Heritage Foundation (GStA PK), VI. HA family archives and estates, NI Carl Heinrich Becker, no. 4682

p. 132: nilo – Agentur für Fotografie

p. 134: left: bpk / Museum für Islamische Kunst, SMB; right: bpk / Museum für Islamische Kunst, SMB / Emil Bieber

p. 137: Federal Archives, Military Archive, Freiburg im Breisgau, Germany: BA-MA RM 40/214, 99: H. Humann to Admiralstab, Berlin 10.7.1916

p. 138: ullstein bild – Gregor Harlip

p. 143: left: collection of Lonny von Schleicher; right: Federal Archive, image 02-14090, Photographer: Georg Pahl

p. 145: left: Federal Archive, shelf number: B 145 image-P046304, photographer: Carl Weinrother; centre and right: Municipal Archives of the City of Potsdam (copyright-free)

p. 146: left: Official Gazette of the Reichsverband Deutscher Offiziere no. 19 of July 5, 1935, p. 553; right: collection Lonny von Schleicher

p. 148: bpk / Luftbild Berlin GmbH